Harriette G. Brittan

Scenes and Incidents of Every-Day Life in Africa

Harriette G. Brittan

Scenes and Incidents of Every-Day Life in Africa

ISBN/EAN: 9783337309107

Printed in Europe, USA, Canada, Australia, Japan

Cover: Foto ©Andreas Hilbeck / pixelio.de

More available books at **www.hansebooks.com**

SCENES AND INCIDENTS

OF

Every-Day Life in Africa.

BY HARRIETTE G. BRITTAN.

"Believe on the Lord Jesus Christ, and thou shalt be saved."—ACTS xvi. 31.

"How then shall they call on him in whom they have not believed? And how shall they believe in him of whom they have not heard? And how shall they hear without a preacher? And how shall they preach except they be sent? As it is written, How beautiful are the feet of them that preach the Gospel of Peace, and bring glad tidings of good things."—ROM. x. 14, 15.

SECOND EDITION.

New-York:
PUDNEY & RUSSELL, PUBLISHERS,
No. 70 JOHN-STREET.

1860.

Dedication.

TO MY BELOVED PASTOR,

REV. J. A. PADDOCK.

It is meet that to one, to whom I owe so much of what I possess of spiritual life, the first efforts of my *pen* for the spread of the Redeemer's kingdom should be dedicated. You, dear Sir, know how these scenes were first penned, as letters to loved ones at home, and that it was from reiterated assurances that they might be useful and interesting to the public at large, that they have now been published. This work has been entered upon and prosecuted with many doubts and fears. I can not expect it to be received by a critical public, as it has been by loving friends; but you are fully aware of the motives that prompted this undertaking: an earnest desire to promote the best interests of Africa; to spread the Redeemer's kingdom, and the elevation and regeneration of our common humanity. These being the motives, I trust there are many who will forgive the lack of skill, or other deficiencies in the work—looking upon it, not with a critic's, but a Christian's eye, believing, as I know *you* will, "she hath done what she could."

Harriett G. Brittan.

CONTENTS.

CHAPTER I.
AT SEA.

Parting—Slave Trade—Sunset—Storm—Friendless—Escape—Composant—Salute—Kroomen.................. 13

CHAPTER II.
MONROVIA.

Kroomen—Mr. Wilson—Landing—Kroo Philosophy—Schools—The Drivers—Miss Killpatric—Sail again................... 24

CHAPTER III.
CAPE PALMAS.

Church—The Asylum—Our Pets—Sunday—Hoffman Station—Daily Life.. 37

CHAPTER IV.
CAVALLA.

Lepers—Cavalla Examination—The Feast—Boys' Examination..... 53

CHAPTER V.
RETURN HOME.

Baptism—Mr. Wilson's Arrival—Asylum Examination—The Bishop Arrives—Christmas Eve—Christmas Day—Escape.... 60

CHAPTER VI.

SUNDAY-SCHOOL ANNIVERSARY.

Work—Native Class—Old M'Lede—Father Scotland—New Year's Eve—New-Year's Day—Fever—The Will..................... 68

CHAPTER VII.

SCHOOL.

Saturday—The Vincennes—Witchcraft—The Dinner Table—Correction—Liberian Uniform—The Children—Communion Sunday—Our Household—Food—Auntie Dade—Ocean Eagle—News from Cavalla......, ... 80

CHAPTER VIII.

THE WEDDING.

The Eagle Sails—The Lake—Cavalla—Daily Fare—Baptism—Little Thomas—The Hospital..................................... 100

CHAPTER IX.

TEST.

Love Feast—The Horse—Wah—The Boat—The Snake—Saturday Interruptions—Grawah—Insects — Saturday Evening—Sunday —Wah — Sacerdillo — Convocation—Good Friday—Change—Easter Sunday—Travelling—Want—The Well—Visitors..... 112

CHAPTER X.

DADE.

Witchcraft—Saturday Afternoon—Wounds—Sickness—Moonlight —Prayer—Lowliness — The Bodia — Cannibals—Atonement—Self-denial—The Well—Begging—Daily Duties—Surgery—Heroism — Sassa-wood—Surgery—Sick Man—Cannibalism—French Emigrant Vessel—Cruelty—Cold.................... 136

CHAPTER XI.

SASSA ORDEAL.

Valentine—Wounds—Thomas—The Bishop's Arrival—Communion—Life—Rum—Missionary Meeting—Salt—Joy—More Joy—Work—Illness—The Examination and Wedding—Birth-day—Baptism—Sassa—The Invitations—Doda-lu—Centipede—Sad News—The Kwi—Time—The Funeral—Ignorance—The Accepted Invitation—Consumption........................ 16

CHAPTER XII.

ULCERS.

Climate — Company — Strange Ideas — Singing — Beauty—Sassa Triumph—Fish—Fever—Harry Bacon—Text—Cape Palmas—New Friends—Carriage—On Board—Travelling—King Weir—Lucie—Reveries—Stores from Home—Transmigration—Rumors—Music—A Pleasant Day—Dauba.................... 194

CHAPTER XIII.

ENTHUSIASM.

Letters—Josephine—The Garden Graves—The Missionary Box—The Girls' School—Patience—Superstition—Cape Palmas—Mount Vaughan—Home—Cruelty—Crazy Man—Nye—Beauty—Marriage—Amusements—Sickness—The Earthquake—The Comet—Generosity—Strange Vessel—Music—Cares—Superstition—The Army—Letters—Fish—Faith—The Sabbath Law—Letters—Harriett—Penalty—Justice—Legends—The Mermaid—The Witch—Church—Sickness........... 226

CHAPTER XIV.

MONROVIA.

Visitors—Sunday School Celebration—Patience—Speeches—Uncle Simon—Company—Sunday — St. Paul's River—Drivers—A Curiosity — Poverty — The Mite — The Creek — Leopard—Travel—Feasts—Pleasure — Monrovia—The Stevens—Christmas Day—Sunday—The Congoes—The Gospel—Sickness—Friends—The Ship—Bassa Sinoe... 282

CHAPTER XV.

HOME.

Mrs. Gillet—Ordination—The Magic Lantern—Illness—Funeral—
Departure — Passengers — Sierra Leone — The Gambia—The
Juju—Cruelties—Drunkenness—Teneriffe—Madeira 332

INCIDENTS AND SCENES
OF
EVERY-DAY LIFE IN AFRICA.

Chapter First.

AT SEA.

PARTING.—How many scenes of ship life have been given again and again to the public eye; in all there is much that is similar, and yet how varied! The vessel seems like a little world of itself—far away from all others; yet the hopes and fears, the joys and loves, of so many centre in her. Following our little bark, we knew were the thoughts and prayers of many, oh! how many, of God's dear children. We were a little band of eight missionaries, from three different branches of the Church on earth, but belonging, as we all hoped, to the one great spiritual Church of the Redeemer. And what confidence it gave us to feel that prayers for us were being wafted on every gale. I pass over the scene of our parting; none but those who have felt it can understand the missionary's farewell to his loved ones—the mingling of joy and sorrow; it is a strangely sad, yet blissful parting.

SLAVE TRADE.—We have morning and evening worship in our little cabin. Unless obliged to be on deck, all the ship's company attend, except the man at the helm. I hope our presence may be a blessing to them; and while thinking of the poor heathen at a distance, may we not forget those around us. The mate brought us a flying-fish this morning, which had been killed by striking against the man at the helm. It is a beautiful little creature, of a deep bright blue. Its wings are very delicate, and perfectly transparent. Our mate was telling us an adventure of his early life—a sad one. He shipped on board a vessel bound for the African coast, ostensibly to obtain a cargo of camwood; but it, in reality, was a slave ship. He and some of the other sailors had no idea what the vessel was till they reached the slave coast, or what was the species of labor they would be required to perform. The horrors of the fearful trade are too well known for me to recapitulate them here. He, poor fellow, could not get inured to them, and he loathed himself for the very acts he was compelled to perform. At length they had succeeded in obtaining two hundred and eighty, about one third of their cargo, when a British cruiser hove in sight.

"The poor negroes," said he, "were stowed away, like cattle in pens, under the deck; and to hear their groans, moans, and yells, was perfectly dreadful." The slaver was chased by the cruiser for five days, and then, finding escape impossible, the captain ran her upon the rocks, and, taking to the small boats, he and the crew escaped to the shore. Whether the poor captives were rescued by the British, or most miserably perished, he never knew. The crew, to avoid detection by the natives, sought singly for safety. He wandered down the coast for four hundred miles, feeding on berries and roots, till he came to a Portuguese seaport, where he obtained a homeward passage. Whether any of his comrades escaped, he never knew. So sometimes even in this world, God permits the "wicked to be snared in his own net." This poor man said he believed if he should ever be entrapped in such an undertaking again, he would throw himself *overboard.*

SUNSET.—This evening, what a magnificent sunset we have had! It puts all my powers of description at defiance. Two of us were sitting together on the deck, and we called to mind that it was the hour of our little prayer-meeting at home. We sang together, and then engaged in silent prayer for a few moments—remembering "that prayer is a great triangle, the base connecting distant friends on earth, the apex being formed by our Father's throne." We then sat and watched that splendid scene, exclaiming—

> "Loose all your bars of massy light,
> And wide unfold the ethereal scene."

And, truly, I never so fully realized what must be the glorious reality of the heavenly city, as I did in witnessing that sunset. "Eye hath not seen, ear hath not heard, nor hath it entered into the heart of man to conceive, the glories which He hath prepared for those that love Him."

STORM.—The captain was called up at four o'clock in

the morning: a heavy squall was coming on, and we soon felt its terrible effects. It lasted about thirty-six hours. To look out, from the deck, the scene was sublimely awful. The waves rolling in mountains, the dense leaden clouds (from which the rain poured down in torrents) coming so close to the water that you could hardly discover where one began and the other terminated; our little vessel pitching and tossing from side to side, every sail furled close, the helm lashed hard, and we left to drift entirely at the mercy of the winds and waves. All that human hands could do, the captain had done, and now we must rely entirely on the strength of an Almighty arm. I never heard a single fear expressed; all seemed to feel that our Father "was at the helm," and that He who once spake to the raging billows, "Peace! be still!" yet "holds the winds in His fist and the waves in the hollow of His hand;" and we knew that without His permission not a hair of our heads could perish. Outside, the scene was grand and terrific; inside, spite of the awe (not fear) we all felt, the scene was so ludicrous, that every few minutes there would be a merry peal of laughter. We did not profess to have any spiritual mediums on board, yet our heavy oak table was lifted out of its sockets, which were nailed to the floor, and was seen performing most remarkable gyrations through the cabin. It would have made the fortune of a spiritualist, and all done without the intervention of any human hands, and even against the human will, following the luckless wight who happened to be in its path so swiftly, that he seldom escaped without a squeeze; and so obstinate was it, that our united efforts were needed, not to make it move, but to make it keep still. Benches and chairs were turning somersets; trunks were flying about in all directions. As to ourselves, seat and all, we would occasionally take a flying leap to the other side of the cabin, frequently putting ourselves into one another's arms. Our different steps and manœuvres were such as a dancing or posture master would strive to imitate in vain. At night the storm seemed more fearful still. The deep, impenetrable darkness around us; the noises sounding louder and harsher; everything in the cabin dashing about; the doors rattling and knocking; the loud roar of the winds and waves; while every beam in the little vessel seemed to creak and groan, as if in pain. "Those who go down to the sea in ships, who do business in great waters, these see the wonders of the Lord." At length the storm ceased, and again tranquillity reigned on the bosom of the mighty deep. "Oh! that men would praise the Lord for His doings to the children of men."

FRIENDLESS.—Last night I heard a sad tale—but how many there are like it. I had frequently noticed our second mate, so very kind and attentive, when he had any opportunity, doing little acts of service. I always spoke kindly to him. Last evening it was his watch on deck—I went up for a little fresh air before retiring. He placed a seat for me, and then lingering near, I commenced a conversation with him. Poor fellow! his heart was overflowing. He told me that I was the *first lady* who had ever spoken to him—what women he had ever known had been of the lowest order. I said something about home. Home! home! he knew not what the word meant. He had no home. His mother had been dead six years, his father only a few months. They were both drunkards. At the age of five he was turned into the street to get his living as he could. He begged, and in summer slept in the markets and under carts, &c.; in the winter he would occasionally find a sleeping-place with one of his companions, or he would beg enough to pay for a bed—sometimes finding where his mother and father were, and sleeping for a week or so with them. At length he picked up a few pennies, bought some newspapers, and set up in that business. From his papers, with the aid of the other boys about him, he taught himself to read. At the age of fourteen he went to sea. For three years he suffered much, but now he has been a sailor for nine years ; he does not like it, but at first " necessity knew no law," and now he feels that he is not fitted for anything else. He is a very fine steady young man, very ambitious, and desirous to improve himself. The captain takes quite an interest in him, and is teaching him navigation. I have promised to lend him some books, as he has none, and would like much to read. Poor fellow! he feels as if he was like a waif cast upon the waters, without friends, or home, or any to love, or feel, or care for him. I hope we may be able to benefit him, and let him feel that some of his fellow-creatures take an interest in him, and, above all, I hope we may show him that he has a Friend above, who ever cares for and watches over him. Poor fellow! his has been a hard fate, but I hope brighter days are in store for him.

ESCAPE.—What a proof have we had to-day of God's watchful providence and care of us! I was lying very sick on the sofa (for though a month out, I still suffer much) alone, all the rest were on deck, when suddenly I heard the most fearful screams. I rushed on deck, and found Miss Ball had fallen overboard. Our captain was in the forward part of the vessel; he heard the steward scream "some one overboard," and shouted directly to the man at the helm to lay-to, for them to get out the boat; but by that time he saw that Miss Ball was hanging on the side. There was a rope swinging on to the boom, which the mate, providentially, had placed there only that morning, and, as she fell, she had caught that. Had the accident occurred the day before, there would have been no hope, as at that time we were going very fast, and, for several days, sharks had been seen playing round the ship. The captain and mate were over the side of the vessel in a minute, and had her on board directly. But, oh! the agony of that minute. She did not lose consciousness till she was on deck. The second mate was tearing up the steps, and with them he intended to leap overboard and try and swim to her. But the captain says, if she had once been in the water he thinks there would have been no hope of saving her, we were going so fast. May we have grateful hearts for our God's unnumbered mercies.

COMPOSANT.—A heavy thunder-storm last night, in the midst of which the captain called us up, to see what he called a composant; it was a large ball of brilliant light, that appeared to be slowly climbing the rigging, and at length settled on the top of the mast. After this, we saw a number of them at different times, but we never could arrive at any determination as to what they were. At one time we thought they might be masses of decomposed animal matter, or some species of phosphorescence blown on board by the storm; but on the sailors climbing to find out, they would put their hands on the very spot where the light was, and could feel nothing, but the light would shine on their hands. We came to the conclusion that it was some species of electricity, but what we could not tell.

SALUTE.—One of our lady passengers was awakened last night by a very affectionate salutation from a black gentleman; but he happened to be of the swine species. He broke out of his pen, and in the middle of the night came rooting about for something nice, and so walked into her state-room, and put his cold nose in her face, she sleeping in the lower berth. There was a great uproar, as the lady had not bargained for so affectionate a greeting to the African coast. The captain was soon at work, trying to drive the gentleman out, but the more he drove, the more the pig would'nt go; he was chased round and round the cabin, but at length, after affording us quite sufficient laughter and merriment, he was expelled.

KROOMEN.—A ship very near us all day. In the evening we were watching the rising moon, all sitting on deck, and feeling quite sentimental, when we heard a very strange noise, like some one crying out for help. The man at the wheel shouted, "A man overboard!"

The captain sprung directly to the side of the vessel, and there, on the top of the water, was a dark object nearing us. He knew that none had fallen overboard from our vessel, and he did not suppose, if any one had fallen from the other, that they could have sustained themselves so long above water, particularly as there appeared to be no lack of sharks in this vicinity. In a few minutes the shouts became louder, and we found that they must proceed from several human voices. The captain immediately concluded that it was some Kroomen come off from shore to be hired by him. These Kroomen are a race of seamen, who live all along the coast. As soon as ever they discover a vessel on the edge of the horizon, they put off for it in their canoes, hoping to be engaged by the captain; every vessel on the African coast being obliged to engage a number of these men to perform all the manual labor while she stays on the coast, loading and unloading the vessel, &c., &c., as white men can perform very little labor here. All the harbors, likewise, on the whole coast are so bad, that nowhere can vessels come nearer than two miles from shore, all the loading and unloading being done by small boats. These, also, must always be manned by Kroomen, on account of the shifting sand-bars, rolling surf, and sunken rocks, with which they only are familiar: they, in fact, are the pilots of the coast; therefore, as they are most expert seamen, and no vessel, not even a slaver, can by any possibility do without them, they are never enslaved; and to distinguish them from other tribes on the coast, they have (both men and women) a long black mark down the face, from the top of the forehead to the tip of the nose. This is something like tattooing; it is done in childhood, and is indelible. They also sharpen the two front teeth to a point, like dogs' teeth. They are a tall, well-formed, athletic race. Generally, when a captain engages a set of these men, he keeps them with him all the time he is on the coast; they receive better wages and food than they can otherwise obtain, and when he discharges them, he writes them a certificate of good behaviour. This they call a book (any writing is a book), which they show to the next with whom they wish to engage. Our captain, not wishing the company of any of these gentry till we should reach Monrovia, made no attempt to wait for them; but they redoubled their efforts, making the most unearthly noises and yells. In a little while they reached the side of the vessel. There were three men in a little canoe; it seemed like a scollop-shell, so small, exactly in shape like an Indian snow-shoe, pointed at both ends. One of the men was employed all the time baling out the water. The captain shouted to the men that he did not want them; but one of them kept calling out all the time, "Book! captain, book!" and, spite of all efforts to prevent it, he caught a rope, and was up the side of the vessel like a monkey. His costume, like the rest of the Kroomen, consisted of a cloth around the loins, and an old hat; this, being the only dry spot, is where "the book" is generally carried. He presented a large paper parcel to the captain, which, on examining, proved to be a package of letters the captain of the other vessel wished us to post for him at Monrovia. A polite message was returned; but, before leaving, the Kroomen wanted " a dash," (a present.) They are great beggars. They wanted either rum or tobacco. Upon finding we had neither on board, they were quite disgusted, but upon the receipt of a little biscuit and meat, they disappeared in the direction of the other vessel. Long after they had disappeared from our sight, however, we could hear their harsh cries and discordant yells, which it seems was singing—though, truth to say, I should never have supposed it. So, I suppose, we are introduced to Africa.

Chapter Second.

MONROVIA.

KROOMEN.—At three o'clock to-day we came within sight of Cape Mesurado, behind which lies the town of Monrovia, and soon commenced such a scene of excitement as I never before witnessed. When we were still several miles out from land, the water began to be dotted with black specks, and, in a short time, we perceived that they were the canoes of the Kroomen, each straining vigorously to be the first to reach the vessel. In each canoe is a headman; he is the best dressed—perhaps he will wear a shirt and pantaloons. He presents his "book" to the captain, which he carries either in his hat, or in a little tin box around his neck, and the first one whose testimonials are satisfactory is immediately engaged. He instantly takes charge of the vessel, pilots her to her anchorage, and engages, and is responsible for the conduct of the other men the captain may require. The vessel anchors two or three miles from shore, and even the row-boats can seldom approach nearer than a dozen or twenty yards from the beach, and everything, including live stock, has to be carried on shore, in the Krooman's arms, through the boiling surf. Our captain has engaged Jack Frying Pan at half a dollar, or the worth of it in cloth, and five others at a shilling a day. They often have very curious names, given to them in jest by the sailors with whom they have worked. These names they have cut out, or carved on large ivory rings, which they wear as bracelets.

Mr. Wilson.—In about an hour after we anchored, we perceived a boat pushing off from the shore. In it was the custom-house officer, a colored gentleman, and the Rev. Mr. Wilson, a white missionary, belonging to the Presbyterian Board. He knew we were expected, and came to see if we had arrived, and to give us a warm and Christian greeting. We never shall forget his kind and affectionate welcome. He made us feel at once that he forgot not the injunction, "love as brethren." That is one beautiful feature of missionary life—there is no distinction felt of sect or denomination, all are "one in Christ Jesus;" they feel that there is "one Lord, one faith, one baptism, one God and Father of *all*," and they are too anxious to point the poor darkened souls to the true way, to stop themselves to quarrel about the *appearance* of the different shrubs, flowers, and trees in that way. It is impossible to tell the effect of such a greeting to a sad heart, and from a stranger, too. It is one of those bright spots in life, which time or change can never efface. Mr. Wilson remained on board with us an hour or so, and made us promise to spend the day with him to-morrow on shore.

Landing.—The captain expects to lay here at Monrovia for several days; he says we may have the boat to go on shore whenever we like, and if we will only let him know in time, he will always go with us to take care of us; he is very kind. About ten o'clock we announced our readiness. The boat was drawn up alongside, and we prepared to descend. The captain went down with each lady. Clambering down the rope ladder made us feel very dizzy, and rather fearful. After he had assisted all the ladies, the captain left the gentlemen to manage for themselves, and they very much amused as well as somewhat frightened us by their unsailor-like manœuvres. We had Jack Frying Pan, and four stout Kroomen, to manage the boat, and they commenced a species of singing or yelling, keeping time to their oars; one improvising something in praise of one or all of their passengers, and the others coming in with the chorus.

The scene, as we near the town, is very pretty. On our right is Cape Mesurado, a lofty promontory, stretching a long distance into the ocean, covered from base to summit with trees of most luxuriant foliage; peeping out from amongst them, at the very top, is the white lighthouse, looking very pretty from amidst the surrounding trees. Back of the Cape lies the town; we can scarcely see it from the water. On our left, stretches a long line of low, sandy beach, with here and there a stately palm-tree lifting up its head, looking even more tall from the surrounding flatness. Immediately in front of us is a narrow beach, on which the Kroo-town is situated, the mouth of the St. Paul's River coming into the ocean just at its side. Back of the town thick foliage again appears, while between the shore and ourselves extend a long line of breakers, looking very beautiful, indeed; but when we recollect that they lie between us and the land, and that we must pass through them 'ere we reach it—and imagination portrays to us a good ducking, if nothing worse—we could readily dispense with the additional beauty they add to the scene. But here they come now; sit still—keep quiet. There! we can but admire the skill with which we have been piloted over those enormous breakers, without even a sprinkle. And, look! there are crowds of men, women and children on the shore to greet us: many of them, in addition to their ordinary attire of a simple cloth around the loins, having a string of beads, or a piece of string, with from one to eight leopard's teeth attached, worn around the neck. Many of the women, too, consider themselves very much ornamented by white stripes on the face and body, formed with a species of pipe-clay. It, however, serves to make them look ghastly. There! our boat is aground, and we are about twenty yards from the shore. Our boatmen spring out into the water, and shouting, "Come, daddy—come, mammy," lift us, with apparently the same ease that we would a little child, and carry us on shore. It was amusing too, to see tall men, like our gentlemen, carried in the arms like overgrown babies—and our first salutations to the shores of Africa were merry peals of laughter. How different to the sensations we thought would pervade our minds when we should first set foot on that darkened land, where we all expected to suffer sickness, weariness, toil and privation, if not death—hoping to aid in her redemption! But a sense of the ludicrous, for the time, overcame all other feeling. The Kroo-town here is a collection of houses, placed without regard to regularity or order; they are small houses, about sixteen to twenty feet square, the sides formed of plaited bamboo, with branches of the plantain laid on to form the roof: the roof overhanging all round, so as to throw off the water. In some houses there is an attempt to form a piazza. The door being quite low, you are compelled to stoop very much to enter. This door serves as chimney and window, as well as door. We passed through the town, followed by troops of men, women and children, and climbing up a steep hill, entered Monrovia. Mr. Wilson had come to meet us, but somehow he had missed us; soon, however, we saw his bright, beaming countenance, and felt the cordial pressure of his hand. Poor man! he was alone; his wife and child had been compelled for a time to leave him, to seek health in their native clime; and his colleague, the Rev. Mr. Williams, had lately had a very severe illness, on which account he had gone on a short voyage. On the top of the hill stands the city of Monrovia, the capital of Liberia. The houses are disconnected from each other; and, whether built of brick, stone, wood or plaster, are all very much defaced by the effects of the climate. The streets are very broad, and covered with grass; but having no horses or vehicles of any kind, there is nothing to destroy it. There is no such thing as a paving-stone to be seen; so in walking through the streets you are like walking through a beautiful green field, shaded by the orange, cocoa-nut, plantain and banana trees, that grow in the gardens. Mr. James met us: he is a colored gentleman, one of the first missionaries in Liberia. (When I use the word gentleman, I use it in its true acceptation, meaning an educated and refined man; and the true Christian is always a gentleman. He has charge of the school here, and he conducted us to his house. Mr. Wilson boards with him. This house, which is a sample of many, is built of rough, unhewn stone, like some of our old-fashioned country churches. You enter by the front door into a large room, used as a dining-room. The floors of all the rooms are covered with matting. Close to the front door, as you enter, there is a narrow staircase that leads up to the parlor. The staircase never has any carpeting. The parlor is a large room, plainly but neatly furnished, always with a broad piazza in front. The bedrooms all open out of the parlor, from which they are divided by plain, wooden partitions, sometimes painted, but more frequently without either paint or whitewash. Generally, there are no rooms below, except the dining-room and offices, as it is preferable to sleep and live as high from the ground as possible. The people here dress very handsomely.

We went with Mr. Wilson to see his house, where he lives: it is the mission-house; but having no lady there, he and his colleague take their meals at Mr. James,' though they live at the mission-house. It made us feel very sad when we went into the bedroom, to see the little vacant crib, (its dear little occupant having gone home with its mother in pursuit of health), and to remember that we should have no dear little pets in Africa, as no white child can live here. And I think we at the North show a far stronger aversion to the colored race than even the Southerners do. Many of us would far rather kiss and fondle an ugly little black dog, than we would bestow the same kindnesses on a little human being, endowed with an immortal soul, which we hope and pray may live with us forever in eternity, because that human being is of a different color from ourselves. How strange, how inconsistent is man!

This is the warmest season of the year, the thermometer at ninety-two; it rarely exceeds that, but we have a most refreshing sea-breeze. The climate of this country is very even, rarely exceeding ninety-two, and never hardly going below seventy-two. After being again most cordially welcomed, and made to feel at home, Mr. Wilson brought us some oranges; they were larger than any I had ever seen, but as green as the greenest apple, yet perfectly ripe. They were very delicious. No fruit must be eaten here after sunset; it is considered unwholesome. At dinner-time we again adjourned to Mr. James'. We had an excellent dinner—the table beautifully laid—plenty of silver, napkins, &c. Two little boy-natives waited at table, and did it exceedingly well. The natives are becoming civilized, by being servants; and they are quite willing to act as such, even for very small pay, as they obtain in that way much better food than they do at home. We had many different kinds of vegetables, all new and strange to me, but I thought them all good; for after so many weeks of seafare, everything tasted nice. About five o'clock we returned to the ship, as we did not wish to remain on shore after dusk. Sleeping on shore one night is enough to give the fever, and we did not wish to take it till our arrival at our own homes; but a good night's rest on shore was a great temptation. We had to be carried in the same way from the shore to the boat that we had been in the morning. We reached the vessel greatly tired, but very much pleased with our reception, and I hope with hearts filled with gratitude to our heavenly Father.

KROO PHILOSOPHY.—Mr. Wilson came on board early this morning, and brought us a quantity of limes and oranges. He looks very unhealthy; but says his appearance is a fair specimen of all the whites we would see on the coast. He and Mrs. Ogden sang very sweetly together.

I asked one of our Kroomen (who spoke a little English), *Jim Upside-Down,* " How many wives have you, Jim ?" He answered, " O, me five, mammy." " That's wrong, Jim; you ought to have but one. God's book says man have one wife." " Oh, mammy, that no country fash.* S'pose now, mammy, me but one wife; she be cross sometime; she have palaver;† she no cook me my rice; what I do den? But s'pose I go have tree, four wives; the first one be cross, den 'noder cook me my rice." Such is their philosophy. A man's wealth and position in society is estimated by *the number* of his wives.

SUNDAY.—We went on shore to church to-day. Our own little place of worship being closed, we went to the Presbyterian—our ministers, who were on board, preaching. We were all very kindly invited to Dr. McGill's to dinner—Mr. Wilson to be with us. In the church, the

* Fashion, custom.   † Quarrel, dispute; serious talk about anything.

colored clergyman, the Rev. Mr. Henning, read the hymns beautifully, and offered the closing prayer. His prayer was excellent. Sitting in that little church, this morning, after passing through the disgusting scenes of Kroo-town, as I saw the decent and well-dressed congregation, and compared them with those we had just seen, I could only think, "What hath God wrought!" Though white ladies are great strangers here, yet there was no staring, no looking round, but as devout behaviour as I have ever seen in the house of God. As I glanced through the window, and saw many of the poor, half-naked savages passing along, and then looked inside, the tears coursed down my cheeks. I had to lean my head down, and to thank God, oh! how heartily, that He had granted to me, one so vile and feeble, the glorious privilege of coming forth to bear the "lamp of life" to these poor darkened ones. I thought, if our dear friends at home could only see all we had seen to-day, instead of mourning our loss, their very philanthropy or love to humanity (if their love to God and His glory, and the eternal welfare of immortal souls, would not do it,) would make them willing that their loved ones, as missionaries, like Howard, should have the glorious privilege of helping to restore and elevate the human race. After service, the people crowded round us, to shake hands, and thank us for coming among them to help them. We were very much pleased with Dr. McGill and family. The Doctor received his education partly in England. He is considered a very efficient and able physician. He and his family are quite light-colored. After service we again went on board. So ended our first Sunday in Africa.

Our gentlemen have commenced their labors. God grant that faithfully and truly they may preach and teach Christ crucified.

Dr. McGill is a gentleman, and his house, in all particulars, well appointed.

SCHOOLS.—Two of us went on shore to-day. We visited the school under the care of Miss Williams. (She is a young colored lady, attached to our mission, a cousin of Dr. McGill.) She has a very nice school; about fifty bright, intelligent-looking children, all shades of color, from pure white (at which I was much surprised) to the most jetty black. In their spelling, little ones of seven years of age were spelling long words, such as "hydrostatics," &c.

We then went to the high school. It was the time of the school examination, previous to breaking up for the holidays. They were here being examined in grammar, and the children did great credit both to themselves and their teacher.

We then called on Mrs. Crummel. Her husband is one of our colored clergymen. She is very dark, but a lady in mind and manners. Indeed, we have been very much surprised at the good breeding of all we have met here. Rev. Mr. Crummel was educated partly at Cambridge, England, and she was with him there. They mixed in the best society; indeed, they received great attention there.

THE DRIVER.—To-day I made an acquaintance which I could very readily have dispensed with. It was the

African ant, called the *driver*. They seem formed to be the scavengers of Africa. They devour everything of the animal kind that is already dead, and even attack the largest living animals, when at all disabled, eating them up entirely, and leaving nothing but well-cleaned bones. Rats, mice, and all small vermin, have no chance with them. If they once enter the house, the human beings have to desert it; and then they never leave it till every living thing of every kind is entirely demolished. A poor man was left here a short time ago, sick in bed, and shut up in a house alone for a few hours. When his friends returned, they found him dead, and almost completely eaten up. I have read that in some part of Africa it used to be the mode in which they would deal capital punishment on an offender, just to bind him and lay him out in the grass, in the track of these ants, and in a few hours his bones would be bleaching in the sun. The inhabitants here are often very glad to have a visit from the *drivers ;* for it is only to leave the house to them for a few hours, and every species of vermin is destroyed, and then they take themselves off to another quarter. I was in the garden walking, when I felt such a dreadful bite. I ran immediately into the house, and I found four of them upon me; and by what they made me suffer in those few minutes, I could readily imagine how possible it was for thousands of them to destroy any living thing. They are about half an inch long, a dark brown, their fore claws resembling those of a lobster; and with these they can make you feel. I have no desire to renew my personal acquaintance with them.

Miss Killpatric.—Miss Killpatric, an Irish lady, a missionary of the Methodist Church, who has a school at a station up the St. Paul's river, about twenty miles from here, having received letters, and hearing of our arrival, came down to see and welcome us. She said it did her so much good to see faces from home.

All missionaries are truly, and indeed, one family. So isolated from all the world, they love the more dearly those whom they may meet far, far away from home. They all have the same hopes, and fears, and aims; the same joys and sorrows; the same labors and rewards, and they "love as brethren." We asked her to come and spend the day on board with us to-morrow.

The next day I had a very bad headache, and was quite sick. I could not enjoy Miss Killpatric's society in consequence. I suppose we went about too much in the sun yesterday. Mr. Wilson slept on board. How pleasantly he talks, and encourages us in the prospect of our work; but he gives us such strict charges to be careful about our health. God give us hearts to labor.

Sail Again.—Mr. Wilson slept on board again last night, and we weighed anchor this morning, after sending him ashore. Our company, I believe, has cheered his loneliness. He had been threatened with an attack of fever, but now feels a little better. He had recently received a letter telling him they were hourly expecting the death of Mrs. Payne. She is dying of consumption. She has been a faithful laborer here for eighteen years, and now she is joyfully anticipating her home. Probably, ere we anchor, her little bark will be safely moored in the *harbor* of eternal rest.

We see many Kroomen out fishing. The captain bought some fish to-day; they were as small as flat-fish but somewhat the shape of a mackerel, of a beautiful coral color, and delicious flavor. I could not learn their name.

Chapter Third.

CAPE PALMAS.

THE breeze has freshened. We may possibly arrive at home to-day; *home*, it will be for some time, possibly, my *long home*. Some of the Kroomen who came alongside told us Mrs. Payne died last Friday—sad news for us, but her home is now in the skies.

About three o'clock we anchored off Cape Palmas, but full two hours before we dropped anchor, a Krooman brought a note to Miss Ball from Mr. Hoffman, saying he " hoped the vessel now in sight might prove to be the Ocean Eagle; we were expected in her; and if so, he begged warmly to welcome us, and state how long and anxiously they had been looking for us, and how much they would rejoice at our arrival." None but those that have been circumstanced as we were, can know the feelings we experienced at receiving such greetings. Mr. Hoffman is our missionary at Cape Palmas. For some time, in addition to all his other duties, he has had charge of the Girls' Orphan Asylum. I hope we may relieve him of some of his cares. My labor, for the present, will be among the Liberians, who are mostly liberated slaves, and their children; a class of people in whom I feel deeply interested. The Orphan Asylum is not for the natives, but exclusively for the orphans of Liberians. I am to be their teacher. For my own part, I am willing to labor wherever the Bishop shall see fit to place me.

About four o'clock we bid adieu to our ocean home and started for the shore. But who shall tell the agitation of our feelings as we felt that now, indeed, we were about to enter on our glorious work—that we were privileged to lend our feeble aid for the redemption of Africa? Cape Palmas runs out into a point, and the Orphan Asylum is situated directly on the point. It is beautifully located. The point is very high, but you can descend to the water's edge by a winding path formed in the rugged rocks; at the base of the point these rocks jut out in broken pieces into the sea, the waves forever foaming and bursting upon them. As we neared the shore, we saw the girls from the Asylum run down the path, on to one of the higher portions of the rock, and stand watching our approach, and when we came near enough they began to sing some songs of welcome, waving to us, and some of them dancing up and down in their delight at our arrival. The landing was some little distance further along the beach. There Mr. Hoffman was waiting for us, who gave us such a warm greeting he made us feel at home at once. With him was the Rev. Mr. Gibson, one of our colored clergymen; he is a very fine man. He very politely offered me his arm to help me up the hill. We Northerners, who are so bitterly opposed to the oppression of the Africans, by our proud reserve and hauteur, wound the feelings of the free educated black much more than the lash does that of the slave. There is no reason that we should become amalgamationists, but we should treat every one as our fellow man, and a gentleman, as such, no matter of what country or clime he is.

When we reached the Asylum the children were all ranged in a row, to receive us, looking so delighted and happy. When we entered our room there were flowers beautifully arranged and everything speaking a welcome to us. Mr. Hoffman sent off a note immediately to inform the Bishop of our arrival. Cavalla, the station where he resides, is about twelve miles from here, beyond the boundaries of Liberia, entirely in the heathen territory.

Church.—After tea, feeling much refreshed, Miss Ball and myself went out to church with Mr. Hoffman. Wednesday evening, being lecture-night, Miss Hogan felt too fatigued to go with us. The little church is quite half a mile from the Asylum, and it seemed a long walk, particularly as there is a very steep hill to climb. The cape is joined to the main land by a sort of isthmus, quite narrow in some places, so that we hear the constant beat of the waves on the rocks, during our walk.

How beautiful our church service seemed that night, and I do think there were some grateful hearts there. How we wished our friends at home could have known of our arrival, that they might have joined with us in the grateful song of praise. After service, our colored friends crowded around us to give us their welcomes and congratulations. May our lives here testify our *gratitude* for God's mercies.

THE ASYLUM.—Though we had thought it would be so delightful to sleep on shore, yet we were all too much excited; but our coffee refreshed us much this morning. There is coffee enough grown here for home consumption, and it is far superior to any I have ever tasted. They are in hopes soon to raise enough to export. I am sure it would bring a good price.

I find we are on a lovely spot. The cape is a high promontory, running out into the water quite a distance, and the land to the right, forming part of a circle, makes a very pretty bay—a small river from inland opening into this bay—across that river and along the shore are several little Kroo-towns, with a background of dense foliage. Immediately back of the Asylum, which stands by the side of the lighthouse, on the brow of the hill, and has a splendid look-out to sea, are a number of the houses of the colonists, with their little gardens in good cultivation, (we have a fine garden at the Asylum.) Then comes the isthmus, a very rocky, sandy bit of land—a Krootown used to stand there, but since the late war between the colonists and the natives, the natives have been compelled to remove the town across the river. It was a great annoyance, as the church standing on the other side of this little neck of land, where it is more thickly peopled, those who lived on the point were always obliged to pass through the town to go to church; and this, on a Sunday, was particularly disagreeable, as they disliked that their children should witness the fearful desecration of the Sabbath. It is pleasanter now, it is removed. We have a number of cocoa-nut and other trees around the house, but it having been so recently constructed (indeed, it is not quite

Orphan Asylum and Lighthouse.

finished yet), they are younger and fewer than we could wish, but that a little time will remedy.

We were awakened very early this morning by a loud talking and jabbering outside our window. Upon looking out upon what we should call our back-yard, what a strange sight presented itself! about a dozen men, women and children, hanging about, talking as fast and as loud as possible. Though the adults always wear a cloth around their loins, the children, until the age of twelve or fourteen, rarely, if ever, wear anything at all upon their persons, save at times a string of beads or a string of grass around their loins, or neck, sometimes with one, two or three leopard's teeth attached. In the yard were several women beating rice; this is the chief food here, and among the poorer classes they have little else, both colonists and natives. For beating the rice they have large wooden mortars, and two women stand on opposite sides with very thick heavy pestles, with which they beat. After this it is emptied into large basket sieves, and tossed, for the wind to blow away the chaff. There being so many to feed in this house, the work is going on the most of the time. Besides these, there were other women carrying stone for the completion of the building—all burdens are borne on the head.

We received very kind notes from the Bishop and Miss Williford to-day. They pleaded excessive fatigue, and sadness consequent on their recent bereavement, as an excuse for not coming to meet us; but hoped, as the next week was to be the school examination at Cavalla, we would go down there, and we should receive the warmest welcome.

We have arrived in good season. The children in all the schools have a public examination half-yearly, at Christmas and midsummer, and then they have holiday for three weeks, and those who have homes or friends visit them at that time if they wish.

Mr. T. Thompson, a young colored man who is studying for the ministry, has been teaching the girls here in the absence of any ladies, but he is very glad to resign his charge, as he is very anxious to pursue his studies. The holidays just commencing, I shall have a little time to get my things straight before school duties begin. All our friends from on board ship spent the day here today. The missionaries all along the coast have learnt the injunction to " use hospitality one to another, without grudging."

Miss Ball has left us to go to her home at Cavalla, where she is much needed. She went in a hammock—this is the usual mode of conveyance. A long pole, to which the hammock is swung, is borne on the heads of two of the natives—a flat piece of wood being fastened to the ends of the pole, where it rests on the head—under this, however, they first place a sort of pad, formed of leaves. I should think it a very unpleasant mode of conveyance, as you must all the time feel as if you are making beasts of burden of your fellow-creatures. The Bishop and Mr. Hoffman have each of them had a horse made a present to them. But, poor things, they suffer, too, as well as human beings in this climate. At present they are going through their acclimation, and must be used very tenderly.

Our morning and evening worship is held in the

school-room; and a bell being rung, some of the natives always come in—sometimes it is one and sometimes it is another—and they always behave with great propriety. A number of them are Christians. Truly, the field here is white for the harvest; and we must pray more faithfully that "the Lord of the harvest will send forth more laborers into His harvest." Mr. Hoffman has a service every Friday at Mount Vaughan, about three miles from here. The two gentlemen from on board the ship are gone with him to-day. Mrs. Ogden is with us, helping us to get our rooms a little in order. The other ladies have not come on shore to-day. The house is constantly crowded with natives. One woman has come to "dash" us a fowl (to dash, is to present); but they always expect to receive, in a few days, a *dash* in return, far more valuable than the one they present. The animals of all kinds here are very diminutive; there are very few cattle, or domestic animals, of any sort. Mr. Hoffman has a cow; neither cows nor bullocks are larger than Shetland ponies; but they are very pretty. The calves are not larger than good-sized spaniels; they come from the Mandingo country. The chickens, also, are very small.

We are trying to get a little to rights, but the things from the ship come on shore very slowly. My matting has just arrived, and two of the native men are putting it down for me. They do it very nicely. They are Christians—Scott and Eastburn. As I look round, those words constantly come up: "What hath God wrought!" May I labor diligently in this vineyard. But I already feel the effects of the climate—such lassitude and debility, as if I could hardly stand or move. This must be shaken off; it will never do to give way to it. But I believe my long and severe illness on shipboard has enfeebled me very much, instead of the voyage invigorating me.

OUR PETS.—Miss Hogan and myself have each selected one of the elder girls to be our attendant, in our own rooms, and we shall, in return, teach them the lighter and finer kinds of work—nice needlework, &c., &c. They are both members of the Church, and very good girls. *Artee*, Miss Hogan's attendant, is a very pretty, light-colored girl. She stood as godmother, a few Sundays ago, for a little infant (the child of a native Christian) who was baptized. She seems thoroughly to understand her duty. *Julia*, my girl, is very black, but very good-natured, and understands the Grebo language; and I want her to go with me as interpreter to the native towns, which I hope, if God gives me health and strength, often to visit.

Mr. Hoffman called me out of my room this morning; he had something to tell me he knew would make my heart glad, or, as the natives express it, " make my heart lay down." He told me that the boy who is supported by our Sunday-school, and to whom we had given the name of Christopher Lippet Paddock, had appeared for a long time to be deeply serious; indeed, he could not doubt of his being really a Christian. He is now very desirous of baptism; and Mr. Hoffman thinks him a very suitable subject, in every way fitted for the reception of the sacred rite. Two others, from the same station, are to be baptized to-morrow with him (the station he is at is about five miles off), here at our little church, St. Mark's. It is his wish and Mr. Hoffman's that I should stand with him, as one of his witnesses. How pleasant this will be—my first Sunday at my African home. Is it not good news for our Sunday-school? May God enlarge their hearts and their means more and more in this good work.

Mr. Hoffman has also two little pets here, which he has taken expressly, he says, for Miss Hogan and myself to take care of. They are two little boys, about five years old. *Wah* is a little deaf mute, but so bright; he is a brother to the little deaf and dumb boy Mr. Hoffman sent to America, and who is now in the asylum, under the care of Mr. Peet. The other, *Dayo*, is a little Grebo boy, the son of the head man of a town about six miles from here. Often Mr. Hoffman had noticed him when he would preach in that town. At length the child appeared to become very much attached to Mr. Hoffman; and one day he followed him, and would not leave him. And the father willingly giving his consent, Mr. Hoffman brought him home with him, where he has since remained. He is a regular negro—flat nose, thick lips, &c.—very ugly; but he is a dear little fellow, very gentle and docile. Miss Hogan said she liked *Wah* best; so she has taken him for her boy, and I have taken *Dayo*. He cannot yet speak a word of English; so I have everything to teach him. May grace be given, that he may be trained up for God. Strange to say, the children, too, have specially attached themselves to us, as if they knew of our arrangement. Perhaps, unwittingly, there may be a difference in our manner to them. I cannot find a minute in the daytime to write home; I have to do it after I retire for the night. A bad habit, this, in a climate where we require so much rest.

SUNDAY.—We could perceive it was Sunday morning, even before we were out of bed—the deep calm of a Sabbath morn, instead of the clatter of other days, prevailing. Nothing now was to be heard but the breaking of the surf upon the rocks, at the base of our mount. We had prayers, at which a great many of the natives attended. I like Mr. Hoffman's plan of conducting prayers so much. In the morning, after singing a hymn, he repeats a verse of Scripture, and makes a few remarks on it; then each one present repeats a verse in rotation, and he makes a few remarks on each. In this way the children acquire an immense amount of Scripture knowledge. At evening worship, he selects a portion of Scripture and explains it. We breakfasted at eight. Immediately after which, Mr. Hoffman went off to preach, or teach, in one native town, and Mr. Thompson, our colored teacher, who is preparing for the ministry, and boards with us, went to another. At half-past nine all the children collected in the school-room, neatly dressed, where they practiced different hymns and chants till it was time to proceed to church.

Our friends from the vessel met us, and together we went to church, which is a long walk in the heat of the day in this sultry clime. It is not so hot as we frequently have it in America, but there appears to be something very debilitating in the atmosphere, that oppresses one with a constant feeling of weariness. Our church is very small, and much crowded; it needs enlarging very much. Two schools of native boys attend here; one from Hoffman station, directly across the river, under the charge of George Harris, a native, who is studying for the ministry—a very fine man; the other a school five miles off (they walk in every Sunday to church). As yet it has only six boys, three of whom are to be baptized to-day. Their teacher is a native—John Farr. Thus these *first fruits* are beginning to sow the seeds of a glorious harvest.

The dress of these boys, as of most native Christians, consists of a shirt of colored cotton, and a strip of printed calico about a yard and a half long, the full width of the calico. This is neatly bound with some bright color, and tucked in round the waist, hanging down to the knees, or below. The teachers, and others, as they advance in civilization, assume more the dress and appearance of Christians. How exquisitely beautiful appeared our services to-day. It would be impossible to describe my feelings when I went forward to stand as the chosen witness of one who had lately been brought "out of darkness into marvellous light"—one whom our own Sunday-school had been the means, under God, of placing in his present position, as "a child of God, an inheritor of eternal life." The candidates do not yet thoroughly understand English. The service, and its nature, had been previously thoroughly explained to them in Grebo, and the questions were put to them by their teacher (as Mr. Hoffman's interpreter), who stood as one of their witnesses, in that language; and the answers were given most slowly and distinctly, in the same. "May God perfect the good work thus begun in them." C. L. Paddock is about fourteen, a fine, nice-looking boy, of great promise. The other two are older; they, also, are very fine boys; but I shall always be likely to take a warmer interest in Paddock. I feel as if this had been one of the happiest days of my life. Nothing would tempt me to return home. I hope, if it is God's will, to live, and yes, to die in Africa! In the afternoon we went to Sunday-school. Every alternate Sunday Mr. Hoffman preaches over the river, in the afternoon, at Hoffman station. His labors are very great. In the evening, Mr. Gibson (our colored clergyman) preached a most excellent sermon; and so finished our first Sunday in our new home. Walking to that church three times a day is too much. I hardly know whether I am really ill, or whether it is only the effects of the climate on me already. I must fight against it; but my head aches all the time, and a constant aching pain in my limbs troubles me; but I must not complain.

We are still busy getting our rooms in order, but we have such constant interruptions. We, each of us, have a nice large room, very airy; they all open on a fine piazza, that runs all around the house. These piazzas are not only great luxuries, but they are absolute necessities in this hot climate. We feel completely at home, and amongst warm friends. Every day we receive a kind note from the Bishop, or one of the ladies at Cavalla, inquiring of our welfare. Each morning, directly after prayers, Julia brings *Dayo* up into my room, and I am trying to begin my instruction to him, she interpreting to him for me. This morning I made her tell

The Devil-House, Cape Palmas, W. Af.

him that the great God who made him lives in heaven; and that he must pray to him to take care of him. I then made him kneel down beside me, and say after me, "Pray, God, take care of *Dayo*, and make him a good boy." Julia explained to him what he was doing, and the meaning of the words. I made him repeat this over several times, till he could pronounce each word right. I then got a picture book, and showed him a horse, dog, &c., till he knew several words. Such was my first lesson, which I hope to repeat, a little at a time, several times a day.

HOFFMAN STATION.—Our friends came from the ship to go across the river to visit Hoffman station, where Harris resides. The captain kindly lent us his boat, and we soon reached what Mr. Hoffman calls his flower garden, "buds of promise," both literally and spiritually. Harris has a very pretty little house, surrounded by a most beautiful flower garden, arranged with excellent taste. There is a native town close by, from which the boys are collected in school. We first went into Harris's house. His wife is a deeply pious, devoted woman. She was a native, educated at the girls' school at Cavalla; she collects the women from the town on Sunday afternoon, and once in the week, to teach them the things pertaining to God; and at other times she teaches them to sew. She is doing a great work among them. After paying a short visit to Sophia (Harris's wife), we went to the boys' school, followed everywhere by a tribe of women and children. About thirty boys were here, all natives, conning their lessons under the care of another teacher, also a native, whom Harris has occasionally to assist him. They read very well, both in English and Grebo, and recited their lessons in English. Mr. Jack then asked them many questions in Bible history, through an interpreter, and we were all much astonished at their aptness, and the extent of their information. We have been constantly surprised at the state of progress and improvement going on. It must have been a work of pure, implicit faith in the first labors here; but so much of the fruits can be seen, that though still a work of faith, yet now there is abundant evidence of the result. From the school we proceeded to the native town. This is a cluster of huts, from one to two hundred in number, perfectly circular, varying in size from fifty to a hundred feet in circumference; the roof rises into a perfect cone, thatched with the long branches of the banana, plantain, and bamboo; these are from twelve to twenty feet high at the highest point. The roof extends several feet beyond the sides of the hut. The floor is made of clay, beaten very hard and smooth, and generally kept very clean and neat. In the centre of the hut are three short, upright pillars, formed of hard clay, about a foot high, put very close together: these form a triangle, between which the fire is placed, which is seldom extinguished; and on these their iron pot (their only cooking utensil) rests—the smoke, after circulating freely about the hut, at length finds its way out by the door. Some of the more wealthy will have one or two boxes or chests, and a low chair, strangely constructed. They sleep on mats, with a block of wood for a pillow. These blocks serve for seats, in the day, and the mats are then put up on a sort of rack, made under the roof, where, also, they generally have a pile of wood stored away. Those of the richer part, too, will have a quantity of pitchers, dishes, plates, &c., hung round the sides of the hut; they have a way of boring a hole through the plates, &c., without cracking them, and then, passing a string through them, they can readily hang them up. We went into several huts, and were struck by the cleanliness prevailing everywhere, both inside and outside. If there is any litter or rubbish allowed to accumulate, the woman receives the name of a bad housekeeper. The women all expressed pleasure at seeing us, coming out of their huts to shake hands, and hoping we would come often to visit them. At a little distance, their towns resemble a large field of hayricks. There is a nice little church going up here, of which Harris, I believe, is to be the pastor, after he is ordained. At present, Mr. Hoffman and Mr. Gibson alternate in preaching to the natives, wherever they can collect them. After our return, I went off and slept on board ship; Mrs. Ogden persuaded me, she felt so very lonely—so, far away from all our friends and loved ones, we became very much attached to each other, and we were very happy together on board.

DAILY LIFE.—We came on shore very early this morning; the gentlemen going with Mr. Hoffman to Spring Hill, the station at which Paddock resides. Mr. Hoffman goes there once a fortnight, to examine and instruct the boys, and to preach in the towns. Though the missionary's work is one of love, yet it is a *labor* of love. The captain has been very kind to us, in helping us put up our bedsteads, and unpacking our furniture, &c. In fact, from the commencement of our voyage, he has shown us every kindness and attention in his power.

When I came home this morning, Mr. Hoffman and Mr. Thompson both welcomed me as warmly as if I had been an old member of the family, away for a long time. Mr. Hoffman thanked the captain for his care of me, &c., as if it was really his charge now to look after us, and care for us; and I believe he feels so. God has given us a new home and family circle. In the evening, Mr. Hoffman went to preach at Mount Vaughan; Mr. Thompson conducted family worship: he appears to be a very serious and devout young man.

Mrs. Ogden comes on shore every day, to give the children singing lessons. They are improving very much; and she has promised, while we are away, to continue her instructions. I find I love her more each day; it will be hard to say "good-bye" when the vessel leaves, but it will be a week or two, first. These partings are very painful, but so it ever must be. I sometimes think it would be good for missionaries to be possessed of a cool, calm, impassible nature, and then they would not suffer so much by the rupturing of these ties; but, so far as I have seen, they are all warm, ardent, and endowed with very strong affections—better so, perhaps, else they never would gain the love of those poor souls whom they seek to win.

Chapter Fourth.

CAVALLA.

The examination of the girls' school is to take place to-morrow, at Cavalla, so we started this afternoon for that place. Our fellow-passengers did not go with us, though the Bishop cordially invited them, as they dare not sleep on shore; so we started, Miss Hogan, Mr. Hoffman, and myself, each in a hammock, borne on the heads of two men, with two others for each hammock, to relieve. Besides these, there was a company of about twenty men and boys, carrying loads down for the Bishop. Our road lay, for about nine miles, along a narrow ledge of sand, thrown up between the ocean and a beautiful fresh-water lake. In some places this sand, that divides the two waters, would not be more than a hundred yards in width; in others, it would be nearly half-a mile. The sand is very fine, dry, and loose, which makes it very hard travelling, as the foot sinks into it at each step. The easiest mode of reaching Cavalla would be by the lake, if there were boats; but there are only the canoes of the natives, and they are rather dangerous, and, unless you have a very large one, you are sure to get wet—and at this season of the year the natives use them fishing. I wish I could give a correct description of the scene, as we journeyed along.

On the one side the sea rolling in, with a heavy surf, the spray dashing high in the air, and forming myriads of tiny rainbows; on the other side of us, the calm, beautiful lake, varying in width from half to three-quarters of a mile; on the opposite shore the hills forming a beautiful background, covered with the most luxuriant vegetation, crowned with the loftiest palm-trees. (All my preconceived notions of Africa, as a dead, level, sandy plain, have completely vanished.) Then imagine ourselves riding in very uncomfortable but truly picturesque style, followed by a number of men, women, and children—our train changing occasionally, as we passed through or by the different towns, one set being tired of gazing at us, and making room for others to take a peep, and satisfy their curiosity. Hammock travelling is decidedly uncomfortable; we were very tired remaining so long in one position. The reception we met with on our arrival was such as would have warmed the coldest heart, and cheered and revived the most home-sick, which we were very far from being. The mission-house and church, and school-houses, all stand within one enclosure. Here the Bishop has a beautiful flower-garden, and in one corner of this, those who have laid down their lives here, sweetly "sleep in Jesus." The church is a very pretty little building; it is not yet finished, although service is regularly conducted in it, in the Grebo language. The boys' school-house is in course of building, also. The one they at present occupy is in very bad condition, and very unsafe. The whole of these premises are literally in a grove of cocoanut trees, which give a most delightful shade, as well as looking so beautiful, and being so useful. Most of them were planted by the hands of the Bishop. A great part of the work, in the construction of the church and school-house, has been the labors of the Christian natives, under the direction of some colonist carpenters, masons, &c. Just back of the mission-house is the Christian village, on the mission premises. This is a collection of houses, built somewhat in American style, where the Christian boys who have been educated in the school, having married Christian girls, reside. They, all of them, have some trade, or means of earning a livelihood, and here they live very comfortably. These little houses are very clean and neat, with many articles of American manufacture in them—tables, chairs, &c., &c. May this be the beginning of a mighty city, where Christ shall be king. There are five native towns surrounding the mission premises, the huts coming up to the very gates, so the Bishop is directly in the midst of his people; and may the Christianity there exhibited be like leaven, "which shall leaven the whole lump." The Bishop and Miss Williford look very unwell.

The house is full of natives, all the while coming and going. They come in, sit awhile, shake hands, and stare at you, or, as they say, "look you," and go away again. The doors are never shut till ten at night, and they are allowed to come and go as they please. The Bishop hopes it may tend to elevate them, even to observe our customs and manners. The only time you can be sure of being alone is when you are eating. Their "country fashion" is never to look at a person when eating; therefore, at that time they always leave.

LEPERS.—I have seen a great many lepers in Africa. They are most disgusting objects, poor things! The flesh turns white in spots, and then the joints gradually rot off. The disease is not as painful as many others. At the time a joint drops off the place is sore for a little while; that is all. There is one man, who comes a great deal to the Asylum, who has lost all his fingers and toes. He is a pitiable object. This disease is hereditary but not infectious.

CAVALLA EXAMINATION.—The girls' school was examined to-day, and I had no idea that these poor degraded natives had such power and capacities, which only need developing. They have very powerful memories—their proficiency in grammar astonished me. There was one little class of four girls that had only been in the school about six months, who could read in the Grebo Testament, and spell hard words, and are learning to read in English. They have been taught by a native teacher. It is almost incredible, but their memories are excellent. The girls' school-house is a separate building, but close by the side of the mission-house. The school-house is very nicely fitted up, owing to the kindness and liberality of friends at home; and there are many nice maps around the walls. It is a very large room, and it is used for Sunday evening and week evening services. Back of the school-room is a large eating room, with two long tables and benches. And the matron's little room is here also, so that she may be always near the girls. Mrs. Gillet, the assistant teacher in the school, is also the matron. She is a native woman,

but a most trustworthy, devoted Christian, and has the
temporal and spiritual interests of the girls at heart.
Over the school-room is the dormitory. It is divided off
into a number of rooms. There is a bedstead in each
room for the larger girls, but they seldom use it—pre-
ferring to sleep on the floor with the others. They each
have a mat and a blanket; these must be neatly rolled
up and put away in the daytime.

THE FEAST.—On the day of the girls' examination
the Bishop generally has a feast prepared, of which all
the school children, boys and girls, the Christian villagers, and head men of the town, and the native
Christians, are invited to partake. The carpenters with
their boards had prepared a sort of table, that reached a
long distance on the grass, under the cocoanut trees.
We stood on the piazza watching the scene. It was exceedingly pleasant, yet very grotesque. On the table
was a profusion of such things as they like best: rice,
palm-butter, cassadas, salt beef, some salt fish, plantains,
cocoanuts and bananas. There were long benches set on
either side. But it was pleasant to see here the courte-
ousness and politeness that Christianity bestows; the
natives from the town huddled in, men and women,
each striving who first could obtain a seat. The men
and women from the Christian village walked quietly up,
arm in arm (almost the only time I ever saw them do
that, by the way,) to the table, and the men saw that
their ladies were seated before themselves, with every
mark of politeness. The old men from the towns were
dressed in all sorts of costumes. Some with old coats

with brass buttons, and a black beaver hat; this last, with a bright colored umbrella, is the height of their ambition; if they only have these things they are " proper gentlemen." One man had a cloth around his loins, and over this an old coat of a navy captain, with the buttons and epaulettes, and a commodore's hat. He did think himself fine, and he strutted about, the envy of all beholders. Others had long red, yellow, or blue gowns, made like a flannel gown, down to the feet; some with all these colors, in stripes—they could be seen at a distance. Many, both men and women, had heavy brass armlets and anklets, sometimes as many as a dozen on the arm or leg; these clinking together made a great noise as they walked. (Many of the little children, also, wear these, in default of any other dress.) The Bishop asked a blessing, and then they all fell to, like hungry wolves; probably many of them had tasted nothing before that day, as they often have but one meal a day.

The influence of Christianity has done much to elevate the heathen in all the towns around. In the towns in this vicinity, the Bishop has induced them to plant cocoanuts—for though they flourish, they are not indigenous to the soil. The natives are very much attached to him—they came from thirty miles around to express their commiseration with him on the loss of his wife.

All are so kind to us, the new comers. If Christian love can make earth so happy, what must heaven be, where there is no discordant or jarring sound permitted to enter?

Boys' Examination.—The boys were examined to-day, and presents distributed to the children of both schools. The boys' examination, like the girls', was excellent; Miss Ball had brought out a doll, dressed, for each girl—many of them had never seen such a thing, and their delight was great; even girls, seventeen and eighteen, were as delighted as the youngest child, and the dress of the dolls was a subject of great wonderment. The boys' studies were grammar, higher geography, philosophy, &c., &c. But in all the schools the Bible, and Bible history, are, of course, the principal study. To me it is truly an affecting sight, these poor heathen apparently so ready and willing to hear God's word. Oh! that " great might be the multitude of preachers," they welcome us with such warm demonstrations of pleasure; take hold of our hands and clasp them in both of theirs, and look so pleased to see us. The Bishop appears to be very unwell. I hope he is not going to be seriously ill.

Chapter Fifth.

RETURN HOME.

We returned to the Cape to-day, in the same way in which we left—in our hammocks. It was very hot in the sun. We had intended to leave Cavalla very early in the morning, but there is no such thing as hurrying the natives—they have no idea of the value of time—so we did not get started till after twelve o'clock. Think how strong they must be, to carry us, or any other heavy burden, for twelve or fourteen miles, and then return the same day, without exhibiting any symptoms of fatigue.

The Bishop appears to have signs of pleurisy, and spitting blood; the trials and fatigues he has gone through lately have completely exhausted him. They have all been advising him to take a voyage down the coast to Corisco, with our good captain. He does not doubt but that it would greatly benefit him, but fears he will not be able to leave. This atmosphere must be very injurious, for everything that is left unused for two or three days becomes coated with mildew.

On our arrival we found Mrs. Ogden giving the children a singing lesson. She is very kind, and so loveable. Mr. Ogden has received a note, by some Kroomen, from Mr. Wilson. He is so feeble that the doctor has ordered a voyage, and as he had some business for the mission

to transact at Corisco, he has concluded to go down there in the Ocean Eagle; so he will come down from Monrovia in a little sloop. And if the Bishop goes, too, they will have a pleasant little company, as Mr. Wilson and he are old friends

BAPTISM.—My journey in the heat of the sun did me no good, yesterday. I am very feverish to-day. I went to church in the morning, but had to rest quietly at home this afternoon and evening. The captain has taken our friends from the ship down in his boat to Cavalla; they started very early, so as to be in time for church. They much wished to see our mission in all its phases. A little babe, the child of George Harris, our native teacher at Hoffman Station, was baptized to-day. Miss Hogan stood as sponsor; and when, at these times, I think of our favored land, and the great neglect that oft prevails there, I fancy I hear our Saviour's words, " The Queen of the South shall rise up in judgment against this generation."

MR. WILSON'S ARRIVAL.—Very busy making rosettes out of pink and white glazed muslin, for the Sunday-school anniversary, which is to take place next Saturday. There will be about three hundred children present, from the different schools under Mr. Hoffman's supervision. He wishes rosettes made for all, as they think much of even such a trifle.

This will be a busy week to us; in fact, we have not had a moment to ourselves since our arrival, and though we appear to be doing nothing, we are learning our work.

Mr. Hoffman is attending the examination of the school at Mount Vaughan, to-day. Where the teachers are natives, and in fact in all the schools, these semi-annual examinations are absolutely necessary, to mark the progress, and to be sure that the word of God is made the basis of all that is taught. Mrs. Ogden and the Captain insisted that I should go on board with them and spend the night, thinking the sea-breeze would refresh me, which it did very much. Just after I left, Miss Ball arrived, to stay a few days with us, and attend the examination of the schools here. As we were rowing toward the vessel the Captain pointed out a distant sail. "There," said he, "that is Mr. Wilson, and after I have put you ladies on board I shall go and look after that little craft, as I know it must be very comfortless on her, and if Mr. Wilson is there, he cannot go on shore to-night, so I shall bring him on board with me." He did so, and about eight o'clock we were all at tea in the cabin. Mr. Wilson was much pleased with the captian's attention. He said the accommodations on the little sloop were very bad; he had slept on deck, as it was impossible to go below, and he had eaten ham (which he had cooked before going on board) and crackers out of a wash-bowl—forcing himself to eat, though loathing it—pleasant things these for a sick man. But missionaries expect such things, and though they feel them, they do not complain.

ASYLUM EXAMINATION.—The Captain took us on shore before prayer time this morning, as the girls at the Asylum were to pass their examination to-day. We found Miss Ball quite sick ; she had considerable trouble with her bearers, and they detained her a long time on the road, in the sun.

A number of the more respectable part of the colonists came to observe the improvement in the children. At noon we had an intermission for a time, and a lunch prepared, of which all present were invited to partake. The afternoon I spent like an uneasy spirit, wandering about from the school-room to one sick-room or the other. Mr. Wilson, Miss Ball, and the Captain, have all high fever—the effects of exposure, for the Captain over exerted himself a day or two ago, working in the sun, constructing a raft of the timber he has to leave here. He had to set to work himself to show the others how. It is very hard to be strictly prudent here, and yet we must be so.

The Bishop has come to the conclusion that it is absolutely necessary, and his duty, to take the voyage; so we expect him here to-morrow. We have the house full constantly.

THE BISHOP ARRIVES.—The boys at Hoffman Station were examined to-day. Mr. Hoffman, Miss Hogan, and our friends from the ship went. Mr. Wilson and Miss Ball were both very unwell in the night, but were better this morning, and needed a little nursing, so I am taking care of them, and trying to do a few stitches toward making some banners and flags. The Bishop arrived quite late in the evening. I opened some preserved peaches I had brought from home ; he said it was the first thing he had eaten with a relish for weeks. Any thing from home tastes good here.

CHRISTMAS EVE.—This is Christmas eve, and the weather is intensely hot, it is the warmest season of the year; we can scarcely realize it is so cold at home. The house full of company again all day. It is no small item in a missionary's expenditure, the number of guests he has to entertain. But that is one thing in which he cannot possibly curtail; it is one of his greatest pleasures, as well as his duty; and, especially with the poorer part of his visitors, he must let them see that he has a regard for their bodies, or how will they believe in his love for their souls. What a magnificent scene moonlight is in these tropical climes. I have been standing, for a time, on the piazza, no sound to break the solemn stillness but the ceaseless dash of the waves; and then I thought that on just such a night as this, eighteen hundred and fifty odd years ago, the "glad tidings of great joy" were announced to man, and I could realize the scene as I never had done before; then looking up, the graceful waving of the long leaves of the cocoanuts caught my eye, and these words came into my mind, "and all the trees of the field shall clap their hands." Oh, that multitudes of grateful hearts might everywhere respond, " The Lord is come, the Lord is come!"

CHRISTMAS DAY.—Christmas day—glorious Christmas. Oh, that some dear to me might this day be born into the kingdom of God's dear Son! and that in their hearts they might sing, "Glory to God in the highest." How sweet it is to think that all over earth's domain, from some part, throughout each hour of this day, will ascend that noble song from Christian hearts, " Glory to God," and "peace on earth," and man will join with angel choirs "to sing redeeming love," and each hour of this day, the sacred feast of the "true passover" will be celebrated by some of His faithful followers, of "every nation and kindred, people and tongue." How much such days bring loved absent ones to mind—but we shall soon meet to part no more. After writing a few warm greetings to those at home, I went out into the breakfast-room and found Mr. Wilson writing his loving remembrances to his wife and child. Miss Hogan and some of the girls went very early to see what they could do in decorating the church, but, though the shrubs and plants are green all the year round; we have no evergreens, such as those we have at home, therefore, what they did put up withered, even before the service was over.

The service was very long but I enjoyed it much. We had adult baptism, confirmation, and the Lord's Supper. There were fifteen confirmed, five with the Kroo-mark upon them. When laying his hands on the natives the Bishop pronounced the prayer "Defend O Lord," in Grebo. He says the Grebo has become so familiar to him that he can preach in that better than in English. It is a joyous sight to see these poor natives gathered in, and to feel that there is "One fold and one Shepherd." The church was so crowded, that they even had a number of benches placed outside the door. We had about seventy communicants, about one third of these natives, so "mightily grows the Word of God, and prevails." Well may the cry go forth from here, "Come over and help us." "Who will come up to the help of the Lord against the mighty?" Here, in all this region, are but two white "heralds of the cross," and though they are gathering in the fruit, and sending it forth to scatter the seed broadcast yet these converts from heathenism need yet much training and much oversight in their work.

We sat down, twelve of us, to dinner at first, and about twice as many afterward, teachers and scholars, who had come in from distant stations. At half past three there was a missionary meeting. They collect here, even in this poor little place, where money is so hard to be had, about ten dollars a month, to send the Gospel further on, to those who are sitting in darkness. May all learn that it is indeed "more blessed to give than to receive." At seven o'clock we bade a long good-bye to our friends. The captain expects to sail very early in the morning. Shall we ever meet again? God only knows. Our lives are in His hands, and to Him and His service we are devoted, in life or death. But these partings are sad. If we have few friends, few ties here, yet:

> "We love the better those
> Our Heavenly Father sends."

ESCAPE.—Early this morning we had a great fright. We went to view the last traces of our vessel, when we were startled to see she was not yet gone, but with all sails set, she was driving full upon Dead Island, a horrid reef of rocks that stretches to our left. With what intense anxiety we watched her, and saw the great hurry on deck, but when she appeared close on the rocks her anchor was dropped. We then went into breakfast. The captain came in in a few minutes, and said, that "after weighing anchor the land breeze blew so strong, he was very much afraid that they would be dashed on the rocks; the vessel would have to lay there till the sea-breeze sprung up, which it generally does about ten o'clock." He had come on shore to attend to a little business he had forgotten the night before. About ten o'clock a fine breeze sprung up, and we saw the little ship move from her moorings. For half an hour we watched with great anxiety till we saw she was in safety; though we had felt that it was almost impossible for anything to happen to her; she had too many good people on board, and was freighted with too many prayers. But this is a fearfully dangerous coast. There is lying here, on the strand, the remains of a vessel that, about three months ago, was anchored here, and, in broad daylight, the force of the current and the wind tore her from her moorings, and she dashed, head foremost, on the shore; nothing could save her, though, providentially, no lives were lost.

Chapter Sixth.

SUNDAY-SCHOOL ANNIVERSARY.

This is to be the Sunday-school anniversary. The different schools are to meet at the church, have some exercises there, then come up here and go down on the rocks, under the Cape, and have refreshments. Our old cook, "Auntie Dade," is busy making some gingerbread, and cooking meat and short-cake. The meat has been sent to Mr. Hoffman, with considerable plain cake, from some of the wealthier of the colonists. This will be a great treat to many of the poor children, who scarcely ever taste anything but rice and palm butter. We have prepared all their rosettes and banners, and Mr. Hoffman and Miss Hogan went down to the church with our children, while I prepared the refreshments for them on the rocks. Miss Ball has gone home to Cavalla. I had scarcely completed my arrangements when the children appeared. I heard the sound of their voices, singing sweetly before I saw them. They came down in perfect order over the rocks, over three hundred of them; it was a pleasant sight, and each school quietly took the place assigned for it, and then the children seated themselves on the rocks, and waited patiently till they were served. Though many of these children never saw a bit of cake but once a year, and some of them had never seen it before, yet they waited with the greatest patience, each for his turn to be served; there was no pulling, or pushing, or snatching, or seeking to get more than their share. No, all was done decently and in order. Their behavior was a model of propriety. The scene was very pretty; the rocks beautiful and jagged. The surge constantly rolling and breaking on them (to me the roar of the ocean is perfect music), and pouring in through the fissures, formed little ponds around, in which, at times, you can find some very pretty shells. Then the costume of the children was so strange; there was the half-naked little boy, and the young colored lady bedizened out in her choicest finery, beads, laces, &c., showy and gaudy. On the top of the rocks the beautiful cocoanuts waved their plumed heads. It was a wild, strange, beautiful sight, never to be seen but in such a clime. After their refreshments the children sung very sweetly, and then departed to their homes, some of them having five miles to walk.

Work.—Now we shall commence our work—to teach the Word. Mr. Hoffman gave notice in Church to-day, that a class for adult females, those who cannot read, or only very imperfectly, will commence this afternoon at the Asylum; Miss Hogan will take charge of it. On Monday we shall have a class for the native women, which we shall take charge of alternately (Miss Hogan, however, soon took its entire charge), and a Bible class will be commenced on Thursday for adult females, teachers and others, who may feel the need of more thorough knowledge of sacred Scripture ; of this I am to have charge. I attended Sunday-school this afternoon, and I find, in doing so, it will be impossible to attend evening worship ; the distance being too great.

NATIVE CLASS.—After dinner to-day our native women came to be taught, but Miss Hogan had forgotten, and had let Julia, our interpreter, go out, and one of the others only understood a little Grebo, so we could have but very little conversation with them. However, for to-day, we just let them understand that we wanted them to come every Monday, so we might teach them "the things of God." There were nine of them ; several of them the wives of the Christian natives, and very willing to learn. As we could not teach them this afternoon, we thought we would amuse them. Mr. Hoffman has a very large music-box, in perfect order ; and I showed them some daguerreotypes, with which they were much amused ; but when Miss Hogan brought out the model of a railroad-engine, which, by winding up, will run about the floor for several minutes, their delight knew no bounds. They jumped, clapped their hands, laughed, sat on the floor, and performed the most grotesque antics ; but when it would move towards them, would scream, jump on the chairs, and appear greatly frightened. They say, "white man can do everything but put the breath into a dead body." Afterwards, we had a teachers' meeting ; the teachers, or some of them, from three different schools, were present. Mr. Hoffman wants to give a number of gowns to some of the old native men on New Year's Day, so, in the evening, I was busy trying to make one.

OLD M'LEDE.—My poor little boy, Dayo, is gone away to-day; I quite miss him. For several days I have noticed a sore place on his head, and thought it was occasioned by a wound, but Mr. Hoffman told me that it was a disease perfectly unpronounceable to me, and that he thought he had better go home to get cured, as he did not know what to do for it, and his friends probably did; they cure it with some herb. This morning his father came in, quite unexpectedly, and he said he must take him home for two or three weeks, and as soon as he was well, he would bring him back. Poor child! he came running to me in great distress, and, by gesture and speech, tried to make me understand that he could not leave me. We all thought, however, he had better go for a little while, and so he was taken off in great trouble. I really have become quite attached to him. On the day of the examination of the school here, I noticed a native woman with a darling little child, (yes! though black, a little darling), perfect in form, about three years old—it was her little grandchild. I could not help noticing both the old woman and child. Upon inquiring of Mr. Hoffman who they were, "That," said he, "is M'Lede; remind me, and I will tell you about her." I forgot it, till yesterday, when she came to be taught among the other women. I asked her, "Where is your little one?" She said, "Me left home." I told her when she came again, she must bring her with her, as I loved her. She said, "Her mother, my daughter, be stranger here, (that is, she is on a visit here), but she go away next day (to-morrow) home in the bush, and she take *Boah* with her, but me bring her see you first time"—(before she goes.) I told her to do so; so, to-day, the old grandmother, the mother and the little one came to see me. Old M'Lede is apparently a true Christian. Mrs. Scott has written a pretty little history of her, which is published—she was a demon woman, or devil doctress, but she has cast all aside for Christ. Truly, "the Word of God is mighty to the pulling down the strongholds of sin and Satan." I asked the mother, when the child was old enough, would she send her to school. "Oh, yes! Oh, yes!" (they are very ready in promising, whatever the performing may be) "so soon she be big enough, I send her you way from the bush—you teach her 'bout *Nyesoa*," (God.) I then brought her a little doll, but it frightened the child, so I gave her some beads instead. A little act of kindness finds its way here, as elsewhere, to the heart. Mr. Hoffman and Miss Hogan are gone out to the service at Mount Vaughan. I did not go, for, though feeling otherwise very well, I have a great aching in my limbs; they say it is Africa striking me. A number of the girls are away, spending the holidays with their friends. Mr. Thompson also being away, I had to conduct evening worship.

FATHER SCOTLAND.—We are anxiously looking for letters now from home. The first thing I do each morning is to look out and see if there are any vessels in sight. The *Stevens* is daily expected from Baltimore. I have just received a very kind note from Miss Williford, wishing much I would spend a week with them at Cavalla, before school commences; but I have been obliged to decline, for I have so many things yet to do, I feel as if I cannot spare the time. There is so much writing to be done here, as no verbal message can be sent, you almost require to sit with pen in hand. Mr. Hoffman has gone to Cavalla, to stay all night. He intends to do so once a week during the Bishop's absence. Mr. Toomy* wrote me a very pretty little note, accompanying some shells he had picked up for me. This afternoon I went to see Mr. Scotland, an aged dying Christian. He sent me word yesterday he would like to see me. He is in an old dilapidated shanty; the furniture consists of a few boards, knocked together, elevated about a foot from the floor, to serve as a bedstead (the straw bed we made for him on our first arrival); a little bench, on which is placed two Bibles, and an earthen jar for water. He is dependent for food and care on his neighbors, as he is perfectly helpless. How much we need a hospital here! It is one of the things for which Mr. Hoffman labors and prays. A woman who was near brought me a little stool, and I sat down beside him. He was perfectly delighted to see me; told me " that he had served the Lord for forty years; he had been a Methodist preacher for many years; he had often preached three times a day, though he could never read a word; he would get some boy to read to him several chapters in the Bible, till he got hold of just the text that would suit him." I was very much surprised at his familiarity with the Word of God. He could tell me where to find almost any passage. I could not but look at that poor old man, with his few privi-

---

* His little history is written elsewhere.

leges, and think of our own more favored country, and those words: "They shall come from the east and the west, and sit down in the kingdom of God; and ye shall be cast out." And as I looked at him, in his want and penury, and witnessed his happiness and his implicit faith, and saw how near home he was, I felt he was really to be envied. Who can doubt the power of Divine grace? I read to him and talked with him on the glories of the resurrection, and the mansions our Saviour has prepared for those who love Him; and then left him, with the promise of soon seeing him again. He is almost blind now. He begged me not to forget him in my prayers. He is dying of old age. No one knows how old he is.

New-Year's Eve.—The last day of the year! Very probably, ere another year closes, I shall have done with time and shall have begun eternity. "Lord, teach me so to number my days, that I may apply my heart unto wisdom." What a time for self-examination and prayer should the close of the year be! In the eyes of the world we may appear to be better and more devoted Christians than we ever were before; but "God seeth not as man seeth," and in His sight we may be far less acceptable. "Search us, oh God! and our thoughts, and see if there be any way of wickedness in us, and lead us in the way everlasting." Mr. Hoffman brought me such a kind little note from Cavalla. What would this earth be without love? A dreary waste. I have finished my gowns for the old men. My Bible class was to commence to-day, but being holiday time, all the ladies were so much engaged, it has to be deferred till next week.

New-Year's Day.—New-Year's day! Very, very hot. How constantly the subject of death is in the mind here. This year may I live each day as though it would be my last, and daily may I go humbly to the throne of grace, saying, " Lord, what wilt Thou have me to do?" and then, " whatsoever my hand findeth to do, may I do it with all my might." I have dedicated myself wholly, " body, soul, and spirit," to my Saviour's service. Oh! that He would receive, accept me, love me freely, and " seal me to the day of redemption ;" and, if it please Him, that here He would give me souls for my hire, use me for His glory on earth, and afterwards receive me into the mansions prepared above.

I have been writing home. We must get our letters prepared, even though they may have to wait months before we can send them, as there is no knowing any day when a vessel may stop on her way home.

We had a very pleasant service in church this morning, and a very good congregation. Both Mr. Hoffman and Mr. Gibson gave us a short address.

We always put away our work, and retire to our rooms at ten o'clock. After that, is the only time when we can really have a few minutes of undisturbed quiet, for writing letters, journals, &c., &c. It is not a very good time for our own health, but it is almost the only time. I have often heard the remark made, that it is a wonder missionaries do not write more interesting accounts and letters ; but people would wonder no longer, if they could see the wearied state, both of body and mind, in which they are when they do sit down to write. There is a constant care, and anxiety for immortal souls, impressed more deeply by the conviction that your time may be so short. I often look at Mr. Hoffman, and think of the words of the apostle, in summing up his labors: "That which cometh upon me daily, the care of all the churches." In the Bishop's absence, of course, his cares are much increased.

FEVER.—I have put the finishing stroke to my room to-day—covering my big trunk to form a settee. My new matting, and clean white curtains and cloths, make all look so neat and nice. It is a great comfort to have a pleasant room, either in sickness or health. I have had a chill, and an intense aching in my limbs, to-day. I am glad my room is all right, for I think it will not be long before I get the fever. They say it is best to have it soon after arrival here. Mr. Toomy has been spending the evening here. I like him very much.

My anticipations were realized. The day after writing the above, though feeling very badly, I went to church, but became so much worse that it was with difficulty I reached home. A doctor and nurse were immediately sent for. At the end of the sixth day my fever was broken, and I was pronounced convalescent.

I found the Saviour true to His promise: "I will be with thee." I had always had an intense horror of death, so much so that I often wondered I should have courage to come to such a clime; and once, some time ago, I had spoken to my dear pastor on the subject, fearing I could not be a Christian; but he had kindly encouraged me, telling me "That I must not expect dying grace in my hours of health and strength; that dying grace was for dying hours; and that the promise is, "*As thy day*, so shall thy strength be." And I found it so; for "He is faithful that promised." I had no fear; I was perfectly resigned to His will, and was in a very happy frame of mind. The last night, however, before my fever broke, was a sore one to me. My disease was at its height; I could not sleep. I was not exactly delirious, but I had no control over my thoughts. I was in a sort of waking nightmare. I knew I was very ill, and that my thoughts ought to dwell on the love, the precious atoning love, of the Redeemer: His blood shed for me, my own utter worthlessness, and the joys He had purchased for me; and yet, instead of these, the worst thoughts were occupying my mind—the most strange and wicked imaginations; such things as I had never before conceived possible, were floating before my brain. Every little while I would be recalled to myself; and as I would be conscious of the greatness of my iniquity, I would utter a deep groan. My nurse would come to ask what she should do for me. For an instant I would be aroused, in terror, lest I had given utterance to my sinful thoughts; but in a moment I was off again. It was a fearful night; I shall never forget it. Towards morning, rousing for a few minutes, it suddenly struck me that it must be Satan who was putting these blasphemous ideas into my mind, to draw me away from God; and then, as if in a picture, came up before me the scene in the "Pilgrim's Progress" (which I had not read since I was a child), of Christian in the "Valley of the Shadow of Death," after his fight with Apollyon. Here evil spirits, which he could not see, were whispering to him blasphemous thoughts; and it gave him much trouble, as he imagined these suggestions of the evil ones proceeded from his own heart; but at length he vanquished them with his weapon, All-prayer, and soon he was out of the valley. This was all pictured so clearly to my view, I thought, perhaps, it was the same with me. Immediately, I commenced praying so earnestly to my Saviour, that if these things proceeded from my own heart, He would "cleanse the thoughts of my heart by the inspiration of His Holy Spirit;" and if they were the suggestions of the evil one, that He would conquer the powers of darkness, and bid them depart. Whilst I was still praying, a deep, sweet sleep fell upon me, from which I did not arouse till late in the morning, when my fever had left me, and danger was considered past. Surely He is a hearer of prayer; He not only rebuked the evil one, but the disease also. A week from that time I was able to sit up, and receive letters from home. Letters! none but those who are far from home, and loved ones, in a heathen land, can ever know their value. During my illness, Miss Ball came up and remained a few days with me, and I had every care and attention. How much have I to be thankful for! Mr. Thompson had to commence with the school, as I was yet too weak.

THE WILLS.—We have a little light-colored boy boarding with us. I employ myself an hour every evening in helping him with his lessons. Matthew is one of five children; all very light, pretty, and well-behaved

Their mistress sent them out here, with their father and mother, about three years ago. Their parents both died within a few weeks of their landing. The children are maintained by their mistress. She wishes them brought up as ladies and gentlemen. The little girls come to the Asylum to day-school, but she pays their board elsewhere. She did not wish them to do the housework that the girls do here; and, of course, as they were here, no difference could be made between them and the other children. I do not think it is wise to give them such high notions; it would not hurt girls to know how to do a little housework anywhere, but particularly in a new country, where the industry of its inhabitants must be its wealth. The other boys board elsewhere, but go with Matthew to the high school. Their mistress dresses them not merely nicely, but elegantly. Matthew takes his meals with us, and is quite a little gentleman. Mrs. Thomson, a colored lady, took tea with us to-night. They call her the "Mother of the Mission." She came out here and commenced a little school twenty-six years ago, and she has labored faithfully ever since. Hers is an infant school. I wish she had the apparatus for it.

Chapter Seventh.

SCHOOL.

Kind invitations from Cavalla again. They think a little change will be beneficial after the fever, and they say I must not think of going into school yet for two or three weeks. But I think a journey down there will try my strength much more than school. I mean to begin, for an hour or two, to-morrow, so I must decline the invitation. Neither of the ladies are well. If they should become worse, then I should look upon it as my duty to go there. Miss Ball has considerable fever. We unpacked a box of presents sent out for the girls—books, dresses, &c.; very acceptable. Many, many thanks, to the kind friends who sent them.

I am going to have sewing-school for the girls (there are twenty-six) three times a week, in the afternoon. I commenced to-day. My eyes trouble me very much; I believe it is always one of the effects of the fever.

They are better at Cavalla, to-day; Mr. Hoffman has gone there to superintend affairs. Mrs. Scott, who was formerly a missionary here, has sent the girls a present of a dress each, and I mean that they shall make them themselves, the elder helping the younger. It is a little trouble, however, cutting and basting for so many. After sewing-school, my Bible class commenced;

I had fourteen present. May I be taught of God, so as rightly to teach others. I find I must "go softly;" I have not regained my strength yet.

Good news! Miss Ball's attack of fever was very short; she is up to-day. I have been looking over the girls' books with Mr. S. Thompson, as I expect on Monday to relieve him of his charge. I went down on the rocks and picked up a few shells, but was very much tired; one is always weary here.

Up in the store-room, looking for school-books. We have been marking a set of new shirts and cloths for the boys at Hoffman Station; and I have been teaching Julia to darn stockings. She is a good girl; she is desirous of improving, so she may become a teacher.

I have begun my regular school duties to-day. Monday being washing-day, ten of the elder girls remain out of school to do the washing; they wash everything for their own use, bedding, table-cloths, &c. I remained in school till half-past one; at half-past two we dine. I had the elder girls in the school-room for an hour, for an arithmetic class, then to the store-room to sort books, and arrange lessons. We had a very heavy thunder-storm; it was truly grand. By half-past six it is quite dark, we then have prayers; and by the time tea is over, it is eight o'clock—then, with helping Mat, and a little sewing or reading, the day is gone.

All my girls in school to-day; they seem to be very obedient, good girls. Mr. Hoffman invited me to go to Mount Vaughan with him this evening, but I thought I had better wait another week, before incurring the fatigue. An English and American vessel have both been at anchor here for two or three days; it is pleasant to see them; we hope to send letters home by the American.

One of the ladies of my Bible-class came to-day to ask me to trim her bonnet for her. I was very busy, but still I feel that it is by little acts of kindness we must win them to us.

A very bad headache to-day; in school till four o'clock, then to my Bible class; it has now increased to eighteen. Kind little notes from Cavalla, but did not have time to answer them. Mr. Hoffman has a prayer-meeting at Mount Vaughan to-day.

We have a prayer-meeting at the Cape every Friday afternoon. The mornings here are sometimes very damp and cool, even in the hottest part of the year. A little flannel sack is very comfortable.

SATURDAY.—How can I tell the multiplied and multifarious occupations here on Saturday. In the first place, it is the great day for the natives to come in to trade—that is, to sell rice, chickens, cassadas, palm-nuts, &c.; and they must be paid with tin cups, tobacco, pipes, or cloths—this is the small change; tin pans, wash-bowls, &c., being the larger coin. Then the teachers from the stations, the workmen about the buildings, the poor pensioners on the mission, come to purchase, to beg, to settle accounts, &c. It is a perfect levee all day. None of these occupations belong to me, but there is often a little to do in helping others, talking to those who come, and such like. I received and answered two little notes from Cavalla. Miss Ball is well enough to go in school again. Helped to prepare and mark more cloths and shirts for the boys of Harris's station. After dinner, Mr. Hoffman started for Cavalla; he will stay there over Sunday; when he goes, he always stops and preaches at one or two of the towns on his way. In the afternoon, Lavinia came up to me: she is a young woman I have promised to assist to read and write; she can only come to me on Saturday afternoon. After she was gone, I was taking a turn or two on the piazza before dusk, watching a vessel coming in, which we supposed a man-of-war, when I was very much startled by hearing my mother's voice calling me; it sounded as plain as I ever heard it. How powerful is imagination! The young men here have a Saturday evening prayer-meeting—Mr. Thompson leads. To-night they have been forming a young man's Christian association, on the plan of that in America. Each young man, a member of the Church, promises to devote whatever spare time he can afford to purposes of benevolence—visiting the sick, the afflicted, and the heathen, not leaving it all to their pastor, but each one striving what he can do for the promotion of God's glory, and the good of mankind. They are each to give in a monthly report of their labors. Sixteen have joined to-night; may they be blessed in their efforts, and not grow weary in well-doing.

THE VINCENNES.—We had a very heavy thunderstorm last night. The ground is very damp, so they would not allow us to go to church, as it is very bad to get wet here. The vessel we saw last night is the

American frigate Vincennes. Several of the officers came on shore, and having packages for the Bishop and Mr. Hoffman, they came up to the Asylum, but without any idea that there were any ladies at the mission; they, however, seemed much pleased, and four of them remained, as it was just dinner-time. They had been strolling about all the morning, trying, some of them, to purchase fruit, vegetables, &c., and were very much surprised upon being told, even in the heathen towns, that, it being Sunday, they could obtain none; if they would wait till to-morrow morning, they would have plenty; this they could not do, as the ship sailed at four o'clock. They appeared quite astonished at the decency and respect for the Sabbath everywhere observable, and at the accounts of the good work going on among the natives. The doctor had gone to church, and was much pleased with Mr. Gibson's sermon. We wished it had been any day but Sunday, as then they could have visited the schools, and themselves seen the work that was going on; but I think they saw enough to prove to them that the Gospel is doing a mighty work. It is not pleasant to have company on Sundays, but we must follow the Apostle's injunction, " Be careful to entertain strangers ;" and we must only try that our words and acts are becoming the sacredness of the day. We were sorry Mr. Hoffman was not at home, as he could have given them much more information regarding the work here than we could.

WITCHCRAFT. — Letters from home to-day—such a treat! all well, thank God. Mr. Hoffman has returned,

and told us of a scene which has taken place at Cavalla; it was a trial by the *gidu* or sassa-wood ordeal. But first I must remind you of the custom with regard to sassa-wood among the natives. I shall say as little of this, and other similar customs among the natives, as possible, as Mrs. Scott has recently published a very interesting work, called "Day-Dawn in Africa," which gives a very full account; therefore, mine would only be a repetition, and might even to some appear to be a plagiarism. When any one dies, unless it is a very aged person or young infant, the death is always attributed to witchcraft, it being believed that every one possesses the power of witchcraft, if he or she only choose to exercise it. Therefore, most frequently, on the death of an individual, some person is accused of the deed—oftentimes the nearest friend of the deceased, as father, wife, or child. The accused person is immediately seized, and compelled to pass through the sassa ordeal, unless they can make good their escape to a neighboring town, where, as in a "city of refuge," they cannot be touched. But the odium of being a witch is so great, that they very frequently return, and, in the presence of a few friends, take the poison. This poison is a decoction made from the bark of the gidu-tree. The bark is pounded in a mortar, and from two to three quarts of water poured upon it, the whole of which the wretched victim is compelled to swallow. Its properties are nàrcotic; and, without being aware of it, the executioners go the right way to prevent its taking effect; for the moment it is swallowed, they seize the victim, not allowing him to rest a moment, but drag him from place to place, till he either falls dead, or his stomach rejects it, and he vomits freely. In the latter case he (or she) has a grand triumph; dressed up in all the finery they can collect, they go about to all their friends, generally followed by a train of their dearest friends, singing and dancing; and at every house they go to they expect some present. But if the person dies, the body is dragged on the beach, where it lies in the sun till the family can provide a bullock, which, after being devoted to the Kwi, is killed and divided among all the people in town, all rejoicing and exulting that "the witch is dead," his death being a sure sign of his guilt. Formerly it was not allowed for his nearest relations to mourn at all; but now that is permitted, though they are looked upon with contempt for so doing, it being asserted that they ought to rejoice that "a witch is dead." The body is then taken up, and thrown somewhere in the bush along the shore. It is not permitted to be buried in the common burial place. It is a very singular fact, that on the administration of the gidu is the only time when God, or Nyesoa, is invoked. At that time, the one who administers the dose, holding the bowl in his hand, looks towards the east, and calls upon God to assert the guilt, or vindicate the innocence, of the accused, by the effects of the poison. The victim takes the bowl, and does the same.

This is often used as a means of personal private revenge, as any one may accuse another of witchcraft. Therefore, they live in hourly fear; no one is safe. Now for Mr. Hoffman's story. On Saturday, at the Christian village at Cavalla, a native Christian, who had taken a heavy cold on a recent expedition up the river, died of hasty consumption. His friends in the town instantly accused a fine looking man, whom I have frequently seen here (who speaks English very well), of being the witch. They caught him Saturday night and made him take the sassa; but he recovered. On Sunday afternoon Mr. Hoffman was standing on the piazza when he saw a great crowd on the beach, and perceived that there was a " palaver" of some sort. He immediately went down to see. There, in the centre of the crowd, sat a man and woman, no relations, but both accused of having practised witchcraft on the deceased. They were firmly guarded. The man sat with his head hanging down, in an attitude of great despondency. The other, a fine, noble looking woman, sat in perfect composure, as if determined to brave it out; though there was an old woman, apparently her mother, sitting by her in great distress, every few minutes giving vent to her anguish in loud screams, flinging her arms around her daughter, crying and sobbing, and, by word and gesture, imploring compassion for her daughter. The young woman, with her hand, would try to still her mother and gently put her away from her; though, it was evident, a great struggle was going on within. Immediately in front of them a man had just set down a pestle and mortar, another had a huge piece of the sassa bark, that he was beginning to break into the mortar, while two boys were bringing large jars of water from a neighboring stream. In these cases the missionary never dares to interfere, otherwise than by persuasion; " it is their country fash," and they believe it to be right. As Mr. Hoffman passed in among the crowd, a little girl, one of the best scholars at the school at Cavalla, caught hold of him; she was crying most bitterly. Mr Hoffman asked her, " What was the matter that she was in such distress?" She said : " It is my brother's wife they are going to kill, and I love her so much. Mr. Hoffman began to talk to them on the wickedness and folly of their proceedings, they listened to him quietly, but still went on with their preparations; when suddenly a detachment of young men from the Christian village appeared, headed by Kade, the son of the former king, now a Christian and a great spokesman. They, with Mr. Hoffman, represented to the people that as the deceased was a Christian, and died in the Christian faith, they had no right to accuse any one of causing his death, and at length, by their arguments, they succeeded in obtaining the release of the accused and carrying them off in triumph.

THE DINNER TABLE.—The headman of one of our towns dined here to-day with us. Each town has a headman or petty chief; they are subordinate to a king who rules over a number of them conjoined. Mr. Hoffman said there were few he could ask, but this one could behave himself decently at table. He speaks English tolerably. One of his sons is, apparently, an earnest, devoted Christian. The old man is a very tall, large man, with grey hair and beard. He had on one of the long gowns I had made, a red flannel cap, with a black tassel, and a black beaver hat, and truly he was "a proper gentleman." At dinner he sat with his chair so far from the table that he could hardly reach. He used his knife and fork, and spoon, a great deal better than I had supposed. He would strike his fork into a sweet potato, and bite off all around it. When we had nearly dined, Mr. Hoffman passed him some bread. He said : " No, me no take, me be full ;" a minute after we had some toasted cheese, molasses, &c., brought in ; he immediately took some, eating the cheese and molasses together, which he appeared very much to enjoy ; amusing us very much by his ineffectual efforts to say cheese ; the nearest approach he could make was " keese."

CORRECTION.—To-day I had to perform the feat (a great one for me) of whipping one of the children. I did not think I could ever do such a thing, but she well deserved it, and I found nothing else would do. I want to attach the idea of shame and disgrace to a whipping, so as to inflict it only in extreme cases when all other measures had been resorted to in vain. I cannot bear punishment, when it can possibly be avoided ; but, I think, when it is done it should be thorough. I suffered a great deal more than the child, for I had a nervous chill after it. Mr. Hoffman is quite unwell, he has had to send for the doctor this evening ; it is an attack of intermittent, so we have it each in turn.

My Bible class increases—two fresh scholars. What a rich mine the Bible is ; the more it is worked the more treasures we find.

Our old gardener, an old man of sixty, was married to-day. He was very much disappointed that Mr. Hoffman was too unwell to perform the ceremony.

LIBERIAN UNIFORM.—Mr. Hoffman is very sick to-day. It has been the general parade of the Liberian Militia. The French, some time ago, sent the Republic a present of a thousand suits as a uniform. It consists of a sort of tight jacket or vest; very full red Turkish trowsers that come about to the calf of the leg, where they are met by leather leggins; a very wide blue sash, tied at the side; and a red cap with black tassel. All the suit was made of flannel. They looked very much like the pictures we see of Algerines. This afternoon went to see Father Scotland. He is in a most miserable but happy condition. I then went to see another poor man, whom they call Red Jackson. He is as white as a Portugese, and has dark, sandy-colored hair. He was a hard-working, industrious man, and he was breaking rocks, when a piece of "poison rock," as he calls it, struck his leg, and for two years he has had a dreadful leg, so much ulcerated and swollen.

How much we do need a hospital. There is a little house close to the Asylum that is to be let for a very low rent. Mr. Hoffman is thinking of putting the old gardener in this house and removing old Father Scotland, if he can, up here, so that he may be a little better taken care of, and he hopes it may be the beginning of a hospital. I do not think that near so many immigrants would die of the fever, when they first come out here, if they had better care and attendance.

THE CHILDREN.—Oh! how much money is wanted here. I pity the poor colonists so much—there is very little doing here; I do not know how any of them contrive to get a living; it is true they live mostly on rice, but the difficulty is for them to obtain a bit of clothes or furniture. But we must hope " there is a good time coming" for Liberia. As her inhabitants become educated, enterprise and national ambition will soon follow, and then the natural resources of the country will be developed. The missionaries here do all they can, for both the temporal and spiritual needs of the people; but the field is vast and the laborers are few.

Dayo's father came to see me to-day. He was, or seemed to be, perfectly delighted to see me well again; he took both of my hands in his, and shook them warmly. He said, " Dayo cry every day to come back to mammy." He calls *me* mammy; it is with them a title of respect, like mistress. I told him he could come home if his head was quite well. He said it was, and then went on to say, " Mammy teach Dayo American fashion, no country (none of our country) fashion; you teach him things of God—make him be God-man" (he meant Christian), and he, himself, is a heathen. Surely God has put it into his heart to wish his child to be a Christian. As to little *Wah*, the deaf and dumb boy, there is no such thing as keeping him. He will be here for a week, perhaps, and will be kept clean and neat, then he will start off to his mother or somewhere else. Everybody knows him and is kind to him; his mother rarely knows where he is; perhaps he will not be back here again for two or three weeks, and then he will come so dirty, having worn the same shirt and cloth all the time he has been gone. He is such an interesting little fellow—so bright and sharp, and so imitative. He has learned the alphabet on his fingers, and one can readily make him understand what one wants. He is very affectionate. I have undertaken, also, the entire charge of another little one. George Harris, our native teacher, across the river at Hoffman Station, has a little one named Virginia, after the late Mrs. Hoffman (whose memory is held very precious), she is about three years and a half old. He very much wishes her to be brought up in American customs and habits—not to learn the ways of the little heathen children among whom he lives. So Mr. Hoffman very kindly offered to give her her board here if I would undertake the charge of her, which I willingly consented to do, as I love children very dearly. So my family is growing—I have already a little boy and girl. May they be children of God. I feel that it is a fearful responsibility.

COMMUNION SUNDAY.—Neither Mr. Hoffman nor Miss Hogan was well enough to go to church. I was the only white person in God's house, or at God's table. How much I thought of home to-day. About dusk a band of my little ones came up to my room for me to talk to them, Sunday evenings I have all the children who do not go to church, in the school-room, and read and talk to them for an hour or so.

OUR HOUSEHOLD.—Mrs. Harris brought over little Virginia to-day. She feels badly at parting with the child. Julia is to wash and dress her for me, and have her to sleep with her. I shall teach her to call Julia aunt. And I have now assumed the responsibility of taking charge of and educating her. Mr. Hoffman is better; he is out of his room and with us again. I must tell you how our household is employed: Mr. Hoffman's cares, charges and duties are so numerous and varied that they baffle my powers of description. Miss Hogan attends to the house-keeping, gives orders to the girls about their various duties, &c., when they are not with me (for, besides the washing and ironing for themselves, they keep the school-room, and all their own premises, clean and neat); she sees to the clothes which they wear, &c., and I look after the sewing. She attends to the purchases (no small item), keeps the accounts of the Asylum, cuts out, and sees that the clothes for the boys at Hoffman and Spring Hill stations are kept in good order; attends to the giving out of books, &c., for the different boys' schools in the vicinity; besides, she attends to all the visiting that has to be done; as I am not strong enough to walk but very little, she must do that, (a very important part of mission work for both.) When I have not strength to go over to visit the heathen towns, she does. My own duties I have related. Then we have twenty-six girls of all ages, from seventeen down to five. I have told you their employments. Mr. J. Thompson boards with us. He is studying for the ministry, and helps Mr. Hoffman with his accounts, which are very troublesome and voluminous, every tin cup or pipe having to be set down. The accounts here have to be kept for eight or ten different stations, and the Bishop, or in his absence, Miss Williford, has as many, or more, to see after at Cavalla. It is a very laborious work. The missionary's life is one of labor, but he is well assured that "a rest remaineth," and he always feels "It is better to wear out than to rust out." Then Mr. Thompson preaches and teaches at the different towns, two or three times a week. He is perfectly familiar with the Grebo language. He holds prayer meetings. Then comes Matthew, I have already told you who he is. Then there is Mrs. Andrews, she is general housemaid for our part of the building; she was house-keeper before our arrival. She is a widow, her husband was killed in the late war between the colonists and the natives. Her children, a little boy and girl, live here at Mr. Hoffman's expense. People at home, when they pay a missionary's salary, have little idea how many are supported out of it. Then there is old Aunty Dade, our cook, who does the cooking for all the establishment, and is " dimensibly" tormented by them natives, who are always hanging about her kitchen, and will wait patiently for hours in the chance of obtaining a mouthful. Then comes Eliza; she used to be a scholar in the Asylum, but now is a sort of matron, and helps in the sewing, under Miss Hogan's supervision. Then there is old Mr. Smith, the gardener, and he takes care of Mr. Hoffman's horse. Virginia, Dayo, and *Wah* (when he is here), bring up the rear. So you see our family. May they all be one family in the household above.

Food.—Only two months to-day, since our landing here. I can hardly realize it, so much has happened; and we are now as much at home in our regular duties, as if we had been here a year. My little Virginia appears to be very docile and tractable, but very timid. Mrs. Andrews came to me to-day, very earnestly praying me to take her little girl; she would give her up to me entirely; if I would only take her, she would be so thankful. I told her I could not, I had quite enough on my hands. I do feel very thankful to succeed in gaining the love of the people here. May my every effort be to promote their good. My health now is very good; I have an excellent appetite. The girls' dining-room is under the school-room—a nice large room, paved with brick, with closets at either end for the dishes. I will give you their bill of fare. For breakfast, rice and salt fish. For dinner: rice, fresh fish, (if to be had), if not, salt beef or pork, with (sometimes) cassadas or sweet potatoes—occasionally, chickens or palm-butter. At tea, rice and molasses. On Sunday evening, bread. Palm-butter is a very wrong name; it gives an incorrect idea of this article of food. The palm-nut, as it is called, has a hard, meaty substance on the outside. These nuts are boiled for some time, and then poured out of the pot, liquor and all, into a large mortar; it is pounded for some time, then the liquor is strained. What remains is thrown away as refuse. The liquor is about the consistency of arrow-root, of a dark yellow color; this is highly seasoned with the native peppers, and is again boiled over. It serves as a soup, and is a great addition to the rice, particularly if it has a bit of fresh meat or chicken boiled in it—foreigners become very fond of it.

My Bible class interests me very much; I never enjoyed that part of God's word so much before. A large vessel in the offing. We like to have them here; it reminds one of home. My little boy, Dayo, has just arrived. I was busy making a dress for Virginia; he wanted to know what it was; I told him, and told him she was to be his little sister, and he must love her very much. I wish I could find time to write in the day, I am always so tired at night, but it must be then, or never; for if I have a moment in the day-time, I am so subject to interruptions that it is impossible to write. The lime-ade is very refreshing, for our drinking water is so warm. Fancy water, when it is brought directly from the spring, having to be put into earthen jars, to stand some hours in the air before it is at all fit to drink. We have an excellent fruit here, called the sour-sap; it is quite green, as large as a very small water-melon, tapering to one end, more in the form of a pear. This is cut in slices; the inside is about the consistency of an orange, of a beautiful pure white, with large, black seeds interspersed. It can be eaten with a spoon, or a fork; being so juicy, it is very refreshing.

Two English vessels lying out here. The captains have been up to see us and brought us some late English papers. Mr. and Mrs. Harris have both been very ill indeed, a sort of cramp colic; they were taken very suddenly, and, for a few hours, we much feared the result. It must have been something they had eaten. They would have been a great loss to the mission, but "God is good."

AUNTIE DADE.—It has been a very wet day, and having a little fever again I have had to lie on the bed instead of going to church. It is very amusing to hear our old cook talk, she uses such long words. She is a very pious, good woman, but talks "*dimensible.*" While I was on the bed, to-day, she came in. She is very fond of me. She began talking: "So, Honey, you'se sick again; I'se sorry, but we knowse it's the portionable lot of all mortalities. What does that most magnificent Book of all books say? that man is born to troubles as the sparks flies up'ards; but, Honey, I wishes all sparks did fly up; but my kitchen smokes so dimensibly that the sparks flies out oftena than they flies up; my old eyes knows it 'cause they feels it. But, Honey, you'se tremensibly hot, your fever am avaraging; but you'll get well, Honey, just demark my words." Then, with a great deal of gesture and many flourishes of her hands, "Honey, you was to come here, the Almighty, the Great Lord, sent you. A bark was launched, it was loaded with a most profusely precious cargo," meaning the missionaries; "it was wafted on the mighty deep and the *Great Positionabler* placing himself at the helm guided it safe to the great land of darkness; and now, my baby, do you think he is going to let any one on 'em die? No, I tell you he won't; and now, Honey, when you writes home to your mother, just you tell her that there is an old lady here, in this dark land, in the kitchen, and as long as she lives your mother's baby shall want for nothing, that she can do for her, so she may make her mind easy on that."

This afternoon I sent for Dayo to come to my room. I wanted to give him something. He did not know what I had called him for, so the moment he entered the room he came and knelt beside me and put up his hands thinking I had called him to come to say his prayers; as that is, generally, the first thing he does on entering the room. Mr. Hoffman is well enough to preach again to-day.

OCEAN EAGLE.—The Ocean Eagle has arrived to-day with the Bishop; he is much better for the voyage. Mr. Wilson does not seem much better. He expects, when he reaches Monrovia, to find that business connected with the mission will take him to America. Miss Coffman, of the Corisco Mission, is also returning for her health. Miss Williford is so feeble we all think she ought to go, too. The Bishop has gone down to Cavalla to see if she will go, and as he is obliged to go to Monrovia, on diocesan duty, for a month or six weeks; if Miss Williford leaves, I shall have to go to Cavalla, to stay with Miss Ball, till the Bishop returns. I have just got into my regular routine of duties here and love them. But *instability* is written on all earthly things, particularly in this land, and we must be ready to go or stay, as duty calls.

NEWS FROM CAVALLA.—Miss Williford has concluded, at all events, to go to Monrovia, and perhaps to America, so I must prepare to return with Miss Ball to Cavalla. She will be up with all the rest, as we are going to have a wedding here on Thursday. Friday the vessel sails. Mr. Hoffman and Miss Hogan are to be married Thursday afternoon. The ceremony is to be performed by the Bishop in our little church, St. Mark's. Mr. Wilson appears very ill; I cannot bear to look at him.

We received a note before breakfast this morning. It was from the Bishop sending for the doctor, Miss Williford having been taken alarmingly ill. The captain says he will put off sailing a day or so if there is any prospect of its benefiting her. None of the people here have the least idea of the wedding. I think Mr. Thompson begins to suspect, as I asked him to-day to get me, tomorrow, all the flowers he could muster. He looked hard at me for a moment, and then smiled very significantly, and said he would do it. A little fever again to-day. I have a low fever on me almost all the time.

Chapter Eighth.

THE WEDDING.

A NOTE from the Bishop this morning. Miss Williford much better (inflammation has not set in as was feared), so he will be here this afternoon. I have been very busy to-day, in school all the morning; then I went to adorning the parlor with flowers. Mr. Thompson brought me a great many, and Mr. Harris sent me a large basket full. Notice has been given of the wedding, so that all who wish to see their pastor married may be present at the church. I made a wreath of geranium-leaves and little white flowers to put over the bride's veil. The Bishop arrived just at dinner-time. He came on horseback. Miss Ball followed, much later, in a hammock. Miss Williford is so much better, he intends to go on to Monrovia, but she will not attempt a voyage. She thinks she shall progress better under the doctor's care. It will not be necessary now for me to go to Cavalla. I saw that all the girls were dressed in their white dresses. Pinned a bouquet on each of them. Saw that the gentlemen were all brushed and cologned, and by that time Miss Ball arrived; we were all waiting for her. We then proceeded to the church. It was very full. After the ceremony, we all returned home to tea, and passed a very pleasant evening.

The Eagle Sails.—The captain intended to weigh anchor early this morning, but no breeze sprung up till toward night. Just at dinner-time there came a messenger, in great haste, from the doctor, begging the Bishop not to go to Monrovia, as Miss Williford is much worse again, and he fears she will not live. The Bishop instantly had his trunk brought on shore, for it was on board the vessel, and he started directly, on horseback, to Cavalla. Miss Ball could not obtain bearers. She feels very much troubled that she cannot get them. The Ocean Eagle got off this evening. We went down with them to the beach. I felt very badly at saying good-bye. Mr. Wilson looks very ill, and he has been so kind to me. I hope when he reaches Monrovia he will find that business calls him home. I think he needs his wife's tender care.

The Lake.—Mr. Hoffman had just been enabled to engage four bearers for Miss Ball, when he received a note from the Bishop. Miss Williford is slightly better, but wishes me to go down there with Miss Ball. Mr. Hoffman said there was a large canoe on the lake, and if we would go by that, the four bearers would be enough for us both, as the lake will take us to within three miles of Cavalla, and two men each could carry us that distance. So we determined to go that way. We had quite a large canoe. Now fancy us, if you can, sitting at the bottom, being paddled along by six of the natives. Our umbrellas forming sort of sails. The shores of the lake are lined with mangrove swamps. The mangrove is a specie of the bannian, which throws its branches down, and they taking root again, form many natural arbors. This is one cause of the unhealthiness of the climate. The scenery is very beautiful. Every few miles we came upon a native town. Little did I think once, when I saw pictures of such scenes, that my eyes would ever gaze upon them. The native huts, with little children running round; the women standing outside, beating or winnowing their rice; others in canoes, unloading them of the wood they have just been cutting (for this is all women's work). These have all been faithfully portrayed. Miss Williford was much pleased to see me. While Miss Ball is in school she needs some one near her. She is very low. The doctor will still remain for some days in the house. Hers is not African fever, but a complication of other diseases aggravated by recent fatigue and anxiety. I hope I may be able to add to her comfort. I left Dayo and Virginia in Julia's care. She is very fond of them. I have many of the colonists come to me to take their children, but I have to decline all further gifts. I was very much pleased at the affection displayed by the girls on my leaving the Asylum, though, I thought it probable, I should be absent no longer than a week. While we were in the canoe we had a heavy shower, but our umbrellas effectually preserved us, shedding the rain over the side of the canoe, it was so narrow.

CAVALLA.—Miss Williford very feeble to-day. It seems to be a comfort to her to have me with her. The service on Sunday morning is entirely in Grebo. It is held in the church, though the building is not yet finished. 1

A Native African Village.

remained with Miss Williford. In the afternoon Sunday-school is held in the church. I had Miss Williford's class in the parlor, and taught them there. In the evening there is service in English in the girls' school-room. About a hundred and twenty were present. There were some of the Christian natives, who cannot understand one word of English, and yet they come to most of the services. There was one I noticed, a woman, who can read English perfectly; she had only a cloth about her; and it really was a pleasant sight to observe how well she used her prayer-book, and joined in all the services, singing the praises of Emmanuel.

Slight improvement in our patient to-day (patient, in every sense of the word). Miss Ball killed a small scorpion in her room. Its bite is not much more venomous than that of a wasp. The larger species is much more poisonous. The bats fly about in the rooms very much in the evening, after the lamps are lighted. A boy was here, with a very nice-looking monkey for sale. I was almost tempted to purchase it, to send home, but did not know what I should do with it meanwhile.

Miss Williford is so much better, I shall return home to-morrow, if I can obtain bearers. How good is God to us! We very much feared we should lose her. Her loss would be a dreadful blow to the mission. I had a letter arrive, by the way of England.

It being Lent, the Bishop has service and a sermon in the school-house every Wednesday and Friday morning, at seven o'clock, in English; and on the same evenings, at half-past six, the service in English, the sermon in Grebo—Mr. Jones, the native deacon, alternating with the Bishop, though he never preaches in English; but he reads the service exceedingly well. He has taught the scholars here to sing by note, and they chant very sweetly. I could not but think, at the time, how much more it sounded like worshipping and praising than all the theatrical music we have in our churches, which always seems a showing off of the singers, instead of God's worship. We pray to God ourselves, and surely we ought, also, each one to praise Him. I never heard the responses better, in any church. It is very difficult to obtain bearers, but I believe the Bishop has succeeded in getting some for to-morrow, as Miss Williford is now so much better, she is anxious, as well as me, that I should be back at my work. That must never be neglected, except in cases of absolute necessity. Mr. Dorsen, one of our colonist teachers, at a station about twenty miles below, came in to-night. He is a very gentlemanly man. The Bishop's home, Cavalla, is a perfect caravansary, where all attached in any way to the mission expect to find a home and a welcome. Mr. Dorsen is going to the Cape to-morrow, so I shall have his protection. I am glad of it; I do not like travelling alone. I have no fear, but it is not pleasant.

They are so exceedingly kind that it made me feel a sort of regret at leaving: but Miss Williford having improved so much, I knew duty called me home. Mr. Dorsen came with me. We were again obliged to go on the lake, but this time we had but a small canoe. The leaks, which were many, were stopped with rags, which, not proving very efficacious, I was thoroughly wet through. Mr. Dorsen tried his best to get a dry canoe, and make me comfortable; but I changed my clothes as soon as I arrived, and hope I shall feel no ill effects. I received a very warm welcome from all my dear children, and likewise from my friends above stairs. As we came along, we saw a number of storks and cranes, standing, motionless, on the edge of the lake. They are singular-looking birds.

DAILY FARE.—Back to my school duties again. You wish to know our daily fare. Well, for breakfast we have boiled rice (that at every meal), and either Indian meal, rice, or wheat bread, always hot in the morning; and then we have it cold at tea-time. You know it will not keep long in this climate. The rice bread is very nice. The rice is pounded into very fine flour, so that it resembles our ground rice. This, with salt mackerel and excellent coffee, forms our breakfast. Our dinner: rice and palm-butter, daily. The palm butter I have described. We always have a chicken or two in it. Occasionally, too, we are able to have a variety; sometimes roast or boiled chickens; or, once in a great while, a little fresh fish; or, in a very great while, a bit of fresh meat; but this is very seldom. Then we have ham, and corned beef, and pork, from America. They catch, sometimes, a species of oyster; it is good, though it is much larger and coarser than ours. We have quite a variety of vegetables: sweet potatoes, very good, but quite white; eddo, which, when mashed, is an excellent substitute for Irish potatoes; cassada, which the natives use in great quantities. This is a long, round root, larger than the largest parsnip, and quite white; but its taste is very like a tough stringy turnip. The natives eat it raw a good deal. Then we have egg-plant, plantains—a species of banana, which is either roasted, or cut lengthwise, and fried. Sometimes bananas are cooked in the same way. Then we have ochre, cucumbers, stringed beans, tomatoes, cabbage (very rarely heads), lettuce, radishes, lima beans, squashes, and Indian corn. None of these come to the perfection they do at home, but still they are good. Thus much for dinner. For tea, we have bread, or wheat cakes, molasses, and salt fish. Such is our ordinary fare. We do not starve, you may depend. Puddings, pies, or cakes, are too expensive, as all butter and sugar come from America; nevertheless, on any very great occasions, we can have them. Though we may often long for home fare, yet we make out very nicely, and our friends there do not forget us. They often refresh our memories, and appetites, too, by jars of canned lobster, or oysters, preserves, pickles, prepared mustard, &c., &c; all things rather expensive for the missionary's pocket, but receiving additional relish when they come as tributes of affection, and often so reviving, when suffering from loss of appetite, consequent on fever.

Most of the people lack a spirit of energy and ambition. I am trying to inspire my girls with it, and give them habits of industry. I want the girls to have their time every moment employed. I am teaching them knitting and crochet. Miss Williford gave me four little work-baskets, for my four elder girls. I have had them in my room to-day, lining them, and putting needlebooks, pockets, &c., in them. They look very nice. Saturday

I call my recreation day; but I always have a number of the girls in my room, teaching them various kinds of things. This is voluntary on their parts, but I encourage it as much as possible. I want them to love to be industrious. May God give them willing hearts to learn. Miss Williford is well enough to be about again.

BAPTISM.—How beautiful are our church services. It seems to me that I love them more and more. May their spirit be written in my heart. To-day I stood around the chancel, one of a group of sixteen, consisting of savage, half-civilized, civilized and enlightened; four to be baptized, the rest as witnesses and sponsors. The first baptized was a native woman, the wife of a Christian—and now I believe a sincere, humble Christian—and her little boy, a child of three years old. Her husband stood with her, as witness, and as sponsor to his child. Another was a boy, about fifteen, from Harris's school—and my little boy, *Dayo*, now Thomas. The sponsors and witnesses were composed of Mrs. Hoffman, colonists, native Christians, and myself. Truly, "I believe in the Catholic Church—one Lord, one faith, one baptism, one God and Father of all." I never fully realized the beauties of our holy religion—never felt what a solemn, aye, an awful thing it is to be a Christian, as I do now. Truly, it is good for me to be here. As I looked at the group, so unlike in outward appearance, I wondered with which of that party would " the high and lofty One, that inhabiteth eternity," most delight to dwell. God only knows which heart was the fittest temple of the Holy Spirit. My constant and earnest prayer is for more humility. I never before noticed how very appropriate the Lord's Prayer is in the baptismal service, after the person has been baptized, when we all kneel and together pray to "Our Father." This afternoon, Mr. Hoffman had his monthly examination of the Sunday-school. The schools from Hoffman station, Mount Vaughan and Spring-Hill, were there. The church was full, and it was so pleasant to hear the full responses to all the questions asked on the Catechism and Scripture lessons. I never heard any school—I will not make one exception—respond more fully, freely and perfectly. How much will those in Christian countries have to answer for, if they neglect their precious privileges. As I returned home, I stood for an instant watching the fearful dashing of the waves—how they raged and foamed, and wreaked their fury upon the rocks, lifting their crested heads on high, as if they would overflow and swallow up all before them. But, helpless as man is to stem their tide, as he stands and gazes at them, he knows there is One who "holds the waves in the hollow of his hand;" and who says, "thus far shalt thou go, and no farther, and here shall thy proud waves be stayed." Man can but bow, and wonder, and adore.

LITTLE THOMAS.—It is very pleasant to me to hear the name Thomas, night and morning, when the roll is called, even though it is only a poor little black boy that answers to it. I think I shall love him all the better for his name. He will repeat a little verse now quite nicely in the mornings; I select very short ones

for him. My little Virginia is very timid about saying
hers; she is a dear little girl; I have a few toys in the
corner of my closet, and my two little ones play quite
nicely together. Thomas does not mind what I do for
Jenny (as we call her), but if I take any notice of any of
the other children, he becomes quite jealous; they seem
to grow fond of each other. I have commenced a night
school for adult females; they are so ignorant, and yet
so anxious to learn, and at night is the only time I have;
I shall hold it twice a week, Mondays and Fridays; my
older girls will assist me; and if I can once get it thoroughly established, in case of my sickness or absence,
they might be enabled to continue it. I have plenty
now to do, though all are earnestly desirous of this
school, yet they fear lest I may tax my strength too
much; but I hope God may give me strength for it, as
it is so much needed.

THE HOSPITAL.—I have not been well since I got so
wet in the canoe, but I hoped it would pass off. Yesterday I very imprudently went to church, (we have service Monday and Tuesday afternoons through Lent)
though feeling very unwell; I had not felt able to go on
Monday, and I think it is such a bad example to stay
away, as well as the loss to ourselves, when we can possibly go. I was obliged, however, to go to bed directly.
I came home with high fever. To-day my fever is very
high, but I have attended to all my duties; my head is
very bad when I have fever. This afternoon Mr. Hoffman
sent for the doctor, and quinine is the order of the day.
Mr. Hoffman has taken the little house next door to us.

and has put his old gardener and his wife there; he intends for it to form the nucleus of a hospital; he has strong faith that one will be established here, it is so much needed. The Young Men's Christian Association attended to the removal of old Father Scotland, and he is now here to be taken care of. Mr. Hoffman supplies him from his own table, and maintains him at his own expense; the change in his position and condition is very great; the poor old man seems very comfortable now, and very grateful. My room looks just like what I have always pictured a missionary's room should be; when I am in it, there are several little ones playing about on the floor, while a number are sitting round at different employments; they must always be busy when they come into my room. I wage inveterate warfare with idleness; even the smallest child must be playing busily. What English my two little ones speak, is very correct.

Went into school, though with a very heavy chill on; in the afternoon my fever was very high, and it was my Bible class; at first I felt disposed to give it up, I was so ill, but many of them had walked four miles to attend, and I did not think it right to send them away. My fever excited me, and I believe our class was more interesting than usual. When I returned to my room, I found the vessel we had been looking for so long, had arrived, and a large package of letters and papers from home awaited me; but I was obliged, spite of my eagerness, to lay them aside for a time—I could not see a line. The doctor came in again; he does not think I will have a severe attack; but persons generally have a second attack in about a month or six weeks after the first; it sometimes is more severe than the first, but after that is safely passed, the person is considered acclimated—as far as the white man ever can be in this clime—but he is constantly subject to low intermittents, though rarely giving up to them till his strength is completely exhausted, then he is obliged to seek a cooler country for a time to revive his drooping powers. Mr. and Mrs. Hoffman both very unwell to-day; we are constantly sick and well, but I shall not speak of it again, unless when any one of us is completely disabled for the time. My skin is now quite yellow—a real African

Chapter Ninth.

TEST.

To-day Mr. Hoffman buried a native Christian, an old man; he has for years been persuaded of the truth of the Gospel, and been under conviction, but it was a stumbling-block to him, the having to give up his wives. This is one of their greatest difficulties. Like the young man in the Gospel, who was almost a Christian, but who went away sorrowful, when Christ bid him give up all, and follow him. The wives here are often a man's only property, and it is like giving up his wealth to part with them; it is a good test of his sincerity. To the women, it is no hardship; there is no love; and they become the property of another member of the family. This old man some weeks since, while still in health and strength, gave up all for Christ.

Love Feast.—A love feast to-night at Harris's; I wish I could attend. This feast is held the night before communion, at the house of one of the Christian natives: it is a prayer-meeting, after which a frugal meal is prepared, of which all partake together—the missionary, and generally one of the ladies attend, if able. Their ordinary custom in eating is for the woman to prepare the food, and then taste it before her husband, "to take the witch off," or *to show it is not poisoned.* A host or hostess never eat with their guests, but after "taking the witch off," they leave their guests alone in the hut, and then themselves eat the remains. Now, at the love-feast, after a blessing has been asked, all, men and women, sit down and eat together, to show they have a perfect love and confidence in each other. "Perfect love casteth out all fear." I was much pleased to-day. I expressed a wish before one of the girls for a lime, and before night I had dozens; they grow very plentifully, and, I believe, wild, here; it showed such kind feeling on the part of the children. Had the girls, who are communicants, up into my room, and talked with them of the holy feast to-morrow; they are good girls, I believe.

An English screw-propeller anchored off. Some of the officers came to the Asylum, but I was in school, and did not see them; I should have liked to obtain some information from them, as they are going on an exploring expedition up the Niger.

THE HORSE.—Mr. Hoffman's horse has been sick ever since we have been here; the poor thing died to-day; and as the natives eat every kind of animal food, even though dying of disease, he allowed them to have the remains of the poor horse, as they would have thought it dreadfully cruel of him if he had not. Not knowing this, and hearing a great "palaver," I went to the end of the piazza to see what was the matter—there, on the rocks, where the waves would soon wash away all traces, was a large native, performing the part of butcher, surrounded by a crowd, all fiercely vociferating, (in their ordinary conversation they talk so loud and hard, you would think they were quarrelling,) each eager to get a large piece. Just as I looked out, one man was stalking off, in triumph, with the bleeding leg of the poor beast. I turned away with disgust; it was a sickening sight.

Mr. and Mrs. Hoffman went to Rocktown, one of our stations, under the charge of Mr. Toomy; they stayed all night, but on the way they were caught in a thunderstorm, and had to take refuge in a native hut for several hours. These huts are very unpleasant to be in for any length of time, as they always keep a fire burning that makes it so hot you are soon in a profuse perspiration, and then the smoke makes your eyes ache badly. Father Scotland is happy, and patient, but longing to be in his heavenly home; he loves to have the girls go in and sing for him. Oh, for a hospital! It seems to be Mr. Hoffman's daily cry and desire, his heart is so large. There is a poor girl dying of consumption; he would much like to have her here, but this little house can but accommodate one patient at a time. Many ships passing to-day.

WAH.—Little *Wah* is here again; what a bright little fellow he is! I wish you could take a peep at me in my school-room, surrounded by thirty girls, of all sizes and complexions, from the very lightest quadroon to the darkest negro, with bright, happy countenances, diligently studying their lessons—myself seated at a desk, on a slightly elevated platform. At my feet, at one side, little Jenny, tired of playing quietly with her doll, has laid herself down, and is fast asleep; on the other side of me are two of the very blackest little boys you ever saw, *Wah* and *Thomas*, talking to one another by signs, occasionally appealing to me to settle their little differences, looking at pictures, or plaiting a sort of *flag*. This is a long leaf, that can be split and plaited, when it is made into baskets, &c. These little boys would plait with twenty strands, holding it with their feet; then *Wah* would bring me a slate, and I set him a copy, explaining to him that each letter meant the same as the one he knew on his fingers. At length, I made him understand that the written word "Thomas" was the same as he spelt on his fingers, to mean the name of my little boy; when he comprehended this, his delight knew no bounds. It was a perfect treat to see his expressive countenance, as it lighted up; and his efforts to write were unwearied—he succeeded admirably. We thought old Father Scotland would be gone to-day. As I looked upon that poor, old man, I thought of the mighty change to him from his helplessness and poverty; the moment his ransomed spirit takes its flight, from that poor pallet he will pass to a throne, for all Christians are to be "kings and priests unto God:" and they are to sit down with Christ on His throne, even as he has overcome, and has sat down with his Father on His throne.

THE BOAT.—By the "Stevens," a nice row-boat was sent out to the mission. It will be very good, when the weather is favorable for carrying stores, &c., to Cavalla, as everything is obliged to be landed from the vessels here, and they have a great deal of difficulty in transporting the articles. John Wilson, the colonist teacher of the boys' school at Cavalla, came up with the boat to-day, and was to return with it this afternoon. The Bishop sent me a kind message, that, according to homœopathy, the medicine which makes us sick should cure us, therefore, as it was my journey from Cavalla had made me unwell, a return hither would perhaps cure me; and as the boat would for some time be coming and going, I had better take advantage of it, to pay them a visit for a day or two. I knew he did not expect me to go that very day, but as it was Saturday, and the boat would return on Monday, I just felt as if I should like it, so off I started—and, though unexpected, I knew well I was not unwelcome. Miss Ball looks very white, Miss Williford better than I have seen her since I have been here.

Attended the services in church this morning—all in the Grebo language—a number of natives present; they put on their best clothes (made a little larger than ordinary) on Sundays. A red night-cap is a favorite article of dress with the old men. Taught Miss Ball's class in the afternoon. Many children from the town, who are not in the day-school, come to Sunday-school.

Home again early enough to begin school. We had a nice awning up all over the boat.

THE SNAKE.—Murder was committed last night in our church; Mr. nor Mrs. Hoffman, nor myself, were present. It seems a gentleman, of the snake species, had made his way into the chancel, and being discovered snugly coiled up, some of the people tried to dislodge him; but his snakeship did not like to leave the church, and so wriggled himself into a hole, but leaving part of his tail sticking out. One of the men seized hold of his tail, and tied it tight to the railing of the chancel, so that it could not get away; his body was fast wedged into the hole. He remained thus all through the service, his tail sticking up about two feet. Whether Mr. Gibson or the snake had the most attention of the audience, I cannot tell. As soon as the congregation was dismissed, the men got clubs, and finally succeeded in withdrawing the gentleman from his hole, and despatching him. It proved to be a young boa-constrictor, seven and a-half feet long. During service, he was making ineffectual struggles to free himself; if he had done so, what a commotion there would have been. Mr. Hoffman has had Matha Owen, the poor young girl who is dying of consumption, brought to the Asylum. Mrs. Hoffman has had a room fitted up for her, up stairs; and one of the elder girls has offered to nurse, and take care of her. It is all at Mr. Hoffman's expense. Poor girl! she is near her end. While her poor body is thus cared for, may her soul be led to Jesus. We are all trying what we can do towards St. Mark's Hospital, in the way of subscribing ourselves, and obtaining donations from home. You cannot imagine the suffering here. I would say to all who read this, "the smallest donations thankfully received." Miss Williford received some time ago a Christmas-box from a friend at home, and we all shared —raisins, citron, prunes, figs, pickles. Many thanks, kind friend; there is scarcely one in the mission, scholars or teachers, but has reason to thank you for your Christmas-box. To Poor Matha and Father Scotland the prunes were very grateful. A little gift sent here, blesses many.

The days when I have my adult school, I am very wearied; in school from nine in the morning till half-past nine at night, with very little intermission; but then there is a sweet peace in the heart, when we feel that we have earnestly endeavored to fulfil our Saviour's injunction, " to do to others as you would have them do to you."

SATURDAY INTERRUPTIONS.—Saturday is the only time I ever have to do any sewing for myself. I have had a dress about four weeks trying to get it made; to-day, I determined it should be finished—but patience has to be exercised here. Sometimes, when I feel inclined to be a little impatient at all these interruptions, I pause and think, for this came I forth! Well, to-day, I had just reached out my sewing, and sat down, when poor Matthew comes to me crying with tooth-ache—talked, and comforted him a little bit—got some flannel, and, heating some vinegar and salt, steeped the flannel in it, and putting it to his face he was soon relieved, and fell asleep. Then my little Thomas was quite ill all day, lying on the floor in my room; he had to be dosed, and attended to. Then two of the older girls came to my room for me to show them how to finish a dress for old Auntie Dade, which I had cut and fitted for her; she wanted it for to-morrow; it is love-feast at her church, (the Methodist) so I had just to set to and help them finish it for her. Then Julia came, and told me Paddock wanted to see me. He is a very nice boy; about three weeks ago he was here, and, as he can read very nicely, I gave him a book; he had come to thank me, and to bring me a *dash* of a fowl. He spoke very prettily to me. I was just seated again in my room, when Julia brought me a little note. I had some work to read it; it was from a native Christian, and he was in the other room waiting to see me. He lives at the same station as Paddock does, and helps to teach the boys there; he belonged to the same town as my little Thomas, which is directly across the lake from the mission station, at which he now lives. His name is Proud; he is a very fine-looking man, though disfigured by the Kroo mark. His wife is a Christian, also; she was educated at the girls' school at Cavalla. He has a little infant, his first child, and he wants to name it after me, so he wanted my full name, and he wishes me to be sponsor. He wants me very much to go and see her at *Half Grawah*, five miles down the lake. He is to come on Monday afternoon for me, and bring me back in a nice large canoe. I asked Thomas if he would like to go with me and see his father and mother, if the canoe was large enough; he said yes, if I would be sure to bring him back. I shall take Julia with me, as an interpreter. A week or so ago, Mr. Hoffman was at *Half Grawah*, preaching, with Proud for his interpreter, when, passing one of the native huts, he heard a low, plaintive moaning; on looking round he saw, under the eaves of the hut, which was shut up, a poor little, deformed child, in the last stages of emaciation. It had the head of a child three years old, while its limbs were those of an infant of a few weeks. Two women were standing at an opposite hut, laughing at the wailing of the poor little one; it seemed in a state of starvation, gnawing eagerly a piece of raw cassada, which his little feeble hand had hardly strength to carry to his mouth. Mr. Hoffman asked the women about it; they seemed to look upon the sufferings of the child as an amusement. They told him that the child had no father or mother—his father's sister (his aunt) had care of him, but, being so deformed, he would never be any good; she, the aunt, had now gone away to the *bush* for some days, and thinking the child would be dead before her return, she had shut up her hut, and left him outside with that cassada to eat, knowing if he died while she was gone, the neighbors would bury him. The poor child could not speak, but his low wails were most pitiable. Mr. Hoffman told the women they ought to take him into their hut, and take care of him. They turned away with a loud laugh, at the absurdity of their doing anything for one like that, who could be of no good. Mr. Hoffman then sent Proud across the lake, to Spring Hill station, to get a mat, and lifting the child tenderly upon it, (for, he was so emaciated, the least touch hurt him) they carried him across to Spring Hill, almost fearing he would die before they could get across; there they put him in the kitchen, near the fire, and tried to do everything to make him comfortable. He cannot live, however, but a few days. I asked Paddock about him to-day; he says he is a little better, but all the time utters that low, moaning cry, that is so painful to hear. What is man without God? Savage! savage! But, to go on with my Saturday—it was now dinner-time; then came Lavinia to her studies, then to see old Father Scotland and Poor Matha, and so ends my day. My poor dress must go away for another week.

GRAWAH.—About half-past one, when school was over, Proud came for me. I dressed Thomas up in his best, (a little suit I had made for Sundays) a white shirt and pantaloons, and, taking Julia along with me, we started. Proud had a very large canoe, with boards put in the bottom to keep my feet from getting wet, and a little native chair for me to sit in. These native chairs stand about a foot from the ground, and really are very comfortable. Proud has risen to the dignity of wearing a complete suit of American clothes—hat, coat, pantaloons, &c.; and no gentleman could have been more polite and courteous to a lady, and more careful of her comfort, than Proud was. About two miles up the lake, there is a very large rock that stretches directly across the beach, from the ocean to the lake; this is called the devil's rock. They believe a great devil, or Ku, lives here, and none of them dare cross it, (which they are obliged to do when coming from Cape Palmas by land) without making an offering, however slight, to the Ku. Poor things! it is little they have to give—a pretty shell, a few grains of rice, &c. As we drew near this rock, we heard the most strange, unearthly cries and screams; as we approached nearer, we found they proceeded from a woman; we heard them a long distance before we saw her. She was in the water, and she would rush frantically from the water into the mango-swamp, and then on the solid ground—there she would fall to the earth, apparently in convulsions, foaming at the mouth, &c.; then the same things would be repeated, with such wild screams, gestures and vociferations, I thought she must certainly be a raving maniac. A man was standing near, not touching her: he was her husband; he was only watching that she did herself no injury. Upon inquiring of Proud what was the matter, he told me, "The devil (the Ku) hab her; she soon come be great devil woman—look, mammy, close on them rock live big devil; many men be lie dead there—plenty devils (Kwi) there—(all the spirits of the departed become devils, and they become big or little devils, according to their position in this world)—one devil he come live with this woman, then she come be wise woman." Upon inquiry afterwards upon this subject, I found that among the Greboes there are some people, both men and women, who are called "Deya," or devil doctor. These profess to find out witches, to be enabled to foretell the future, and, in fact, to perform all the charms and spells such people ever have done in all parts of the world. Before they become doctors, however, they have to go through a long preparation. They first become suddenly seized with the idea that they are possessed by a devil, that they cannot get rid of him, but that he will teach and enable them to perform many wonderful things. They do actually appear to have the symptoms that the Evangelists tell us were seen in those possessed by devils; they go into violent convulsions, wallowing on the ground, gnashing their teeth—sometimes, I have been told, falling in the fire, and, as I now witnessed, into the water. When in their lucid state, they will go to a devil doctor to be taught. They have to separate entirely from their family during this time, which varies from one to three years, at the teacher's pleasure. They have to pass through a number of strange ceremonies, but at length their instruction is complete, and they go home, and can set up in business for themselves, where they are held in great respect.*

After watching this poor woman awhile, we then went on to Half-Grawah, my little boy's home. We were taken to the house of the head-man, (Thomas's father). The hut was very large, and clean; and round the inside were as many as fifty plates and dishes, hanging by pegs, stuck in to the side, and arranged very neatly. At one side were a number of jars and pots, made of the country clay. There was no fire in it, for which I was very thankful, as the smoke and the heat are dreadful. The head-man did not make his appearance; so, after sitting and talking with Thomas's mother, and others, for a while, I got up to say good-by. They said no, I must not say good-by, for head-man was gone to get dinner for me, and he would be very much offended if I did not come back and eat his dinner. So I said I would go across the lake to Spring Hill, see Proud's wife and child, and then come back.

There were several men here who understood English

---

* Since writing the above, I have seen a very full account of these people in Mrs. Scott's "Day-Dawn," to which I refer you.

very well, and I had good interpreters in Julia and Proud. I asked Thomas if he would like to remain with his mother, while I went across the lake. But, no! he was too much afraid that I would go away, and leave him. I had given him some tobacco to give to both his mother and father (all smoke here, men and women, and even young children, when they can get it; you cannot give a more acceptable present than a little tobacco) as a *dash* from me, and some beads for his little sister—and he was quite delighted at having these things to present. He was quite the centre of attraction to all the little urchins in town; such fine clothes had never been seen on any little boy before. At Spring Hill the teachers have a very small wooden house to live in, like the houses in the Christian village, at Cavalla—very coarse tables and chairs, but still infinitely superior to everything they had been used to in their own huts. You remember these native teachers are, all of them, those that have formerly been themselves educated in the schools. All the garden, round the house, looked in very nice order. Many young fruit and coffee-trees were flourishing, as yet too young to bear, but giving promise of future harvests. Proud's wife and child, and all the boys, looked well, clean and happy. We went into the kitchen, to see the poor little creature Mr. Hoffman had rescued from death by starvation; but, just as he said, it is impossible to do justice to the picture. A child, probably between three and four years old, with head the size, and limbs the length, of a child of that age, but, oh! so fearfully emaciated and attenuated. His breast-bone protruded like a chicken's, and there appeared to be nothing but the thinnest skin over that and the ribs. His back was the shape of the letter S; but, oh! his eyes—shall I ever forget the expression of those eyes! Immense eyes! starvation, misery, and anguish, were written there. He feels a little better to-day; the food he has had the past few days has given him a little strength, so he can sit up. But what agony the poor child must have suffered, and no "eye to pity, none to help." He moaned so pitifully, it made the heart ache; he does not attempt to speak, but all that can be done for him, is being done now. I thought of that poor little creature so soon to be laid low; and then, that, through the all-atoning merits of the gracious Redeemer, that now fearful-looking object would be beautiful, bright and all-glorious, clothed in white,

> "And with the angels stand,
> A crown upon his forehead,
> A harp within his hand;
> There, right before his Saviour,
> So glorious and so bright,
> He'd wake the sweetest music,
> And praise him day and night."

And, as I turned away, I thanked my Saviour with a grateful heart, that "light and immortality had been brought to light by the Gospel." Paddock seemed much pleased to see me, and promised to look after and tend the poor little boy. I gave him a *dash* of tobacco, for his father. We then re-crossed the lake, to Half-Grawah. We first went into the hut of a native Christian, called Johns; he has lately been building himself a new one. It is very nice and large—oblong, instead of round; and it has a partition, formed of mats (made of bamboo) so as to form a bed-room; in this he has a very decent bedstead. Everything looks neat and comfortable. His wife (of course, he has but one) is a very good-looking, intelligent young woman. After talking with them awhile, we were told our dinner was ready. I did not go to it with a very vigorous appetite, but they had prepared this to show me as much honor as they could express, and I would not refuse and wound their feelings on any account. We were conducted again into the house of the head-man; there a large chest was set out in the middle of the floor, covered with a clean, coarse, tow-cloth. At opposite sides of this impromptu table, country chairs were placed for Julia and myself, and a log of wood for Thomas to sit on. Three little dishes were turned upside down, at our places, to serve for plates—a large iron spoon for each, with the addition of a fork for me. Then there were two covered vegetable dishes, and a gravy dish, with cover and ladle. Johns and his brother stood by, to wait on us. They were Kroomen, had served on several vessels on the coast, and were quite proud of their knowledge of " 'Merica fashion." On another box, beside us, was a pretty little pitcher of water, and some glasses. Our waiters stood quite still, with folded arms, till we had asked a blessing—then they whipped off the covers, with a great flourish. In one dish, was rice; in the other, the fresh fish our host had been to catch, which had been cooked in the palm-butter that was in the gravy-dish. Julia and Thomas enjoyed their dinner very much; I can hardly say as much, though I did

take a little of each, out of compliment to my host.
He never made his appearance till we had finished eating; then, whilst Proud and Johns were eating the remainder, we went outside and talked with him.

Johns' brother, *Prince William*, is a very intelligent man. He has been to sea a great deal. He begged and implored me to take his child, a fine little girl about three years old. I told him I could not; that I had as much as I could do now. But he implored very earnestly " That I would take her and make her a Christian child." How hard it does seem to be obliged to deny such requests. They think I love children (they are not far wrong there), and this is the twelfth child I have had offered to me. Thomas' father seemed very grateful. He told me, " He gave me his boy, as long he live; he be my child, to do what I pleased with him, and he hoped I would make him mind me, and he grow up to be good man." As we returned in the canoe, we saw a poor leper, in a dreadful condition, bathing: dipping himself up and down in the water. It brought to mind the Syrian leper, Naaman.

INSECTS.—We have many petty annoyances here in the way of insects. In the first place, though such a thing as a bedbug is unknown, we have very few flies; you will hardly see one in a week. They are great rarities. Then we have a few, but not many, mosquitoes. There is a little insect that, at times, is quite troublesome, called the tick. It buries itself in the flesh of the feet and legs. It festers and becomes quite sore for several days. Then we have centipedes and scorpions. We do not see them so often, and they rarely injure you unless you happen to put your hand on them, or something of that kind. The cockroaches are a great nuisance. They grow very large, and are as bad as moths for eating clothes, particularly anything made of silk. But the greatest pests are the little ants. They are about the size of the little red ants at home, and they are here in myriads. Anything to eat, or drink, even a glass of water, must be stood in a dish of salt water, if you do not wish it full of them. They are perfect scavengers. Should you kill a roach and leave it, in an hour there will be no trace of it; they will have carried it off. The speed with which they collect round anything is marvellous. Rats and mice we have also in any quantity. I caught a very large rat in my room last night

SATURDAY EVENING.—Instead of reading the usual portion of Scripture at worship on Saturday evening, Mr. Hoffman has a custom of asking the children what has happened through the week, and then of deducing lessons of wisdom from these occurrences. Even in this small place, every Saturday evening, there has been one or more deaths to speak of. To night it struck me this world ought not to be called the "land of the living," but the land of the dying. It is the other world that is the "land of the living." Mr. Hoffman told the children that they had been speaking to him of death, now he would speak to them of life—"life from the dead." To-morrow, again, we are going to have two natives baptized, a man and a woman, and Mr. Hoffman feels that Christ has, indeed, called them from the dead and given them life. How delightful it is to see one after another waking from "the death in sin to a life in holiness." May it thus prove with them.

Sunday.—Again the beautiful baptismal service. May it ever remind us how it represents to us our profession, to follow the example of our blessed Lord. Read and talked to Matha, on the parable of the marriage, explaining to her the wedding garment and the freeness of its gift. Oh! that each Sunday we may travel " a Sabbath day's journey" toward our home.

Wah.—My adult evening class has increased to sixteen. *Wah* has been in the school-room all the evening. We always close with prayer. When we were about to kneel, he rushed across the room, knelt at my side, and taking hold of my hand placed it on his head, and held it there all the time we were in prayer, at the same time looking up, most earnestly, in my face. I do not know what he meant by the action. He is a very bright, intelligent child. I love to watch him. I wish I could know what ideas he has with regard to God.

Sacerdillo.—Mr. Hoffman brought in a large fruit last night about the size of a very large cantelope, only it is egg-shaped instead of round. The outside is a beautiful fawn color. It is called the sacerdillo. Upon cutting it open, in the centre, there is about a teacupful of pulpy substance, with seeds in it, exactly resembling grapes with the skin off—only the seeds are quite soft. This you eat with a spoon. It is delicious. The remainder of the fruit, cut up and stewed, makes a very good substitute for apple sauce, only it is rather sweet. It grows on a vine, which clambers up very tall trees. But, like all parasites, it materially injures that which maintains and supports it.

Convocation.—Mr. and Mrs. Hoffman are gone to attend the convocation, at Cavalla. This is a meeting held three times a year, at different stations, when all the teachers and ministers, from the different places, that can possibly come, are present. Reports are read, speeches made, and all business for the mission attended. Exchanges or removals, decided upon. I could not well be present. It is best for one of us always to be at home.

Good Friday.—Good Friday. Mr. Gibson preached a most excellent sermon, from the words, " He bowed His head and died." It was really a beautiful discourse. Would that every heart in that little congregation could respond " the Saviour died for me." Poor Matha is very feeble. She coughs and expectorates constantly, but will not believe she is near death.

Change.—Mr. and Mrs. Hoffman did not reach home till quite late. They brought me letters from the Bishop and Miss Williford, in which I find several changes have been determined upon at this convocation. Mr. Gibson is to be removed to Monrovia, to take the pastoral charge of the church there. Mr. Crummel, also a colored clergyman, is to come here, to assist Mr. Hoffman, and to have charge of the Boys' High School, which is to be removed to Mount Vaughan. And Miss Ball and myself are to change places. She is to come here to the Asylum, and I go to Cavalla. We should all be willing to go, or stay, wherever we can accomplish most good, and it is thought best, and so we are to remove next week. We have been expecting this some time.

EASTER SUNDAY.—In bed all day, with very high fever, but could rejoice in a risen Saviour.

I have had a nice little note to-day from Mr. Wilson from Monrovia. He is still very unwell. He is going home to America. I hope his health may be improved by it. Last evening we had several of the colonists here to tea. We had a very pleasant evening. My children seem to feel very badly at my leaving them. I shall be obliged to leave my little Virginia here. Miss Ball will take care of her, as all the children at Cavalla are natives, and Mr. Harris does not wish her to mingle with them. Little Thomas I shall take with me, and let him go into the boys' school at Cavalla.

TRAVELLING.—The sea has been so rough, for some days, that the boat has not been able to come up; so after leaving all my things packed, to be sent when the sea is calmer, I started for Cavalla in a hammock, the boy the Bishop had sent up going along to take care of me.

The rolling of the surf to-night was most truly grand. As the waves broke upon 'the rocks, the spray would be tossed up for yards. Truly, it seems to me, Old Ocean is the most magnificent creation of the Almighty hand.

My bearers detained me very long on the road, so that it was eight o'clock in the evening ere I reached my destination. I should have felt quite timid if the Bishop's boy had not been with me. It was perfectly dark, and the last two miles of our road lies through a plain covered with grass four feet high, through which a narrow foot-path has been trodden. Thoughts of leopards, snakes, &c., darted across my imagination, and then the strange, wild cries of the night-birds in the bushes, made me truly realize how far away I was from home, and, to complete the romance, one of my poor bearers slipt and fell, tumbling me to the ground; fortunately, we were neither of us much hurt—just a bruise or two. But the bright smiles, and cheerful, happy faces that soon greeted me, made amends for all fatigue.

To-morrow I shall begin my work among the natives. I do not know whether I shall like it as well as among the colonists, but wherever I am, I hope I may work for God.

WANT.—Miss Ball went to the Cape to-day, and the Bishop started for Monrovia. He probably will be absent two months. I have been into the store-room with Miss Williford, learning the place where everything is kept—books, material for wearing apparel, &c. Then we cut and basted five dresses for the girls. We went into the native town to visit two sick women, and so passed the day.

The people are very poor, and yet very generous, among themselves dividing their smallest possessions. There is no character they appear so much to despise as a stingy one, or, as they call it, "a close hand." And if the missionary wishes to effect any good among them, he must show his kindness by frequent little *dashes;* so I have supplied myself with a piece of dark cotton cloth, some tobacco and pipes for this purpose. Poor creatures, they really suffer very much. A little thing makes them happy. Since the war last year there has been great scarcity of food, and you constantly are met by beggars—placing their hand on their stomachs, they will say, " Hunger kills me," or " Hunger affects me." Money, money, money, how much are we often tempted to covet it.

My little Thomas has walked down to-day from the Cape. It is a long walk for such a child.

There is a French vessel anchored off here with a great deal of rum on board. We see some of the horrible effects of it. It is so very, very wicked thus to destroy the missionary's labor of years.

The Well.—A calm, peaceful Sabbath. I was awakened in the morning by a loud chattering and jabbering, and looking out of my window, a perfect eastern picture presented itself. Our house stands on the brow of a small hill, completely enveloped in cocoa-nut trees, which add much to the beauty of the scene. Just at the foot of this little hill, or bank, the Bishop has had a deep well dug, the water of which is, at present, raised up by means of a windlass. There has been quite a drought for some time, and all the springs in the neighborhood are dry, so the natives from the towns around come to our well for water. I suppose there were as many as fifty or sixty round the well in every conceivable attitude, all waiting with their jars to be filled, while a long string of women, with their jars on their heads, were coming and going. It really was a very pretty sight, and when you add to this, the rolling waves, the white sandy beach, and the deep rich green of the grass and foliage, you may imagine quite a picture.

In the morning Mr. Jones conducted service, in Grebo, in the church. I had two classes in Sunday School, in the afternoon: the one composed of colonists—our house servants; the other, the married women from the native village—all Christians, educated in the school here. These classes I am to have charge of. After Sunday School, Harry, a colonist carpenter from the Cape, who is here building the boys' school-house, came to my room to read and hear God's word explained. He is over fifty years of age, but he is very anxious to learn to read his Bible well. At present he has to spell almost every word.

We had service in the school-house in the evening. Mr. Jones read the service in English, but preached in Grebo. After our return to the parlor, we sang some hymns, and so closed our Sabbath.

VISITORS — There having been so little water lately, the girls are obliged to take their clothes some distance off to a running stream, to wash them. So on Monday mornings, for the present, our school duties are very much shortened. From four to five o'clock in the afternoon the ladies generally sit in the parlor, to receive all the natives who may choose to come " to look them." Formerly they used to be coming and going all day, but it was found to interrupt the time so much, that the ladies determined to receive no visitors in the morning, unless it were sickness or some case of urgent necessity, but always some of them to be in the parlor at that hour of the afternoon, except Saturday and Sunday. They have learnt this; so always in the afternoon we have quite a number here, and they expect us frequently to *dash* them. Poor things! they having nothing, literally nothing, themselves, our little possessions to them appear enormous. We went this afternoon into the Christian village. It consists of those who have been educated in the schools, and have married each other. Their houses all look very neat and nice. In the evening, Henry, the Bishop's factotum, came to me. He is to come an hour to study every evening. There is never any lack of work here.

Chapter Ten.

BADE.

I FIND I get along better with the native children than I supposed I should at first. This afternoon I took one of the older girls as an interpreter, and went to town to visit some of the women. One, a poor old woman named Bade, is a leper—every joint is eaten off both hands and feet. She lives in a very little hut, but she is in a very happy frame of mind. She very rarely can get out, even to church, but she is a sincere Christian, and talks to all her friends who come to see her about God's things. It is very pleasant to hear her talk.

Miss Williford takes charge of the sewing-school three times a week—a great relief to me.

WITCHCRAFT.—Every little while something occurs to remind us we are in the midst of savages. The last day or two, a fine large vessel has been beating up and down the coast, in our sight. To-day she came to anchor about four miles off. *Kade* came in and told us a sad tale about her. She is an English vessel—has been down the coast, and now was on her return home, fully laden with corn, wood, and palm oil. She has a good many Kroomen on board, whom some months ago she took from Cape Palmas to work her on the coast, and now she was bringing them back to their homes, before she proceeded to England. Every white man on board of her, except the captain and steward, are dead. The fever has carried them all off. The captain lies very low, and is perfectly delirious, and the steward just able to crawl about, and give a few directions. They have met with so many disasters, bad winds, and such a number of deaths, that the Kroomen came to the conclusion, that there must be " a witch" on board. They, therefore, accused one of their number of witchcraft. So they took him and tied him up in the rigging, giving him neither food or drink, in that hot sun. Each day they beat him severely. At the end of three days they let him down, tied a rope around his body, and flung him over into the sea—keeping him under water till he was almost drowned. This they repeated three times. They then again tied him up in the rigging — beating and starving him as before—but in two days after he was a corpse. They then flung the body into the sea, exulting that another witch was dead. Thus was this poor wretch tortured for a crime, of which it was utterly impossible he could be guilty. There was one far greater, far mightier, than them all, but whom they knew not. He it is that holdeth the " winds in his fist, and the waves in the hollow of his hand." The victim was the uncle of one of our school boys—a very fine man.

Does it not seem dreadful to know of such things taking place, and, yet, to be utterly powerless to prevent it? We shall send on board, to-morrow morning, to see if we can do anything to help them. Miss Williford has sent information to the Cape to-night, that the governor may send down some one to take charge of the vessel up to the Cape. The Kroomen on board know the coast, and where the vessel ought to go, and where she ought not, but they do not understand steering her. She will have to lay at the Cape, either till the captain recovers and can get men, or till some other vessel arrives, to take charge of her. The captain will be there, too, under the doctor's care. See how daily we have to feel the need of a hospital! Mr. Hoffman came down this evening. When the Bishop is away he often comes to look after us. Two of the girls at the Asylum wrote me pretty little notes, and sent me a quantity of shells they had all been picking up for me. Mr. Dorsen came in this evening also. He brought me a beautiful shell. One of my school girls, also, brought me two nests of the rice bird. They know I am fond of collecting such things. These nests are very curiously built to avoid snakes and monkeys, who are very fond of the eggs and young birds.

SATURDAY AFTERNOON.—One of our trusty men went on board the vessel. The captain was able to speak to him, but he left him, as he said, "just for dead." I always go into the girls' dormitory every night, to see that they are all safe. At nine o'clock a large bell rings, and then I send in a lantern to the girls' school-house, to be hung up in the passage, in the dormitory, between their rooms. At ten o'clock I go in myself, see that they are all safely there, and bring away the lantern; and on Saturday morning every place, belonging to them, is scrubbed. So I look after it to see that it is done properly. Saturday afternoons we always go to town, to visit the women. Miss Williford goes, with an interpreter, in one direction, and I, with mine, in another. To every one we meet, we always bow and say, "*Sande diade*," Sunday to-morrow. The children, too, are all permitted to go to town, but all commissioned to tell to every one that the next day is the Sabbath—God's day. We also have a certain flag waving from the mission house, called the Saturday flag; and on Sunday, there is another waves from the tower of the church. Thus, all means are used to make them "remember the Sabbath day." Harriet Williams, one of the native Christian women, is my interpreter. She is an exceedingly intelligent woman, has been well instructed, and thoroughly understands the teachings of the Sacred Scriptures. I have engaged her to come to me, three times a week, to teach me Grebo. Poor old *Bade*, the leper, is very feeble. The rats trouble her greatly at night. The disease affects every joint, and that appears to attract these animals, and she is never without a very bad sore occasioned by their bites. I have sent her an old dress. I hope it may be some protection to her. She speaks very joyfully of her heavenly home.

SUNDAY.—It is Sunday. After church; this morning, a number of my little girls came into my room; and after Sunday-school, this afternoon, about a dozen of the elder girls came up, wanting me to show them pictures and talk to them about them. While conversing with them, as they all sat on the floor around me, I placed my hand on the shoulder of one of them, and said, "Girls, I do hope you will soon learn to love me." They all exclaimed immediately, "We do; we do love you this time." And I believe they do. They all look so pleased whenever they see me; and the little ones run to catch hold of my hand. I am very glad to observe this, for I always feel that a teacher can accomplish comparatively nothing without having a hold on the hearts of the pupils. I want them to obey me from love, not from fear. Much as I love to talk to them, however, I shall be obliged to tell them I cannot have them come to me on Sunday. I must have a little time to myself and for rest. But it is very hard to deny knowledge to those so eagerly inquiring after it. But prudence, prudence; it is a very hard thing for an impulsive person to learn. Some man has died in town this afternoon. They have been firing guns, as their custom is, all the evening. We were not aware that any one was sick. But it is frequently the custom, when any one is ill, to hide them away. They think the sickness has been brought on by witchcraft, and so the person is concealed that the witch may not be able to exert any further influence over him. Sometimes, the poor sick man (or woman) is hid away by his mother (they have more confidence in the mother than any other relation), in the conical roof; where, to add to his disease, he is almost suffocated. Sometimes he is carried off to a distance; in fact, he is hidden anywhere that it is thought the supposed witch will not guess his whereabouts. Strange it is, that these poor deluded beings, knowing how liable they are, at any moment, to be accused of this crime, and to suffer its penalties, yet, whenever they have a severe quarrel with another, will be sure to utter, maliciously: "I'll witch you." This is always remembered, and should any great evil happen to the party, even twenty years after, the person who has uttered those words is sure to undergo the penalty.

WOUNDS.—We have heard nothing more about the dead man. No sassa-wood ordeal this time. I have commenced the study of Grebo. I fear it will be slow work, however, as I have but little time to give to it. If we allowed the school children to talk to us, in that language, we should get along much faster; but, though that would be for our benefit, it certainly would not be for theirs; it is much more important that they should learn English. Our life here is pretty uniform; plenty to do, and, I hope and trust, willing hearts to do it. Each hour through the week has its appointed duty, that we never have to stop and think, "what next." How much more can be accomplished where there is a regular system! This place would not do for very fastidious ladies, who cannot dress a wound, and whose own feelings are so sensitive that they have no room left to feel for others. I used to feel deadly faint and sick at the sight of a wound, or of blood. But I learnt to look upon it as a purely selfish feeling; giving way to our own weaknesses, instead of throwing them off, and exerting ourselves for the good of the sufferer; I determined, therefore, if possible, to conquer this morbid sensitiveness, and I have pretty well succeeded, though not entirely, as I could wish, yet sufficiently, so as to enable me to render assistance in suffering. We are here constantly called upon to administer healing balm to the bodies, as well as the souls, of these benighted ones. They think the white man can do everything. " He have all wisdom," and they place perfect confidence in his power. Sometimes, however, the sights are disgusting, and we turn away with a sickening feeling. But, then, we must call to mind Him who " went about healing all manner of sickness and disease among the people ;" and we must remember how loathsome and disgusting our leprous souls must be in His eyes, and yet the Great Physician does not disdain, on that account,. to stretch forth His hand to help us. My little Thomas has contrived to cut off part of his toe, and I have had a very sore wound to dress; and this morning a young woman came to me from the town with a finger almost chopped off; all the bone laid bare —it looked dreadful. We have found the most effectual way of treating these flesh wounds, when fresh done, is first to bathe them well with warm water—so as to be sure that all the parts are clean, and then to put on raw cotton soaked in laudanum; it smarts dreadfully for a few seconds, but stops the bleeding, and heals soon. This is bound up tight, and left for two or three days, so the air may not come to it, then it is carefully washed and cerate put to it each day. It soon is quite well.

SICKNESS.—The poor girl has been again to have her hand dressed; it looks better. She seems to feel quite grateful. More little notes from the girls at the Asylum. It is very pleasant to receive them, only it involves the necessity of answering them, and my time! my time! the days are not half long enough for all we want to do.

The vessel that was out here was taken, some days ago, to Cape Palmas. Under kind care and treatment, the captain is rapidly recovering. There is another English vessel just put in there, from down the coast. The captain of that is well, but he has lost all but two of his men. They may have to remain there some time, before they can pick up men enough from other vessels to take them home. It is very sickly this season down the coast. I hope God will preserve our missionary friends there. I am often struck with the absurd reasoning of worldly men; when they hear of the death of a missionary, in this baneful clime, they say we ought to take it as an indication that God does not mean Africa to be Christianized by our instrumentality, and that it is throwing away our lives, in fact tempting Providence, to go there; but there is an old adage, "It is a poor rule that won't work both ways." They never think, however, of applying it in this way, no matter how many lives are lost on the coast in pursuit of worldly wealth—ah! that is nothing—they never think it is a divine indication that they must give up all commerce, all pursuit of wealth here. Now, since I have been here, in a few months—just between here and Lagos—seventeen seamen have perished of fever; not a third that number of missionaries have died in as many years. Do the owners of these vessels think they must never send them forth again? Is not the health and life of each seaman as dear to him and his family, as the missionary's is to him? Is not the fever as acute suffering to the one, as to the other? Is the poor, (often) ignorant, debased and vicious seaman, surer that, the moment he dies, death shall be swallowed up in victory, that he will enter the haven of eternal rest, where all tears will be wiped from every eye? These flimsy pretences to philanthropy, in regard to the welfare of the missionary, are too often made to conceal the entire want of feeling. These persons are generally afraid that their pockets will suffer, and, therefore, they say: "Oh, no! we won't give you anything—we consider it wrong, decidedly wrong, for missionaries to expose themselves to the perils of such a clime." Let these persons carry out their principles, and, as far as they can, prevent all commerce, of every description, with such a clime, and so prevent the sickness and death of so many seamen there; for surely, if it is not worth the missionary's while to peril his life, that he may win the choicest jewels that shall shine in the Redeemer's crown to all eternity, it cannot be worth the seaman's while to peril his, for a little, worthless dross, that will perish with the using.

MOONLIGHT.—Paddock walked up to see me to-day. I like him very much. He said he came to bring me a little of the fruits of his garden—a few egg-plants and some tomatoes. They grow very well here, but very small. I felt quite pleased with this little attention from him. The poor little diseased child is dead; he was very decently buried. He is now safe at home!—safe at home! He had none here on earth, but he has now joined the happy band, to be forever with the Lord. It is a splendid moonlight night; the effect, through the cocoa-nut trees, is very beautiful. But, oh, dear! it is a great fall—after your ideas have been wrought up to the highest pitch of sublimity, by the magnificence of the moonlight on the surrounding scene, and the ever-rolling surf—to go into your room, and descend to the most unpleasant task of hunting cockroaches. I do not know why it is, but there is something repulsive and disgusting about these animals.

PRAYER.—Friday afternoons Miss Williford has a prayer-meeting for the Christian women of the village, and the older school-girls, who are members of the Church. This afternoon, she had a swelled face, so I conducted it for her. She always calls on one of the women to pray in Grebo. I was surprised at the length of the prayer, and the ease and fluency with which it was spoken.—" God will work, and who shall let."

LOWLINESS.—The girls often come to my room, when they think I have a few minutes to spare, for me to show them how to do something. Some of them are trying to make patchwork. In one of the huts we visited to-day, there was quite a little congregation collected. Harriet Williams is an excellent interpreter; being conversant with Scripture, she can explain and enforce all that we say. She generally carries her little baby with her. Children are placed in saddles on the back, fastened on with straps around the waist, and over the shoulder, leaving both arms free. When we go to town, we always put on the commonest clothes we can wear; for going into the smoky huts, and then sitting on a small block of wood on the ground, does not tend either to cleanse or improve your clothing. When I first used to go into their huts, I would sit down on the chest, which you almost always find in them, but I found that the smoke almost blinded me; at length, I tried the block of wood on the floor, and I soon found that in this case, as in most others, "with the lowly is wisdom." When you go home, you must be careful, also, not to touch anything till you have given your hands a good scrubbing, as the hands you have to shake are not always in the highest state of cleanliness, particularly those of the children; and, should you happen to be a favorite amongst them (children are good physiognomists—they soon know who loves them), numbers of these will follow you, each saying, as they stick out a dirty hand, "Tomo kwa"—touch my hand; and they seem quite disappointed if you refuse.

THE BODIA.—The Greboes have a number of customs, that seem to me as if they had a Jewish origin. Each town has a Bodia*, or high priest, who, when he is installed into this office, is anointed, as is also his house. He is the principal man in their religious ceremonies; he it is who offers the sacrifices, &c.; but his office is very undesirable, as he is made accountable for bad weather, failure of the crops, and a variety of other ills that may befall the people; and he most frequently ends his days by sassa-wood, for some imaginary misdemeanor. This office is hereditary in certain families, though not to the eldest son. Any member of the family may be selected, on the death of the old Bodia, to fill his place, and he is

* See Mrs. Scott's "Day Dawn," for full account.

obliged to take it immediately; the position must not be left vacant a day. *Nya*, our gardener, was the son of the old Bodia; and, when his father died, they determined to make him Bodia (he was not then a Christian), but he ran away and hid himself, to escape it—and, as the office must be filled directly, they were obliged to choose another member of the family. The Bodia, and his head wife, never work on a farm; but all the people must pay him a tithe of what they raise. He always carries a monkey skin, as a badge of office; and when he sits down, it must always be on this. He and his head wife must never, at one time, be absent from the hut. It must always be open, and one or other of them present. The fire must never go out in the hut. They have no idea where their fire first came, or how it was obtained, for they say they never were without it. Shall I tell you of one visit we made? We went into a hut, which was quite large, and hung round with plenty of plates and dishes; it had three doors. These doors are merely pieces of the wall or side of the hut, that can be removed at pleasure. The whole of the roof, up to the very apex of the cone, was piled up with wood, arranged very neatly on a frame, made for the purpose. There was a bright fire blazing in the little triangular fire-place, emitting volumes of smoke. As we entered, a bright, pleasant-looking woman, who had been peeling cassadas, with a troupe of little, naked children around her, arose, and came forward to welcome us. She pushed towards each of us a log to sit upon, and then seated herself beside us—one child between her knees, another beside her, and all listened most attentively to the Word of Life, as interpreted by Harriet. At the other door of the house a woman had been standing, beating palm-nuts in a mortar—(these are so large that the women always stand, when employed about this work)—but she, too, gradually stopped her work, and drew near to listen. My little boy, Thomas, is sitting at my feet; he always follows me everywhere, and sits very quietly. God grant, that we may have faith to believe that the Word may take root, "that it shall not return unto him void." Can you picture us? Would that I could not only show you the scenes these eyes see, but that I could fill you with the same earnest longings, the same intense desires for the temporal and eternal interests of these poor people, then, I am sure there would be a full supply of laborers.

CANNIBALS.—These people have all been cannibals. There is, probably, not a man, thirty years of age, who has not feasted on human flesh; it does not appear with them to be a relish for this kind of food, but it is done to show the greatest contempt and derision for their enemies, as it is only those taken in battle whom they thus devour. Many of their prisoners, however, are preserved as slaves. These, in general, are treated well, and are, in most respects, as well off, as any other members of the household. But I have heard that there is a tribe of savages, about eighty miles back of Monrovia, that are regular cannibals, not merely devouring their enemies taken in battle, but feeding on one another. How fearful it is! Miss Williford was laughing at me to-night, and saying, it is such hungry times now with these poor people, that, a little distance back, I should stand but a poor chance, as I appear to be in such good condition. I have no ambition, however, to run any such risk.

ATONEMENT.—How even the most degraded of human beings feel their guilt, and need of an atonement. Among this people they have a custom, before going to war, for the whole tribe, consisting sometimes of several towns, to meet together, and confess their sins to one another—the sins or offences I mean that they have committed the one against the other, perhaps some deed committed years ago. They then make restitution, and offer a sacrifice to the *kwi* (devils); unless they do this, they think they will not prosper in battle.

SELF-DENIAL.—In Christian lands, we can hardly imagine the strength of mind and the grace it requires to maintain a consistent Christian profession among the heathen. Two of the poor Christians, in town, were sorely tempted yesterday. It is very hungry times with them now; and the continued dry weather we are having, makes them fear for their growing crops. A great devil-doctor has been summoned, who, after various incantations, has ordered three bullocks to be offered to the Kwi, in sacrifice. Every man in town is compelled to pay his part towards this, Christians as well as others. After they have performed many ceremonies over this sacrifice, it is divided, and a portion given to each family to eat. These Christians, true to their profession, (though suffering as much from the want of food as others) refused to take their share, as the Bible expressly forbids us to eat meat offered to idols. Was not this a great act of faith and love, probably, far more acceptable to God than many of the mighty deeds performed by Christians in other lands?—An heroic deed of self-denial.

THE WELL.—To-day, I was forcibly reminded of the Scripture account of the strife of Abraham's and Lot's servants about the water. I have told you before that, in consequence of the drought, all the springs are drying up; and the people, from a great distance, come here to the well to obtain water. The scene is certainly very picturesque. I never tire gazing at it. The well is of the simplest construction, covered by a flat platform of planks, and the water raised by turning a crank. It is dug in a hollow—the coarse grass, very green and fresh, around it, and completely surrounded by cocoa-nut and palm-trees, with their beautiful foliage, forming a fine shade, while scores of women are continually disputing and contending for their turn to draw. Twice to-day, Miss Williford has been obliged to go out and settle a "palaver" about the well.

BEGGING.—A poor colonist woman has come down from the Cape, begging. Last week, while she and her child were away gathering palm-nuts, her house took fire; and when she returned, she found it burnt to the ground, with all her worldly goods. The *all* was not much, but then it was her all—and she a widow. We have such constant and unceasing demands on our charity—and really so deserving are the objects—that it

The Fan Palm of Cavalla, W. Af.

is so hard to deny, and yet so hard to supply. The missionary's salary is small, and his heart often large; but if we cannot do much, we can show our willingness by our mite.

DAILY DUTIES.—I gave you my daily routine of labor at the Cape. I will tell you now what it is here. I rise at six o'clock, and read till half-past seven; then we have prayers for the family, in English. Mr. Jones conducting prayers with the children—*all*, boys and girls, (nearly a hundred) meeting in the girls' school-house at seven. We breakfast at eight, then a few minutes to study Grebo. A little before nine, I go into the girls' school-house, up into the dormitory, and all around, to see that everything is neat, and in order. From nine till half-past one in school, without a moment's intermission. When I come out of school, I always find either an orange or some other refreshment placed in my room by the loving hands of our good hostess. Then Julia and Mary, our two housemaids, come to my room for instruction in reading and writing. I am very tired, but this is the only time I can give them. Two afternoons in the week, Miss Williford has sewing-school. I take my work after dinner, go into the parlor to receive the native visitors, (who are numerous) and take my Grebo books to try and study a little, if I can. The other three afternoons, I have my Grebo teacher, and Grebo dictionary to write. The Bishop, three afternoons in the week, preaches in different towns, when he is at home. At half-past six the candles are lighted, and then Henry James comes to me, till tea-time. After tea, prayers;

by this time it is eight o'clock. We get our work, and sit down together; presently, Mr. Bacon will come to me to spell; and Mrs. Bristow, our cook, to Miss Williford. There is another half hour. Then, there is always some interruptions; some of the girls or boys have either headache or toothache. With a household of over a hundred, there is always something wanting. It is impossible to tell the multiplicity of things to look after. We settle to sewing about nine o'clock. At ten, we shut up the house. I go into the dormitory to look after the children. On returning to my room, I write for an hour—journal, letters, &c. My bed generally receives a pretty wearied body; but sleep is sweet. Such is my daily routine. I say little of the employments, &c., of the other missionaries, except as it comes in connection with my own; but every one of us has every moment employed, only I am writing my own experiences. A vessel has anchored off here, to-day; the captain sent us some late papers. It is very rare for a vessel to lay off here, except for the purpose of obtaining Kroomen, as the coast is so bad, it is impossible to land any goods.

SURGERY. — Miss Williford is sorely troubled with boils; she could not go to town to-day. We found Bade very sick; if it were not for the mission, she would die of absolute starvation. The rats gnaw at her, even through her dress. In passing through the town I heard a number of women's voices, uttering something between a wail and a song; and, directly, we saw a number of women and children collected in front of a hut singing (or howling) and dancing. A woman had just been buried, and thus they were mourning for her. While sitting in another hut, we saw a number of men passing, and, among them, one covered with blood, whom the others appeared to be helping. Harriet went out, and in a few minutes returned, and asked me to go with her. In the enclosure of a hut, close by, was the poor man I had just seen; he appeared to be fearfully injured; he was uttering a low, wailing sound, was sitting on a stone, and looking deadly faint. I called for some water, made them give him some to drink, and bathe his face. A man, standing beside him, was shaving his head, with a rough, blunt piece of iron, disclosing four fearful, gaping wounds, any one of which looked as if it might have killed him. He had another dreadful wound, directly across the knee-pan. His canoe had upset, and he had been dashed upon some jagged rocks. He was a Bushman (a man from inland); he had never seen a white lady before. I hurried up home, prepared clothes, &c., and came back. Upon washing the wounds, I had to remove five splinters of bone. I bound up his wounds, and told him to let them remain so, till I opened them. Poor creatures! in suffering, they have no idea of tenderness towards one another. It really was dreadful to see the torture inflicted on him by the way in which his head was scraped.

HEROISM.—Miss Williford not able to be at church to-day. To night Mrs. Gillet, our assistant teacher, had a bad sick headache, and went to lay down. Just as the sermon commenced, however, she came to the door, and beckoned to me. I went to her, and found that one of our little girls, about ten years old, had, during the day, picked up a needle, and had stuck it in the front of her dress, and in kneeling down to prayers, she had leaned against it, and the needle had run into her breast, and entirely disappeared, though upon pressing, we could see about where the head was—it had gone in, point foremost. I took her immediately into my room, and made a slight opening with a needle, but could do no good—it must be lanced. She bore it very patiently. We are fearful lest it should have touched the lungs, as it hurts her every breath she draws. Mrs. Gillet will take her to the Cape, early to-morrow morning, to the doctor.

Mrs. Gillet has come back, with little Sophia. The doctor has probed, but though he once saw the needle, he could not get hold of it. He has put on her a plaster, and hopes that it will work out, without doing her any harm. Mrs. Gillet wanted to leave her, for a day or two, at the asylum, but she would not stay. Think of the poor child having endured that pain, and yet walked twenty-two miles to-day.

Poor Matha Owen died at the asylum yesterday. She sleeps in Jesus. Her end was peace.

Sassa-wood.—Yesterday afternoon a man passed in front of the house, dressed up very fine—a white and red cotton umbrella, (this, in their estimation, is splendid), carried over him by a friend. He was followed by a train of boys and women. This was a triumphal procession—he had escaped the effects of the Sassa-wood. In town they are having a "grand palaver" about the man who was killed on board the ship, that I spoke of, (as if a person is supposed to be a witch, the Sassa ordeal is the only lawful way of trying him), and now this man having escaped, they will try others. Last night we heard a great howling and screaming, proceeding from the town, and we found it was the lamentations of the friends of another man, whom they had caught, and to whom they are about to administer it. Though many innocent persons suffer by this poison, yet were it not for the fear of it, there would be no end to the fearful crimes committed.

I often feel—to wonder at ourselves—the perfect freedom from fear that we have—two white ladies alone, without any gentlemen, with about a dozen Christian men near us, and surrounded by a hungry, almost famishing population of thousands of savages, and we known by them to have in our possession food enough for many weeks (till we get supplies again from America) to support our family of over a hundred. Is it not a wonder that they do not break in and steal it? But we lay down and sleep in perfect peace and safety, knowing that the "Watchman of Israel never slumbers nor sleeps.

SURGERY.—To-day I have been quite a doctress. These things still make me feel a little faint and sick, but I battle with those feelings. First, I looked a little to Miss Williford's boils; but Mary is very good; she attends to her very nicely. Then I put a drawing plas ter on Sophia, and after it had drawn awhile, I could see the needle moving about under the flesh. I probed the wound, making the incision a little deeper, but I could not get hold of the needle. Then the poor Bushman that was injured came. I intended to have gone to him, but he came up into the school-room to me. I had hardly thought it would be possible for him to live. Two of the wounds had fractured the bone of the skull. I removed several more small splinters. I was full two hours dressing and attending to his wounds. I fear now very much about his leg—just on the knee-pan quite a large piece is completely gone. He is a wild Bushman—one who probably would not have hesitated to make a good meal of me, if he had found me back in his country. He speaks but very little Grebo—the girls can scarcely understand him, but he appears very grateful.

I could not help thinking to-day, how the precious Word of God is a rule and guide to us in every position in which we may be placed. I had a number of the older girls in the room, while I was attending to the man, as I wish them to learn how to do these things themselves. When attending to the man's knee, of course he could not bend it, so I had to kneel down to dress it, at which all the girls set up a loud scream of laughter. I am keenly alive to ridicule, even from these poor people, and my first impulse was to spring up from my humble position, feeling that it was a degradation to me, far beneath my dignity, to assume such a position here, when the remembrance of the blessed Saviour's words and example checked me, when he knelt and washed his disciples' feet, and said to them, "If I then, your Lord and Master, have washed your feet, ye ought also to wash one anothers' feet." How hard it is to root out pride from the human heart. Afterwards I opened and dressed a very bad boil on the arm of one of the girls. So much for my surgery. I am getting along bravely. The Bishop is very good with all these things, when he is at home—he is quite a doctor.

I have nailed all my daguerreotypes up in my room. It is so pleasant to feel I can look up and see my friends without having to hinder my time in going to open them.

Our rains have commenced. We seldom have a continuously wet day, but violent storms and hurricanes come on without a moment's notice. It is this that makes navigation on the coast so dangerous. The seaman has hardly time to furl his sails.

I dressed the wounded man again. Really, I am beginning to have some faith in my own skill in that line—all the wounds in the head, except one, from which another small piece of bone had to be abstracted, are fast getting well, and that will soon. His father has sent two men from the Bush country to carry him home, but he thinks he will be able to get along himself, though still very lame.

SICK MAN.—In one of the huts, in town to-day, I found a young man evidently in the last stage of consumption. He had been a Krooman and could speak considerable English. I asked him "if he knew anything of God and Jesus Christ." He said, "Me know a little what Payne (the Bishop) teach me." I asked him if he ever prayed to God. "Not now; me did when me go to school, but now me never do; me want to pray, but now me no *sabby* how." (Sabby is to understand.) I then asked him when he went to school. He said, "A long time pass—much time—me no *sabby* how long, but me only go five—six weeks, and then me be bad boy—me run away; but it no pass me what him tell to me—it here" (pointing to his head). I talked to him some time, and when I went away I told him not to forget to pray. He said, "Me no forget, me can't forget; God's things in my mind all the time." Do not such cases make us take courage to "cast our bread upon the waters, knowing we shall find it after many days."

CANNIBALISM.—There is a man that comes here to the house very frequently. I have had an intuitive horror of him, though I heard he was a Christian. Speaking of him to-day, I found he had been a dreadful man—a great *cannibal;* and he confessed that his great delight had been in tormenting his victim, cutting and hacking him to pieces. He is a striking example of the power of Divine grace upon the heart. "The lion has become the lamb." But his countenance still bears the marked characteristics of cruelty and barbarity, though subdued. He has a dreadful eye. But he has now for years been a consistent Christian.

We heard to-night that two of the tribes up the river are at war, and one of the tribes took three men of the others prisoners. They were immediately killed and eaten! Hungry times here, as elsewhere, are quarrelsome times. May God give to these poor people the bread of life.

FRENCH EMIGRANT VESSEL.—Mr. Ashton and Mr. Cooper, two of our most respectable colonists, came down from the Cape. Mr. Cooper has just been giving us an account that he had from the captain of an English steamer that is at the Cape. It seems a company of Frenchmen have pledged themselves to furnish laborers for Guiana. They have fitted out four vessels, which they have despatched to this coast, under the pretext of *hiring* laborers. But as soon as the poor wretches get on board the vessel, expecting only to be emigrants, they find they are slaves. Well, one of these vessels was lying off Cape Mount, the most northern part of Liberia. She had her full complement of men made up; the captain had just sent his last gang, consisting of about thirty, on board, while he remained on shore to finish his business. But when this last set reached the vessel, (many of them stout, hardy Kroomen, used to the sea,) they found that, instead of being treated as emigrants, they were to be treated as slaves, and the sailors were about to handcuff them. This did not suit them; they knew better. So, immediately they all fell on the sailors, and killed every white man on board, thirteen in number. They then went down into the hold, and found a quantity of poor creatures, all handcuffed, and stowed away—regular slave-ship fashion. They released them from confinement, but could not unmanacle them. When the captain came from shore, they all threatened him with their guns; and having no arms, and not one white man left, he was obliged to hurry back to land. The Kroomen let out the sails, and put out to sea, but had no idea how to steer. After beating about for seven days, the English mail steamer passed near, and seeing this strange vessel, with no colors, and apparently none but blacks on board, they determined to board her. At first the blacks were disposed to show fight, thinking it a French vessel; but as soon as they saw the English colors (God bless England for it!) they quietly submitted. The English soon saw that in all her outfit, &c., she was neither more nor less than a slaver. The steamer took her in tow, sent on shore for her captain, and, as a prisoner, brought him to Monrovia. He was there placed in prison, to be tried; the blacks set at large, each one going on shore carrying his handcuffs in his hand, from which he could not be prevailed to part, as they will make him a grand ornament. Most of the Kroomen will be retained as witnesses, and it is supposed the vessel will be awarded to them as a prize.

The next day a French steamer arrived at Monrovia, and demanded the vessel, the captain declaring she was an emigrant vessel, not a slaver. The British consul refused; upon which the Frenchman said he would fight, and take her by force. But just then an English man-of-war appeared, showing her teeth, very fortunately, or, I should say, providentially, as the mail steamer was obliged to proceed. Upon this the Frenchman drew in his horns. Two days after this, an American man-of-war arrived; upon which the Englishman left the vessel in care of the American, while he came down to Cape Palmas, to look after the captain, with his vessel, who has been detained here so long by sickness. Surely God will bless England, and make her a blessing, so long as she advocates the cause of mercy. Is it to be wondered at that the natives here fear and hate the white man, and distrust his religion?

Mr. Hoffman, we have heard, has been ill all the week, but is a little better to-day. Miss Ball's health still remains miserable. The doctor has told her he believes she will have to return and remain at home. Her constitution, he says, is too robust; the fever takes too firm hold of her. I hope and pray it may not be so; we need more laborers, not fewer. But it is God's work; it will go on. We are looking daily for the Bishop now. I hope it will not be long before he arrives. I am very busy making my scholars review their lessons, preparatory to the examination, which will take place in about a month.

CRUELTY.—These people are not generally a cruel people, even when they are cannibals. They generally will despatch their prisoners at one blow, not torture them. Recently, however, a man went up the river from our town, to trade. He was seized by a tribe, with whom the Greboes are at enmity, and having been himself always a very cruel man, he was fearfully tortured. He was bound to a stake, a fire being kindled at a little distance from him; then, with long, sharp-pointed knives, slices were cut off his body, and roasted on the point of the knife, and then held up and eaten in derision before his eyes. This was continued slowly, for some hours, till finally both arms and legs were cut off, before he expired! May the glad tidings of "good will to men" soon spread in all the land.

I am teaching several of the older girls different kinds

of fancy-work. Such things would meet with a ready sale among the richer inhabitants of the colony, and may be a means of livelihood to them. After the children have been brought from heathenism, instructed in our schools, and civilized, they all want some means of living. We have native ministers, teachers, carpenters, farmers, masons, washwomen, and needlewomen, and they all try to earn a respectable living.

COLD.—The old saying, in ridicule, of "Red flannel waistcoats for the little negroes of the West Indies," is not really so much of a burlesque. This rainy weather they suffer with cold, and nothing is more acceptable to them than a piece of flannel. We are having new shirts made for the younger boys, of red flannel. We have just heard from the Bishop; he expects to be home in a few days. There is a probability of our welcoming more laborers here in the fall. God grant it. We need them much. Mr. Hoffman requires relief; but it is hard to lay by with so much to be done.

Chapter Eleventh.

SASSA ORDEAL.

To-day I have seen the first death by sassa-wood. Last week a number of Kroomen came home, from a long voyage, among them two young men, belonging to our towns. I believe I told you that we were directly in the midst of five different towns, all within a circuit of half a mile. These contain, all together, about five thousand inhabitants. These two young men belonged to different towns, and, on their voyage, they had quarreled fiercely, and one had been heard to say he would "witch the other." This other almost immediately fell, sick, and was brought home very ill. His friends directly, of course, accused his companion of having witched him. And here was shown a strong proof of a mother's love, even in this land. Hearing that her son was accused of being a witch, she was in the greatest agony. He was her only child; a fine, noble-looking young man. He had been away from her a long time, and had received good wages for his services; and though these wages are always taken by the headman of the family (their customs being truly patriarchal), and divided among all the members of the family, yet, by far, the largest portion always falls to the share of him who earns it. The mother was looking forward to spending many happy days with her son; for if there is a human being a man loves here, it is his mother. Think, then, what her anguish must be at such an accusation. She went off, three days ago, privately into the woods; obtained a large piece of sassa-wood, came home, pounded and prepared it, then she called a number of the headmen and others of the townspeople, to see her drink this, to prove that her son was no witch. She drank it all, but rejecting it, again she triumphed. The people, however, were not satisfied. They said it only proved that she had not witched the sick man, but it did not prove that her son had not done so. This morning, Sunday, they seized him very early, and administered the poison. We knew nothing about it, till a little while before service, we heard loud yells, shouts, and hootings, mingled with the most heart-rending shrieks, proceeding from the direction of the town. On going out on the piazza, we saw a great crowd issuing from the town. The man was dead. They had a rope tied round his feet, and so dragged him, several hundred yards, on the beach—directly in front of the mission premises. The poor mother followed the corpse, uttering the wildest screams, and with most frantic gestures: The rest of the crowd, among whom were scores of little children, thus early taught to be unfeeling and cruel, were hooting, shouting, laughing, and pelting the corpse with stones, and whatever missiles came to hand. After awhile the crowd began to retire, leaving the poor mother almost alone in her grief. But how can I portray to you the extremity of her anguish. To me it was heart-rending. She dashed herself about, in the sand, seeming, as it were, to bite the very earth; throwing the sand over herself, as if she would have buried herself with her sorrows. Then she would jump suddenly up, and, frantically, embrace the corpse, pressing it tightly to her; then gently laying it back on the sand, she would fling her arms, wildly, up toward heaven, as if invoking mercy and pity from the clouds. Poor thing! she had no God to invoke. Her grief was hopeless despair. Her loved one was gone from her forever—for, in the spirit land, witches may never mingle with other spirits. They have a separate burial-place, in a swampy part of the bush, where the body is just thrown, not buried. But it must remain exposed, on the beach, till the family has found a bullock. This is first offered, in sacrifice, to the *Kwi*, and then divided among the townspeople. While we were in the church, from whence the voice of praise and thanksgiving was ascending, from native lips, to the precious Saviour, we still, at intervals, heard the distracting cries of the poor lone one, on the beach, who had no Saviour. How my heart bled for her, and never did my prayers ascend more fervently for this benighted land; and I felt, how gladly, had I ten lives, I would lay them down to aid in Africa's regeneration. What are the privations, the toils, the sickness, we endure here, in comparison to the utter despair and heart-rending hopelessness, from which it is our aim to rescue these wretched sufferers?

VALENTINE.—It is Whit-Sunday. Oh! that the Holy Ghost may be poured out abundantly upon us, and upon those committed to our care. Mr. Jones being ill to-day, so we had the services conducted by Valentine, one of our native Christian villagers. He never was in school. He was converted after he became a man, and then he learned to read, and for the last ten years he has been a most humble, earnest, devoted, and consistent Christian. He has the Kroo-mark on his face, but the "beauty of holiness" is stamped there, too. You could not look at that man without feeling that he was a Christian. The Christians all work here. They feel that when they are called into the vineyard, it is as laborers. Saturday is a general holiday, or rest day; none of the men work. On the Sabbath they do—Sunday work. For between our services they scatter about into all the towns, for miles distant, to carry the glad tidings, which has been made known to them. Valentine is one of the most faithful of these.

WOUNDS.—When I came out of school to-day, I felt very bad. I had just flung myself, for an instant, on the bed, when I heard a loud knock at my door; on opening it, there stood a fine looking native I had never seen before. He exclaimed, hurriedly, "Please, sir—maam, oh, come! here be a boy—he cut him hand much, plenty." I went out and found a fine looking young girl, about fourteen (they make no distinction of gender in talking, always addressing a lady either as mammy or as sir-ma'am, putting both together as one word). She had cut off the top part of the middle finger of her left hand. She must have had a very sharp instrument, for it had cut through the nail, leaving about an eighth of it, and through the bone, taking the piece quite off. It was cut perfectly clean through the nail, not the least jagged. Poor child; she did not utter a sound. It was bleeding profusely. The powers of endurance of these people are very strong. The man was very gentle, in assisting me to dress the wound, and I then found she was his wife. "Why," I said, "so little." "Oh!" he said, "he be much good; he grow plenty; me take good care of him; me tank you much, plenty; you make he finger well." They think the Kobi, foreigners, to be great devil men. They can do everything. "They wisdom plenty." Mr. Hoffman came down to-day. He looks very bad. Miss Ball is slightly improving. Our store of rice is almost done, and there is very little to be sold at the Cape. Miss Williford has secured all she can. It is a great anxiety to provide for so many mouths in times of scarcity. We use at the rate of fifteen bushels of rice a week. Well, "our Heavenly Father knoweth that we need those things," and we must trust that "the Lord will provide."

THOMAS.—The mother of my little boy, Thomas, came, to-day, to see him. She is very much alarmed about him, as there is a deadly hatred between the Graway and the Cavalla people, and she is afraid of his being witched. That belief of witchcraft is just as firmly held as any of our doctrines is by us. I consented to let him go home for a visit. I shall miss him much, though. Miss Williford tells me I had better let him go to school, either at Spring Hill or at Hoffman station. She thinks I shall never be able to keep him here now, his mother has taken that notion; she will be forever fetching him away. In that case I had better let him go to one of the other schools. Two of the girls, about seventeen years of age, come in every day to attend to my room. I am trying to teach them to be neat. Already they can make my bed, and sweep, and dust very well. It is an additional care to me, but they are good girls. They are engaged to two of our Christian young men, and I want them to know how to be neat about a house.

THE BISHOP'S ARRIVAL.—This morning, early, we saw a large ship off on the edge of the horizon. I told Miss Williford I thought it looked like a man-of-war, and I believed the Bishop was on board of her. She thought it was nonsense; that I could not tell a man-of-war from any other ship at that distance; and that if it was, the Bishop certainly would not be on board of her. I thought no more about it, but went into school. Just as I was about to close, Miss Williford called to me to close school, and hurry in; that the Bishop, with four other gentlemen, were here. To close school I found was impossible; the announcement of the Bishop being there, drove every other thought out of the children's heads; all rushed to the doors and windows, to obtain a glimpse of him. When I went in, I found the Bishop, Mr. Williams (a Presbyterian clergyman, from Monrovia, the former colleague of Mr. Wilson), and three of the officers from on board the ship. It was the United States ship "Marion." On her way down the coast she had stopped at Monrovia, and finding the Bishop and Mr. Williams waiting to come on, they had kindly brought them, and landed them here. They had come from the ship over five miles in a canoe. The officers on board the men-of-war, both English and American, are always very kind and polite to missionaries. Those who came on shore were very pleasant, gentlemanly men. They remained and took lunch with us. One of them, an earnest Christian, on taking leave, begged to be remembered—where a Christian most wishes ever to be remembered—at the throne of grace. We watched them go on board, and then the vessel soon disappeared from our sight. Mr. Williams will remain some little time with us. His health is very poor. The change may benefit him. As soon as he is well enough, we can give him work to do. Among the missionaries the Church of God is one. Would it were more so at home. Mr. Williams was telling us to-night, that in one of his itinerating excursions, he was preaching in a native hut, at night, to quite a large congregation. The sole light they had was the only kind that is ever used here: a saucer filled with palm-oil, with a piece of rag lying in it for a wick. But this could not be persuaded to burn. After being coaxed by one, and then another, of the congregation, it went entirely out, and they were left in total darkness. He, however, continued his sermon; but he said it seemed so strange to be looking round at his congregation and gesticulating all in the dark. But he was holding out to the people the lamp of life. It does seem to me, if there is any position in life to be coveted, with all its denials, its sufferings, and its toils, it is that of the missionary.

Mr. Hoffman came down to-night. He was at Graway, preaching, and hearing of the Bishop's arrival, he came on. We have had the house thronged with natives, too, all eager to welcome home their dear "Payne." Mr. Hoffman took Mr. Williams home with him, to spend a week. The Bishop's health is very much improved. We have had letters from home. Truly, "good news from a far country is like rivers of water to the thirsty soul." Loving friends are one of God's best gifts to man.

COMMUNION.—Sunday—a lovely day; a true Sabbath of rest. I can from my heart say, "Thine earthly Sabbaths, Lord, I love." The Bishop had the usual services this morning, in Grebo. In the afternoon we had communion. We have not had it before since I have been at Cavalla, on account of the Bishop's absence, Mr. Jones being only in deacon's orders. The communion service is in the afternoon, which makes it just the hour on which it is celebrated, on the same day, at home—the first Sunday of the month. It is very pleasant to feel that our loved ones, far, far away, are at the same time joining with us in "keeping the feast." May it not be long before we shall know that all we love are "compassing God's altar." There are here about ninety natives, who are communicants. They come from the neighboring towns. Their deportment is very serious and devotional. The Bishop has translated the communion service into Grebo, but it is not yet quite ready for use. The Bishop made an address, in English, which Mr. Jones translated into Grebo; and never did the words of the ninety-fifth hymn sound so appropriate:

"And are we now brought near to God,
Who once at distance stood?"

What intense satisfaction it gave to look at that congregation, from among the heathen. Pray that God may pour forth His spirit here, and that these may be "living epistles known and read of all men." How constantly we need to watch against the devices of Satan, who seeks occasion to tempt us in our holiest moments; how we need to have every thought and every act washed in the blood of atonement. While kneeling at the chancel, to-day, a poor old native woman knelt beside me, and the thought came up that, probably, in the sight of our heavenly Father, she was far the most acceptable, as she had certainly made far better use of her privileges than I had of mine. See how hard it is to root out of the mind the idea of *merit*, forgetting that if we both had on the wedding garment, faith in the Redeemer's righteousness, ourselves were entirely covered, and we were accepted through him alone. After service, I was in my room with Lucie (one of our elder girls, a communicant), speaking with her of this wedding garment, when we were startled by loud shrieks and screams. On looking out, we saw a woman running swiftly along, tossing her arms about in the wildest manner, and uttering such fearful cries. Upon inquiry, we found that two of her children were just dead—poisoned! Christians, I leave it with you to say who were the *murderers*. An American vessel was here, a few weeks since, and sold to these natives a hogshead of rum, since which time our congregations have been very much smaller; and on visiting at the towns, it is hard to gain attention to our message. Rum! rum! has besotted the minds of the people. "Shall not God arise to judgment for this?" Oh! it is a fearful crime, for so-called Christians to hinder thus the work of the missionary. They tell us here, that no vessel can trade on the coast to advantage, without rum; and that those who have it make rapid fortunes. Think of ship-owners and captains confessing boldly such deeds, that they have to debase and degrade the poor natives, to intoxicate them, before they can cheat them, or make them sell their commodities at half their value. The little vessel we came out in, carried no rum, and the captain was told he would never succeed. So far, he has done well. God grant him success, that others may have courage to follow in the same path. But to return to my murdered children. Their mother and father had a rum-bottle, which the children often saw them partake of, and appear much to enjoy. This morning, after taking some, they put the bottle away in the chest, but forgot to lock it; they then went off to their farm, leaving these children at home. They got at the bottle, finished its contents, and, on the parents' return, were found dead, with the bottle beside them. This may, perhaps, be for the good of the community, as they have a great horror of death. They would never believe before, that rum is a poison; now they will see its poisonous effects.

LIFE.—This country teems with life; almost every night we have fresh swarms of some new species of insect, attracted by the light. The little red ants are in myriads, being over everything; and at night, we have a species of winged ant, that is very annoying. Then, our spiders are immense. I have seen them with a body as large as a twenty-five-cent piece; they are very ugly Then, we have quantities of lizards, of all sizes, playing about. Some of them are very large, of a most beautiful blue color, excepting the head, which is a bright red, giving them a very singular appearance.

Rum.—A French vessel has been lying out here, selling rum, for some days past. The natives have been in a constant state of excitement, quarrels and "palavers" going on all the time. God forgive the venders of this poison—our poor people! we feel so sorry for them. On this subject, we can have little influence with them, while the rum lasts; the missionary might almost as well cease preaching. To-day, the captain and mate, and four of his men, were on shore. It was very rough going over the bar; the boat was upset, and the mate and two of the seamen were drowned; the rest swam to the vessel. The body of one of the men was found some little distance below by some Kroomen. They took him up, and buried him like a dog, with the exception of just firing a few shots over his grave.

Missionary Meeting.—We have a missionary meeting once a month, when the Bishop reads to us any intelligence received from other parts of the world. To-night, he read to us a short account of the glorious work going on in New-Zealand—"Nations being born in a day." Then Mr. Williams gave us a beautiful address on Ezekiel's vision. I cannot help constantly admiring the oneness of feeling prevailing here in the different branches of the vine. Christ's prayer seems answered,

"Oh! Father, that they may be one, as we are one." And to Christians at home, missionaries would constantly present the request, "Brethren, pray for us!" Yes, all who love the Lord Jesus Christ, uphold them by your prayers; pray, that they may teach Christ, by their holy lives as well as by their doctrines, and that, from their conduct, men may take knowledge of them, that they have been with Jesus. Again, I would urge, pray for them.

SALT.—In one house, to-day, a woman was putting up a large quantity of coarse salt, obtained from the sea-water, by evaporation. She was putting it up in cocoanut leaves, then to be hung up in the hut to dry. It was put up quite prettily; it really looked very ornamental, now while the leaves are green, but that will only be for a day or two.

The people are very fond of children, never hardly correcting them; they let them do precisely as they please, unless they become too outrageous, and then their punishment is most barbarous; they will put red pepper into the eyes of the refractory ones—you may imagine the torture; but, strange to say, after they get over the pain, which lasts several days, it does not injure their sight, as one would suppose.

JOY.—I thank God for his boundless love. It is Sunday. This morning, before going into church, we were speaking on the subject of Christian assurance, and our constant doubts and fears; and, calling attention to the mighty expanse of waters spread out before us, it was remarked that the ocean could as easily bear up the most deeply-laden and the largest ship, as the tiniest little cork that floated on its bosom; and so the ocean of Christ's fullness can as easily sustain the soul that is most deeply-laden with guilt and iniquity, as it can that of the comparatively innocent babe. Who can fathom the unutterable depths of the Saviour's love? Mr. Williams preached for us a sermon, full of Christ, Mr. Jones interpreting for him. During the morning, after service, Mary Bowman, one of the girls I have to attend to my room, came to me, and, with her book in her hand, sat down at my feet. At first, I took no notice of her, as I was busy reading; presently, I noticed that her heart was full; she was crying. I laid my hand on her, "Mary, my child, what is the matter? can I do anything for you?" She looked up at me, "Talk me, talk me." "Well, Mary, what shall I talk to you about? Shall it be of the love of the precious Saviour? Shall I tell you of the solemn vows and promises that were made to-day?" Two of the boys in school (the one, nineteen, the other, seventeen years of age) were baptized to-day; they give every promise of being useful, sincere Christians. I talked to her a long time, though at first I did not like to be disturbed, as I was much interested in what I was reading. But God's Word says, "In the morning, sow thy seed: and at eve, withhold not thou thine hand, for thou knowest not which shall prosper, this or that." For some little time, I have remarked a growing seriousness in Mary, and one or two others, and great attention to the things of God. Those girls have been well and faithfully taught for years: they have head knowledge. I went down to dinner, leaving Mary still in my room; on returning, I found her yet there. She came and knelt beside me, exclaiming, "Oh, I want to be a Christian! I want to be baptized!" I commenced talking to her on the great and important subject of baptism; but we were obliged to hurry off to Sunday-school. There, the children were addressed on the necessity of a change of heart, which subject was very simply, yet beautifully illustrated to them. After school was over, Mary came again to my room; we continued talking for a time, when suddenly she seized my hand, "Miss B., pray a me." "What! Mary, shall I pray for you, or with you?" "Yes! yes!" and she got up, and together we knelt and prayed for that new heart, those precious influences of the Holy Spirit, of which she had been hearing in Sunday-school. We talked and prayed together, till the bell rang for evening service. She asked me to tell the Bishop her earnest desire to be baptized, to confess Christ before men. "Truly, the wind bloweth, where it listeth: and thou hearest the sound thereof, but canst not tell whence it cometh, nor whither it goeth, so is every one, who is born of the Spirit." In the evening, we heard an exquisitely beautiful sermon from the words: "They went, and told Jesus." Oh, what a friend He is! Afterward, we talked together about Mary. Truly, we have "joys that the world intermeddleth not therewith." We all believe Mary to be a good girl.

More Joy.—Another joyful scene to-day. After dinner, Mater came up into my room, and told me that she, like Mary, was minding God's things—that she, too, wished to be taken into God's house, to be God's child. I had a long and delightful talk with her, in her broken English, and prayed with her. She told me that Elizabeth (another of the elder girls) wished to come and talk with me, that she, likewise, was wishing to come forward, and confess Christ. Elizabeth was busy this afternoon, so she could not come to me. I intend to take those three girls alone in the afternoon, and try and make them thoroughly understand the duties and responsibilities of a Christian profession, before they make it. But I really must try and take a little more rest. I am never free from fever three days at a time; and for several weeks I have been so ill, I could hardly crawl about—no one would think it, though, to see me; for, having a constant fever flush, I always look well. On talking to Miss Williford, she says that for many months there has been a growing seriousness and interest in the religion of Christ manifested among the older girls. God's promise is, that "His Word shall not return to Him void;" and the precious seed has been sown diligently here — one faithful missionary after another, planting and watering; and, though much has fallen upon thorny, stony, or barren soil, some has fallen upon good ground, and gives promise of a future harvest. Now, the tender blade is beginning to appear; bye-and-bye, it will be the ear, then, the full corn in the ear. Many of those faithful laborers have gone to their account. They sowed in faith — they saw not the fruits of their toil—but, at the great harvest home, who shall tell how many sheaves of bearded grain, bound up in the bundle of life, will owe their existence to the seed they first planted. We must each work diligently, as though the conversion of the whole heathen world depended upon our individual efforts; while, at the same time, we must feel that " Paul may plant, and Apollos may water, but it is God only that giveth the increase." We should never forget, too, that *He does give the increase* always to faithful planting and watering; but "if it tarry, we must wait for it, knowing that, in His good time, it will come, and will not tarry." God give us grace faithfully to tend and nourish this precious seed that has been planted, and, by God's spirit, appears now to be shooting forth. Truly, truly, it may be a "*fearful* thing to die;" but it is an *awful* thing to live—to live, as we shall wish we had, when we come to die, improving, to the utmost, every talent committed to us.

WORK.—Very ill to-day, but had my different classes come to my room to recite, Miss Gillot taking charge in the school-room. She is very faithful. This afternoon, when in bed, Mary came and peeped into my room and then went away, without speaking, but, in a few minutes, she returned with Meter and Elizabeth. They came in and sat down. "Please talk to us—tell us of Jesus." "Oh! Mary, my child, I am so weary, and my head pains me so badly, I cannot talk to you now." I saw a shade of disappointment pass over their faces, and it instantly recalled me. What! refuse to tell those poor perishing heathens of Jesus; refuse to point them to the Lamb of God; refuse to give to their famishing souls the Bread of Life, which they were pleading for; and I remembered, "Whatever thy hand findeth to do, do it with all thy might, for there is neither thought, device, nor knowledge in the grave, whither we hasten." I took the Prayer Book, and commenced talking to them on the first answer in the Catechism, "in baptism wherein I was made a member of Christ," &c. I tried to explain it to them, and prayed with them. My earnestness in talking produced a profuse perspiration, which removed my headache, so that, after they had gone, I got up, feeling much better. Dear girls, may God's Spirit be abundantly poured out upon them; may He perfect the good work He has begun in them, and may they be as lights in this dark land. At dark Henry and Mr. Bacon came to me for an hour and a half. So, we cannot really afford the time to be sick, for, if we are, our duties have to be neglected, no one being possibly able to attend to their own and ours, too. Our time is very short, and much to be done, " for soon the night cometh wherein no man can work." I thank God daily for granting me the precious privilege of laboring here.

ILLNESS.—A week in bed. I ought to have been there before, but I would not give up. I battled every inch of ground, till obliged to succumb. And now again, with my array of calomel, blue pill, castor-oil, quinine, and ale, a goodly army, I am, at length, coming off victorious. I have had my children in my room, to recite to-day, as we are preparing for examination. The Bishop and Mr. Williams have been away attending the examinations at Mount Vaughan—the Asylum. The

Bishop came home to-day. Our examination, of the girls is to be on Tuesday; the boys on Wednesday. The house is always full at these times, missionaries and colonists all making it a point to be present. So it was thought to be a good time for the wedding to take place then, when all, who would be invited to it, would be present. We are very busy preparing, but I feel very feeble. I fear a relapse, and that would not be pleasant just now. Lucie, one of my girls, brought me a large piece of the sassa-bark. I should like very much to have it analyzed.

THE EXAMINATION AND WEDDING.—I have talked as much as I could, and others have, with the three girls. They are to be baptized on Wednesday evening. I think they are fully prepared, as far as man can see, for the celebration of that sacrament. Truly the light shineth here in a dark place. It is just the dawn, but ere long it will usher in the glorious day. Christ will have the heathen for his inheritance, and he shall reign "from the river even unto the ends of the earth."

Our winter has commenced. The salt winds blow, and though we have not so much rain, yet, from now (the middle of June) till September we scarcely see the sun, just a peep now and then. The atmosphere is cloudy and murky. A thick dress, with the windows closed, is quite comfortable. Our friends arrived to-night in preparation for the wedding and examination to-morrow. How very badly Miss Ball looks.

My Birthday.—Truly I can say "hitherto the Lord hath helped me." I have ended one more year of my earthly pilgrimage. I hope it has brought me one year nearer my heavenly home. How varied has been my experience the past year, yet I think I have realized God's promise, " My presence shall go with thee, and I will do thee good." I have dreaded this examination so much—the idea of having to appear and speak before so many. I know it is done in our schools constantly, at home ; but to me, it is very repugnant. I felt very like a criminal when I went into the school-room. It was full. I suppose all, white and black, must have numbered over a hundred and fifty, and I had to sit before them all, to examine my scholars. I trembled, and my voice faltered so much. I had hard work to proceed. But it was over at last, and I could have jumped, and danced, and clapped my hands, like the veriest child. I was so relieved. By the way, what strange ideas some people seem to entertain of what a missionary is. I suppose they imagine them with constant long faces and gloomy aspects, going about like so many monks or nuns. I just received a letter from a friend at home, asking me how we felt. That she should imagine we *always* felt so good, just as people do on Sundays. Now, I suppose what she meant was that we always feel grave and serious. I wish she could take a peep in upon us sometimes. We have enough; ah! quite enough, to make us thoughtful and very sad, but just for that very reason we feel it more our bounden duty to " cast our burdens all on Christ," and in our daily intercourse with one another, even when suffering severely with sickness, to wear a smiling, pleasant face, and to be as light-hearted and cheerful as possible. This we consider a positive duty we owe to each other. The examination was over at five o'clock. We had trimmed everything and every place with flowers—" God's smiles," as some one has beautifully called them. The ceremony took place in the church, which is just completed, Mr. Hoffman performing for the Bishop the same service the latter did for him a few months since. Who would have thought, six months ago, to see Miss Williford, that she would have ever lived to be a bride? God bless them both, and make them a blessing to this people. Most of our company stayed all night, to be present at the boys' examination. We were obliged to make up any quantity of extempore beds. A mission house should be elastic.

BAPTISM.—I was too tired to sleep last night. To-day the boys' examination has been held. Some of them declaimed very well. One of them recited a speech of Patrick Henry's. It could not have been better. I took those three girls away, for awhile, to my room. We read over the baptismal service, and I was pleased to see they had been studying it, and had made themselves quite familiar with it. They are good girls, so far as man's eye can see. In the evening they were baptized. Mrs. Payne and myself stood as their witnesses. That service grows in beauty, to me, every time I see it. It is a very solemn thing, this turning from heathenism to Christianity. May God give them grace to confess him fearlessly before men. The church is just finished. The chancel rails and pulpit were put up yesterday morning.

Mr. Hoffman preached this evening. We still have a house full.

Sassa.—A sad sight this morning again. Just before breakfast we heard a loud wailing on the beach, and we soon saw a corpse dragged out and cast upon the sand. It was a young woman this time to whom sassa-wood had been given. She died almost instantly upon swallowing it. A very great crowd gathered round her, but, in a very short time the bullock was provided, and the corpse was carried away. How fearful it seems. An hour ago that poor woman was in the enjoyment of full health and vigor, and now her lifeless corpse is cast out unto the swamp, to be devoured by beasts of prey. It is dreadful! And yet when you talk to them about it you can hardly tell how to answer them. "Mammy, it be our country fash. S'pose man bad your country, he hate noder man, he shoot he wid a gun, or he stick a knife in he; what you do wid dat man s'pose you catch he? I knows, mammy, you take a rope, you put him round he neck, and tie he on a tree, till he dies. That your country fash, mammy. But s'pose we countryman, he hate noder, he no shoot—he no take a knife, but he witch he; we no hang he up, but we give he *gidu*. That be our country fash."

Our friends have left us this morning, except Miss Ball (it now being the holidays she can be away from home) and Mrs. Williams. I have had some very interesting conversation with several of the people in town. There are many who think about God's things, but still hold back from making a profession. Can we wonder at it when we see the multitudes, in our own land, that do the same? cannot give up all for Christ, though fully persuaded that they ought.

The Invitations.—Communion service: it is a holy season. Over a hundred native communicants are here. Five communed to-day, for the first time—the two boys and the three girls, from our schools. They have now buckled on the Christian armor. May they never lay it aside, but fight manfully, as good soldiers of the Cross. May their course be ever onward and upward. The customs here at communion season remind one forcibly of the feast in the Gospel. In that, you recollect, three invitations are given—the last when supper is announced: "Come, for all things are ready." With us, except on Communion Sunday, we always have Sunday-school in the afternoon; and that the people may not forget, they receive three invitations. The first is given the Sunday previous. On Saturday, we and all the women from the Christian village, and school girls and boys who are members, go and scatter about through the towns, telling them of the feast to-morrow, and talking to them of it; and again (as they have no regard for time), just before service, some of the girls are sent to the Christian huts in each town, with the message, "Come, for all things are ready."

This morning, the fourth of July, I was awakened very early, by the firing of guns. I suppose there is noise enough of that sort at home to-day. How it took me there. The rejoicing here was occasioned by the completion of a new town-house—a large square house in

African Bridge

the centre of the town, where town meetings are held, "palavers" settled, &c., &c. All the men have to help to build it, therefore it is a matter of great rejoicing when it is finished, particularly, as in this case, when the materials of which it is constructed have to be brought from the woods, at some distance. Miss Ball has gone home to-day.

DODA-LU.—Doda-lu is a native town, about two and a half miles distant from us, where the Bishop goes to preach every Tuesday afternoon. To-day he wished us to go with him; so he engaged men to carry Mrs. Payne and myself, in hammocks, and he and Mr. Williams took it by turns to ride on horseback. We had a most delightful ride. Doda-lū is very prettily situated, on the Cavalla river. Unlike any other towns I have seen, it is completely environed by trees. The scenery all along the road is very lovely; it is a most beautifully undulating country. The Bishop preached in front of one of the houses, in an open space, under the shade of a fine cotton-tree. These trees grow to the size of the oak. They brought country chairs for us to sit upon, while the natives themselves sat on the ground around us, in all imaginable positions. These scenes must be witnessed to be felt. Never, till you are in a heathen land, do you realize, in all its fullness, the "beauty of the Gospel." Two of the girls walked down from the Asylum this evening, to see me. They thought I should have gone up with Miss Ball, to spend part of the holidays there. Finding I did not, they came to see me. They show strong proofs of affection. Mr. T. Thompson also came down, for a day or two.

This afternoon we started to take a little walk on the beach, to see some very romantic projecting rocks a short distance off. In passing through the town, we came upon the "Palava House," recently erected. While we stood looking at it, a Krooman came up and commenced a conversation, speaking English very nicely. Mr. Wilson pointed to some gree-grees, or fetishes (a large stone and two or three bunches of chickens' feathers), in front of the house. The man said, "Me no believe in gree-grees; me want to believe in God's things." In a few minutes quite a congregation had collected around us. Mr. Wilson preached Jesus to them—the man we first met being a very good interpreter. We then went on to the beach, towards the native grave-yard. Just before you come to this, however, you meet King *Wia's* grave. Here there is a native hut inside a large enclosure, beautifully shaded by trees. King Wia is buried inside the hut. On the outside, within the enclosure, seats are placed for the spirit to rest on when it comes to visit the grave. King Wia was a very good native, a kind friend to the missionaries, and one "almost persuaded to be a Christian." There is a stone, with an inscription to this effect, placed there by the missionaries. The hut is completely filled with those things which constituted his wealth when on earth. But every pot, or pan, is broken (an apt emblem). Pieces of rags, &c., are hung all round, as gree-grees. Poor people! We knelt and prayed beside this grave, for the eternal life, the resurrection unto life, of these living ones around us, who are still dead in trespasses and sins. We then passed on towards the general grave-yard. It is an enclosed piece of woods. When any one is interred, a grave is dug a few inches beneath the surface, or else the body is just laid on the ground, and an old canoe inverted over it. In the trees are a great number of monkeys; and though, when found elsewhere, they are killed, and eaten, without scruple, yet these no one dare touch, as it is supposed they may be the habitation of the spirits of the departed. The doctrines they hold are very contradictory; sometimes they assert their belief in one thing, sometimes in another.

CENTIPEDE.—This evening, while sewing, I was startled by the cat jumping suddenly upon me. I started up, and felt a little frightened to see a centipede drop from my dress. He was despatched very quickly. I felt quite thankful to pussy, for though the bite is not mortal, or very rarely so, yet it is very poisonous, and occasions much suffering.

SAD NEWS.—While busy in my room this morning (Saturday), the Bishop came to tell me that the Stevens had arrived, and there were lots of letters for me. Down went my work on the floor, and I rushed into the parlor, and could do nothing else till I had devoured the contents. My father very ill—probably already gone home. Thank God! "a rest remaineth." Mrs. Payne has sad news; the death of a dear and only brother. But God gives her grace to feel that "the Lord gave, and the Lord hath taken away," and she can bless His name. The Bishop has also received the intelligence of the death of a brother of his. "He that rideth on the pale horse does not confine himself to one country or clime; his name is *ubiquity*." Even should our lives be spared to see our own land, how many faces shall we miss. To-day, when I was in town, in two of the houses, I met a number of wild bushmen. They had never been to the coast before. I was the first white person they had ever seen. They were really frightful-looking creatures; they had added to their natural darkness by painting themselves over with a sort of lampblack. Their heads are always most ridiculous spectacles; shaved sometimes in one fashion, sometimes in another; sometimes little circles or oblongs of hair left, and all shaved between. You might fancy they had seen a prettily laid-out garden, the hair representing the beds, and the shaved parts the paths between. At other times one half of the head is shaved; on the other half the hair is permitted to grow about four inches long, and then it is plaited into innumerable tails, that stand straight up and out from the head. It will take their wives from four to five hours to do this for them. I talked to them, through my interpreter, for some time. They had never heard of God. I told them of man's total depravity, of God's holiness, of the Saviour's love, and begged them to come to church to-morrow. They promised me they would. We must constantly sow the seed; the bread cast upon the waters may be found after many days. The people of the coast look down very much upon the bushmen, considering them as vastly inferior to themselves, as indeed, in many respects, they are. Shaving the head, among the Greboes, is a sign of mourning; and, according to the nearness of the relationship, the head is more or less shaven, it being shaved either a quarter, the half, or the whole head.

THE KWI.—The bushmen were at church to-day. The Bishop preached in Grebo. After which, Mr. Williams followed in an address, which was interpreted. Both the sermon and address were on the folly of idols and gree-grees, and the nature of the true God. This people have had the Gospel, in its purity, preached to them for over twenty years; and now God appears to be speaking to them by His providences. Last year, without any apparent cause, the rice, their main dependence for food, after it was nicely headed, withered, and was destroyed; and now the same thing is occurring. It has been looking beautiful, already headed, but it is now all wilting away. It is believed that the spirits of the departed become devils, or demons (*Kwi*), and that it is they who inflict the evils which the people suffer; they, therefore, often offer sacrifices (a bullock, goat, or chickens), to propitiate them. Some great man has died, not very long ago, and, for some supposed offence, they think his *Kwi* is angry with them; so, this last week, they have been offering sacrifices to him. May the scales of error soon fall from their eyes.

TIME.—Mr. Williams has left us in the Stevens. He has gone back, I hope, strengthened for fresh labors. I have had time to write but very little for home. I have sent home my watch, by Mr. Johnston, a merchant (colored), of Monrovia. It is a very singular thing that no watches will keep correct time here; even the very best chronometers will vary somewhat on this coast, and no two watches will keep time together; if you set them alike to-day, they will not remain so to-morrow. About every two or three days the Bishop sets the clock in the parlor right, by the sun, and we keep ours by that. I cannot understand the philosophy of this thing. My watch, since it has stopped, has been a great loss to me, as I have to regulate my school duties, &c., by it, and it may be many months ere it will be returned to me.

THE FUNERAL.—I have just returned from the funeral of a little child, a very fine little boy, the son of one of our Christian villagers. He was about three years old. The father is a carpenter; he made the child's coffin himself. The child has been sick for two or three days, but did not seem to be dangerously ill. He died about eight o'clock this morning, and is just buried now, at eleven. This haste seems dreadful, but it is necessary. We could not but notice the blessed effects of Christianity, if it were only the mitigation of our sufferings in time of trouble. All the relations, of both parents, are heathen; and the wild, despairing grief of the grandmother was a marked contrast to the deep but subdued sorrow of the parents, who could look beyond the grave, to the "resurrection and the life," and feel that their child "is not dead, but sleepeth." Who that has but one spark of humanity but would long earnestly that all men might have the hope of the Gospel. How much of human misery does it soothe and relieve! The Bishop had the service in the house, Mr. Jones interpreting his address into Grebo, then following himself in a short speech—many of the natives from the towns being present. We then went to the grave-yard, a pretty little spot, under the trees; only three, as yet (all children), being buried there. The bell was solemnly tolling all the time. May we also be ready, for in "such an hour as we think not the Son of Man cometh." We heard to-night that old M'Lede has gone home to her rest.

IGNORANCE.—I felt very sorry for one poor woman I met in town to-day. I went into her house, and began talking to her about her children. I then told her it would be Sunday to-morrow, asking her if she was coming to church, and telling her if she did not keep God's Sabbath, did not mind God's Word, He would not bless her; and I begged her to come to God's house, to hear His Word. She said, "No, she would not; that some time ago, she used to go much to God's house, but He had not blessed her; that He had taken away two or three of her people, and she would not go to His house again." Poor woman! how sad my heart felt for her. She seemed to think that by learning the way to eternal happiness, by hearing the good news of salvation proclaimed to a poor, lost, perishing sinner, like her, she was, as it were, laying God under an obligation to her. I fear, alas! that such ideas are not confined to *heathens*.

THE ACCEPTED INVITATION.—I was reading to-day on the subject I recently spoke of: that in many parts of the East it is still the custom, on the occasion of any great feast, to send the invitation many days before;

then, again, the day before the feast, to remind them of it; and again, when all is prepared; and it is a great indignity to refuse to come, after all this trouble. Now, we do hope, with these guests, who come here to the great feast, though they come with little outward clothing, yet we trust they are clothed with the ample garment of the Redeemer's righteousness, and, therefore, are admitted as welcome guests. How many at home have had the invitation, again and again, and have " made light of it," and gone their ways; and these, from the highways and hedges, are brought to the feast on earth, and, finally, will be purified and happy guests at " the marriage supper of the Lamb."

Consumption.—How time flies! So many, many things I had set myself to do during the holidays, and I have scarcely performed a tithe of them; and yet I have been busy, oh! so busy, every moment. It really would not do for us to have too much sewing for ourselves to do. Copying my Grebo dictionary, and studying the language, take every moment of spare time. School has begun again. The children are all very glad at the commencement of the holidays, but they are much more so at their termination. Mrs. Payne received a large box of presents, from kind friends at the South. It came by the Stevens; presents for herself and the school. To-day we were up in the storeroom, putting away some of these things, when, on laying a piece of shirting on the table, an enormous centipede ran out of it, and ran across the table. It was the largest I have seen yet, and one of the most venomous species; but they appear to be as much afraid of us as we are of them. They seldom are the aggressors, but they are ugly things. I was a little surprised at some statistics the Bishop was mentioning to-night; and yet there was no reason to be surprised, when we reflect an instant. He says that four fifths of the children here die in infancy, and four fifths of those who attain to manhood die of consumption. They always have fires in their huts, even in the hottest weather, keeping them up to boiling heat; and now, at this season, it feels quite cool, even with a thick merino dress on. And they will constantly go in and out from these intensely hot huts, into the cold air (that even we feel cold), with nothing but a little cloth around the loins. At night, after sitting round the fire, in a steaming hut, they will go out into the cold air, and there take a hot bath (not cold, or tepid, but hot), and then stand for some time in the cold, damp, heavy dews. Is it a wonder they have fearful coughs and consumption? They are very cleanly in their persons, and this hot bath must be taken by every one every night.

Chapter Twelfth.

ULCERS.

The natives, and many of the colonists also, are troubled with the most frightful ulcers. They are most frequently in the legs. The slightest bruise or wound will produce them. I have seen them with holes so large you might lay a pigeon's egg in them. They will suffer with them for months or years. There is an herb grows here, similar to the plantain, which they sometimes apply; but I never could perceive that it was at all efficacious. There are also a great many lepers; we have several constantly coming to the house. This disease is hereditary, but not infectious; though often, if the leper should come between you and the air, you would perceive a very strong, heavy odor. They will frequently turn white, in large spots or blotches, which give them a very disagreeable appearance. We have, however, to overcome any fastidiousness or squeamishness on that point very soon, though some of the sights are sickening. But then we must remember that they are our brethren, children of one common Father; and we must put away our own feelings, that we may be enabled to " pour in the oil and wine " to others' wounds. We ourselves at first appear very disgusting to those who have never seen a white person before. They think that the reason we are all white is because we are such fearful lepers.

CLIMATE.—Another large centipede killed in the school-room to-day. How soon we learn certain habits. I never think now of putting on my clothes without giving each article a good shake, to be sure that there is neither centipede, scorpion, nor spider, concealed there. I have bought a monkey to-day. *Kade* is going to take care of him, and train him for me, till I can send him home. It surely must be far more healthy in the interior than it is here on the coast, for every animal that comes from there here has to go through an acclimation. I had a beautiful parrot sent me, some weeks ago, from up the river, that I gave to *Kade* to train and take care of. He understands these things. But the poor thing died a few days afterward. I hope my monkey will live.

The Bishop brought me a beautiful little bird to-day. He found some native children ill-treating it, and they gave it to him. It is still alive; but I fear it will not live; it seems stunned. I have placed it on some cotton, in a box, with plenty of air, food, and water. I hope it will recover, for it is a beautiful little creature. It is about the size of a sparrow. Its plumage is a deep glossy black, like the richest velvet, except the breast, which is a splendid red. The bill is a very bright blue.

My little bird died in the night, and by this morning it was half eaten up by the ants. How delightful the accounts we have from home of the revivals and prayer-meetings. Oh! that God would also pour out His Spirit here, that "nations may be born in a day." There is going to be much hunger here again. The rice has been blighted by the winds. It seems as if God intended to show the people that "the Lord reigneth;" and if they will not hear His voice when He speaks to them in love and mercy, he will make them feel His judgments.

COMPANY.—I am alone in my room, and yet I have plenty of company. What, with spiders, cockroaches, scorpions, ants, rats, and occasionally a centipede or young lizard, by way of a change, I have visitors enough. I ought to be lively. I have been trying my hand in the way of stuffing and preparing birds for preservation, but have had to give it up in despair; I cannot accomplish it. I have had two very singular birds' nests brought me, from two hundred miles inland. I shall send them home.

STRANGE IDEAS.—The Bishop has been away for several days. He came home last evening. He had visited a great number of towns, and administered the Communion in one. All the towns appear to be in a state of antagonism; towns not farther than half or quarter of a mile apart, at war with one another. Oh! if infidels could only see the world as it is, without God, they would say, "Give me Christianity, if only for this life!" One woman says she would not be a Christian, because Christians have nothing to eat when they are dead. Another, who really seemed to believe all the doctrines, of Christianity, and to thoroughly understand them would not be a Christian, she says, because then she would not be buried with, and in the spirit land wear, all her brass armlets and anklets, as she does here. Oh! that the Spirit of God may breathe on these dry bones, that they may live. It is, indeed, a labor of faith to teach them. I found a dead scorpion in my bonnet-box. The old proverb of skinning the eels is very good here: "Nothing when you're used to it." Old Dawba, a native Christian in town, is very ill. Poor man! I am so sorry; we all think so much of him.

SINGING.—Sunday mornings, all the children collect in the girls' school-room to sing hymns. This morning, I thought it sounded more sweetly than usual. My room overlooks the school-room, so that I can have a constant oversight of them, and hear all that passes, though the buildings are separated. They were singing "Messiah is king! Messiah is king!" When they came to that line, "Tell how He cometh from nation to nation," such a thrill of delight passed through me, that I was one of those privileged to spread these "glad tidings of great joy" in this dark land. May the numbers be speedily multiplied of those who shall, from their hearts, join in hallelujahs of praise to the great King. One of our lay preachers—for we have many that circulate on a Sunday (this being, as it were, the centre from which the rays of light issue in all directions)—found the people in the town to which he went, giving *sassa* to a man. He had not much of a congregation to hear his message. He tried to stop the giving of the poison, but could not succeed. When he left, however, he thought the man was likely to recover from its effects.

BEAUTY.—How truly has Tupper said, "For the estimates of human beauty, dependent on times and climes, manifold and changeable, are multiplied;" or, to come down to the common proverb, "Tastes differ." I saw a woman to-day with the half of her head shaved, leaving quite a bushy crop on the other side; and then the whole head was dyed with a species of tan, which made it a perfect brick color. She herself was jet black. It looked horrid, and yet so ridiculous. I could scarcely keep from laughing at her; but she thought she was beautiful—"she fine too much."

SASSA TRIUMPH.—Whilst in school, to-day, we heard considerable shouting and singing. It was a woman, enjoying a triumphal procession, after having escaped the deadly *gidu*. She had on quite a large cloth, for a woman; attached to the bottom of this, were a great number of little bells, a very favorite ornament, and a good article of trade. She was loaded with heavy, brass armlets, and anklets, up to the knees and elbows; these, with her bells, made such a noise, that they could be heard at a great distance. Her head was dyed bright red, while, with a species of clay, her face, arms and body, were marked with white stripes. She went dancing along (the dancing consists in a very strange, vulgar motion of the body), improvising a song, in her own praise, while a man walked beside her, holding over her head a red and white cotton umbrella. At a

Portraits of Native Africans at Cape Palmas.

sassa triumph, is the only time at which a woman is so honored as to be allowed to walk beside the man; at all other times, she must walk behind him. We had heard nothing about it; but this woman, it seems, had the sassa administered to her on Sunday; she recovered, but they gave it to her again yesterday, when she also recovered, and now she is having a grand triumph. It is not uncommon, if there is much malignity felt towards the supposed criminal, to administer the poison two or three times before they will consider their innocence to be proven. A man has been known to die from the effects of the fourth dose. They, however, allow two or three days to intervene between the reception of each dose.

FISH.—As I came in from school, I saw a crowd collected on the beach, and, looking out to sea, I perceived about a dozen canoes, apparently joined together, coming in towards shore, at a very slow pace. It seems they had caught an immense fish, with a harpoon, and they wanted to bring it on shore alive, but they could not; and, at length, they were obliged to cut it up, and bring it in piecemeal. It was a perfect God-send to the town. It was so large, that there was enough for a good meal for every one in town. Such a thing is always divided equally among all, no matter who catches it, it is considered town property. They sent the Bishop quite a large piece, and it was pronounced very good. The Bishop said it was a very singular fish, more in shape like a bird; its flappers, or fins, being immense, and like birds' wings. Fever seems on the increase with me again, my head and eyes are so bad.

FEVER—There is one noun that, in Africa, we can never decline—fever; and yet, as a verb, we have to go through it, in all its moods and tenses. A boy, from the station at *Nitie Lu*, was baptized to-day, the first of that tribe—a tribe of cannibals. The Bishop was much pleased with the boy, and his thorough knowledge of Scripture doctrines and duties. He has been instructed only by a native teacher.

Had to give up to my bed to-day. Mrs. Payne brought me a bundle of letters from our friends at Corisco and Gaboon—all well; though all had suffered slightly with fever, none had been severely ill. They are very pleasantly situated, and take great delight in their work. Fernando-Po and Corisco both belong to Spain. She has just sent to Fernando-Po a new governor, and a company of Jesuit priests. They have shut up the Protestant schools, and forbidden preaching; and it is feared they will do the same at Corisco. They have an armed vessel with them, to enforce their authority. Well, we know that with "the madness of men," as well as the raging of the sea, there is one who says: "Thus far shalt thou go, and no farther." The little vessel which brought us these letters, came up to get Kroomen; she returns to Corisco. The captain has very kindly offered to give Mr. Hoffman and Miss Ball a free passage down the coast. They both remain so unwell, that a little voyage will, probably, be of great service to them. They sail to-morrow. I hope they may come back well and strong. Mr. Gibson has gone to Monrovia. Mr. Crummell is now, with his family, settled at Mount Vaughan; he is a very gentlemanly, well-educated man. He received his education at Cambridge, England. He is to take charge while Mr. Hoffman is away. Poor Mr. Thompson! he is so anxious to enter the ministry, and he was studying so hard with Mr. Crummell, and again he is hindered. He must take charge of the school at the Asylum till Miss Ball returns. Truly, may we say, " here we have no continuing city." We must be willing to be removed, or to change our work at any moment, as it is best for the cause; and if we constantly put up that prayer, " Lord, what wilt thou have me to do?" we shall do it cheerfully and willingly.

The children of the schools here are corresponding with those of Monrovia. I think it will be instrumental in doing them all much good. For several days, out of school hours, I have had a number of the girls in my room, trying to write letters; it must be entirely their own work, only I tell them if such a word is right or not. Whilst they are doing this, I am trying to study Grebo; but it is slow work—quite " the pursuit of knowledge under difficulties."

HARRY BACON.—Oh! how the simple faith of the poor and ignorant often puts us to shame. I have spoken of Harry Bacon, the colonist carpenter, who is working on the boys' school-house; he comes to me whenever he can to have a spelling or reading lesson. I was speaking with him, to-day, on the efficacy of prayer, and he said, " Yes, marm, I knows it, cause I'se 'sperienced it. Let me tell you, marm, what the Lord did for this old nigger once, and no one need to tell to me that He don't hear prayer—yes, and answer it, too. I used to live in Georgia, and I had a proper, good, kind master, too, marm, and he gave me a good trade. When I grew up I was a pretty smart workman, so massa he let me hire my time. I pay in his han' so much hard cash ebery week, den I go whar I like, lib whar I like. Well, marm, my wife she b'long to anoder massa, but most de time I was able to lib with her; and sometime I able to earn more money den I gib to massa, and I take home to my wife, and we wery happy." He then went on to tell me his story, but I cannot give it you in his words. His wife and himself were both zealous, devoted members of the Methodist Church. They lived very comfortably together, till their eldest child was fourteen; they had five. At this time, his wife's master dying, left her and her children free at the end of a year, but they were all to be sent to Liberia. Harry immediately wrote—I mean, had a letter written (he could neither read nor write) telling his master of his wife's freedom, and his deep attachment to her and her children, and imploring him to set a price on him, and let him try and obtain that money, so he might go with his wife and family. His master sent him word, that he would not sell him at any price. He petitioned a second and a third time, to no purpose. Well, Harry, with the light-hearted thoughtlessness of his race, thinking a year was a long way off, went on in his usual way, with his little spare money buying little comforts for his wife and children, and putting off the evil day. At length, the time arrived for them to sail. He was allowed to go with them to Savannah, to bid them good-bye. They were obliged to remain at Savannah some days, to wait for the vessel; and there he was compelled to leave them, to return himself to a factory, where he was then at work, thinking he had bid them adieu forever. For two or three days he could neither eat nor sleep, devising ways and means to go with them; but all was hopeless. At length, he heard that for some reason the vessel was not to sail for three weeks. He now again sent a most imploring letter to his master, who, thinking such a thing would be utterly impossible, returned him word that, if he would pay him a thousand dollars before the vessel sailed, he should go. The poor man was almost in despair. Where was he to raise a thousand dollars, in a little over two weeks? However, he sent letters to two or three gentlemen, for whom he had worked, and to one northern gentleman, stating his case, and praying for assistance. That night he felt that he had done all he could, but his case was hopeless. He lay down to sleep, with all his fellow-workmen—one of them had read a chapter in the Bible to the rest—soon all were asleep, but he could not close his eyes; "and," to give his own words, "oh! marm, de blessed Jesus, he was so good to dis poor, miserable sinner, suddenly dar was a purty light in de room, now whar it come from I couldn't just see; and right dar, sitting close aside me, was a mighty fine gentleman. At first I thought it was an angel, but afterward I was sure it was Jesus himself come to comfort me. He had a large book open on his knee; He put his hand on part of de book, and read dese words: "Whatsoever ye shall ask in my name, I will gib it you." I started up, but He was gone. I'se sure it was Jesus, de blessed Jesus, say dem words. No! marm, it warn't no dream, I broad wake as I is dis here minute; dem folks all try to 'suade me it was a dream, but I knows better—I 'spects surely it was Jesus. I knows I'se on'y a poor black man, but, marm, He cares for the sparrows, and I sure He cares for me. Well, marm, I got up 'rectly, and went out into de woods; I wanted to pray big, and I 'fraid I'd wake up dem poor fellows as was tired; so I goes out into de woods, and I did'nt tink a bit 'bout de snakes, or de panters, or any of dem creatures—dey didn't come a bit into my mind. I knelt down dar in that ar' woods all alone, in de dark, and, oh! how I prayed God, for Jesus' sake, not to let my wife go 'way widout me. Well, a'ter praying a good spell, I come back into de house, and lay down, and went to sleep. The nex' day I tell to de men all roun' I was going with my wife; I sure of it, for Jesus tell me so. Some of dem laugh at me—some say: 'Well, Harry, we pray for you, too.'"

Harry's faith did not waver, as day after day passed, and still no prospect appeared of his obtaining any funds —still, to all his companions' questions, and doubting remarks, it would always be, "Yes! I am going; Jesus told me so." He heard no word till two days before the vessel sailed, giving him just time to reach Savannah. Then came the joyful tidings, "You are free!" The gentleman to whom he had written, had interested some northern friends, and the money had been made up and paid. He reached Savannah, and joined his wife only one hour before the vessel sailed. "Yes, marm, God does hear prayers; an' bery, bery wicked will I be, if I eber doubt Him." He and his family are doing well, and making useful members of the community. I was attempting to teach him the efficacy of prayer, and he taught me such a lesson on faith—simple faith, taking God at his word—as I hope I may never forget. What simple, childlike faith, that man evinced. He believed Christ said it, and it would be so. Oh! that we had more of it. We all need to say: "Lord! I believe: help thou my unbelief."

TEXT.—I mentioned, some time ago, that it is the custom at morning prayers for each one present to repeat a verse of Scripture. One of our school-girls is of a very fierce, fiery disposition. Yesterday she got into a desperate quarrel with one of the older boys, and, out of sight of the house, they had a regular pitched battle, in which she came off victorious. This morning, when it came her turn to recite—with a most demure countenance, and a loud voice, so as to be heard by all, both boys and girls—she repeated these words from the psalms: "Blessed be the Lord, my God, which teacheth my hands to war, and my fingers to fight." Of course, there was a suppressed titter ran round the room, for all had heard of the yesterday's battle.

CAPE PALMAS.—I believe I have mentioned that we have convocation three times a year; the ministers, teachers, &c., as many as practicable, being present, and all giving in their reports for the last four months. The meeting convenes on Friday morning, continuing through Saturday, and all remaining to commune together on Sunday. They are very interesting, but as yet I have not been able to be present at one. It is to be held this season at the Cape. Mrs. Hoffman has sent me a very kind invitation to go up there (she feels very lonely, Mr. Hoffman and Miss Ball both away), but I have had so much fever lately, that I do not think it is prudent to incur the fatigue. I do not want to be laid aside again, even for a week. This constant fever is so debilitating, we need to be very careful not to increase it. The Bishop intended going up to the Cape to-day, but he has a very bad boil on his knee, so that he cannot possibly put his foot to the ground. He, therefore, cannot go to-morrow; perhaps he may be able to go on Saturday, but there is not much appearance of that now.

When I came out of school, to-day, Mrs. Payne told me that if I felt at all well enough, the Bishop wished me to go up to the Cape. The change may do me good. The "Ocean Eagle" has just arrived, and will stay a week there. She has brought out Rev. Mr. and Mrs Bushnell, and Rev. Mr. and Mrs. McQueen, of the Gaboon and Corisco missions; and the Bishop wishes me to go and welcome them, and extend to them his and Mrs. Payne's most cordial invitations to make us a visit. The Bishop cannot possibly go himself; he cannot leave his room. He is really very ill. We fear it is something more than a boil; he suffers very much.

NEW FRIENDS.—Early in the morning we started for the Asylum. I took Josephine with me, (one of the scholars); she is a fine girl, and I thought it would be a treat to her. James Barber, our printer (a colonist), asked to accompany me, to take care of me; so we took some breakfast, and started very early. We reached the Cape about eleven o'clock; but before I got out of the hammock, there was such a scene (I had not been to the Cape since Miss Ball and myself had exchanged some months before), one of the girls spied me, and there was such a scream, "Miss B.—Miss B. has come!" and then such a rush as there was, all the children (they had been very fond of me, when I was their teacher), Auntie Dade, Eliza, and all about the premises were round me, dancing, shouting, screaming; you never heard such a noise. They are very demonstrative. Mrs. Hoffman came running down to see what was the occasion of all the tumult, and found I was the innocent cause. I found Mrs. Bushnell and Mrs. McQueen in the parlor; the gentlemen soon came in, and we had a very pleasant day. I found Mr. Bushnell had been kind enough to call and see my mother, before he left New-York, thinking it would give me pleasure to hear from him that he had seen her. I felt very thankful to him. Such little acts of kindness do not cost us much; but how much pleasure they afford. Oh! that the Saviour's golden rule could be more indelibly impressed on our hearts. They left us for the vessel, about five o'clock. They decline making us a visit at Cavalla, as they do not wish to sleep on shore—they fear it. It would not be pleasant to have the fever, shut up in a little vessel; and one night on shore may give it.

Mr. Bushnell is to preach for us to-morrow. There was to have been confirmation, but the Bishop is unable to come. A number of the colonists have been up to see and welcome me; some of my Bible and adult evening classes. It is very pleasant to feel you are remembered with affection. I met Mr. Crummell for the first time. I am very much pleased with him; he is a gentleman, well educated, and refined, I have been bitten by something I do not know what, but the part is very much swelled and inflamed; it is very painful. I am bathing it with arnica.

CARRIAGE.—Mr. Marshall, one of the colonist merchants here, has had a little carriage made that will hold two persons. It is drawn by two of the natives. They are trying to train bullocks to use in it. Mr. Marshall said he was sure I was not strong enough to walk to church to-day, so he, very kindly, sent it up for me. Mrs. McQueen rode in it with me. I never can get over the feeling of repugnance I have at these poor natives being like beasts of burden. Mrs. Hoffman always goes to church in a hammock. Mr. Crummell, with our friends from the ship, dined here, but a storm coming up, they were obliged to hurry back to the ship. The captain is a little feverish. He very much dreads having the African fever. Before our friends left us they persuaded me not to go home to-morrow, which I had intended to do, but to stay and go with them out to Mount Vaughan, and visit Mr. Crummell and his school, which I consented to do, as I have never been there yet.

ON BOARD.—The captain came and told us none of his passengers would be on shore to-day, as they were none of them very well. So he persuaded us to go on board and see them. We did. It was very rough. I was dreadfully sea-sick all day, so I did not much enjoy my visit. I could scarcely hold up my head when the captain put us down into the boat, and till I reached the shore, I was so deadly sick. I do not think I shall pay a visit on board ship again in a hurry. I took Josephine with me. I wanted her to see the inside of a ship, but, poor child, she was almost as bad as I was. Mrs. Hoffman was quite well, and enjoyed her visit very much. Perhaps this sea-sickness may be of benefit to me. My foot is still very much swollen and painful. I cannot think what it can be that has bitten me so. I have seen more of Dr. D'Lyon, and have had more conversation with him now than I have ever had before. He is a young colonist physician, sent out by the Board of Missions as a physician to our mission. He bids fair to be of much use, not only to the bodies but the souls of his patients. He seems an earnest Christian.

TRAVELLING.—How different travelling is here to what it is at home. I am only fourteen miles from my African home, but cannot get there. I was so anxious to go to-day, for the Bishop is really very ill. He sent up for the doctor to-day. It is a large carbuncle he has, and he suffers very much with it. He must have it lanced, and I hope he will find some relief. The men are all away cutting rice, and I cannot obtain any bearers. I hope I shall have better success to-morrow. It has been so very rough that no one, but the captain, has ventured on shore from the ship.

KING WEIR.—This morning the doctor told me he had received another note from the Bishop, and he had been enabled to obtain one set of bearers, and as the Bishop's horse was here, with both a man's saddle and a side saddle, I could go either way I liked. I preferred the horse, for though he had never had a lady on his back, yet I knew him to be a quiet, gentle creature, and that it would be impossible for him to run far on the heavy sands, even if so disposed. After prayers, in the morning, the girls crowded around me, begging me to ask permission of Mrs. Hoffman for them to go part of the way, on the beach, with me. I obtained the desired permission. They thought I was going in a hammock, but when they found that I was going on horseback their delight knew no bounds. Mrs. Hoffman lent me an old skirt, and, she being very much taller than me, I contrived to pin it on so as to make it a very nice riding length. Against we arrived on the beach we had quite a procession after us; the doctor in the hammock, and myself on the horse. When we arrived at the Devil's rock (this is very steep and precipitous, of which I have before spoken), I was obliged to dismount, and my horse was led over very carefully. The doctor had to lead him over, as the natives are all so afraid of him, none but the school-boys daring to touch him. I then rode on a little in advance of the doctor, Josephine walking and keeping up with me, and arrived at Graway a little before him. The natives, particularly the children, exhibited, on my approach, the most ludicrous spectacles of curiosity and fear. While in the town, I was waiting till the doctor came up so my horse might have water, when one of the natives came to me and said, "Mammy, you must come off him horse, and come in house, rest yourself." He spoke very good English. I told him no; it was too much trouble to get off my horse; I would rather go on. "Yes, mammy, he must come in; my father, he King Weir; he go for say so." Well, I was afraid of vexing him, as he is a very fine man; the king of all these towns; so I jumped off my horse and went in; one of the school-boys, who was by, taking care of him. I was all alone; in a few minutes, however, the doctor arrived, and soon we had plenty of company, "come to look us," and completely filling up the door-ways, and excluding every breath of fresh air. I must describe Weir to you. He is a king of several towns, and calls himself a "proper gentleman." He is a tall, thin old man; wears a dirty red flannel night-cap (of these they are very proud), and a dirty blue double gown. This is not his ordinary costume, but he was "dressed up plenty" to receive us. The house in which we were is his company-house, or drawing-room. It is never used except for the purpose of receiving and entertaining visiters. There is never any fire or smoking allowed in it; and everything in it is as neat and clean as wax. I was quite struck with its appearance. There were a great number of boxes and chests arranged around the sides of the hut, several of them piled one on another in places, to serve as a sort of table, and covered with a nice white cloth, on which were displayed, and arranged with very good taste, glasses and bottles of all sorts and varieties, colored and white goblets, tumblers, and wine glasses. Hanging on the walls were scores of pitchers and mugs, plates and dishes, all very clean; while above them again were many bright-colored prints. "Oh! his house was proper rich house, and he was proper gentleman." In one corner of the hut was a low wooden bedstead, on it was a pallet stuffed with plantain leaves; and thrown over it, for a quilt, a very coarse, white country cloth. It had such an air of cleanliness and comfort. In the middle of the hut stood a deal table, covered with a clean white cloth. At either end of this table was a plate turned down, a very bright and clean knife and fork, and a very handsome goblet; a decanter, likewise, filled with fresh water, stood on the table. It was very evident they knew we were coming, and preparations had been made for our reception.

The "proper gentleman" soon made his appearance, followed by a number of other men. The outside of the hut was fringed with children. His son, the young man who had spoken to me outside, came in as an interpreter. We told the king that we were in a great hurry; we could not stay, as we wanted to get home. "Oh! we must stay; he cook some chop (food of any kind) for us, and we must stay, eat him. Some boy he come along in the morning and tell him doctor-man him pass with mammy by and by; then he think he make chop for mammy; mammy must go for stay eat him." There was no help for us, so we waited patiently for half an hour. Then the son took three very large covered vegetable dishes, and went out of the hut, he came back in a moment or two with them in his hand. In an instant the hut and its surroundings were cleared, as if by magic, of all its inmates, but ourselves and the son. The young man invited us to sit down; we did so, and he stood, with folded arms and eyes cast down, while the doctor asked a blessing, he then whisked off the covers with a great flourish. There was rice in one dish, palm butter in another, in the third a very fine chicken, which had been cooked in the palm butter. We tasted and it appeared very good, and after sitting a few moments we got up to go, but we found our host's hospitality was not ended. The doctor's bearers were called to eat what we had not. The rice was put in a large wash-bowl, a great quantity added to it, and the palm butter was poured over it. This was set down on the ground, the chicken placed beside it, and the four men sat on the ground around them, then, with a big spoon, they each helped themselves out of the dishes, and in a few minutes they were cleared. We then were allowed to proceed on our journey. The spoons were used in compliment to our presence. The usual method being for each one to put his hand in the dish, gather up a handful, and, after squeezing it together, with a sudden jerk to toss it into his mouth, when he appears to swallow it without biting. We found the Bishop still very unwell; he cannot sit up yet. The doctor has lanced the carbuncle a second time. I hope he will be able to obtain some rest to-night. But, oh! dear, such a greeting as I had when I went into the girls' school-house. I thought they would have torn my clothes to pieces in their enthusiasm; each one trying to get my hand first, and to shake hardest. It is very pleasant to feel you have the love of these poor heathens. May God give us grace to lead them to Him, to show them the love of the precious Saviour. And now I am back there, in my own room. Truly, I feel it is "*domum, domum, dolce domum.*"

LUCIA.—Would that I had Dickens' powers of description, but I have not, so you must be content with the best I can do.

Lucia went with me to town, as my interpreter, to-day. Well, but first let me describe *Lucia.* I have spoken of her several times, and she is one of those on whom I place a high estimation. Lucia Byrd is one of the girls in our first class. She is a large, stout girl—a member of the Church, and, I think, a sincere Christian. She must be about eighteen years old. She is a very retiring, diffident girl, and you must take pains and wait patiently for awhile before you understand Lucia's character—but when you do know it, you find it something worth knowing. She is a girl of sterling integrity. She was brought to school a little child—but she has never been known to tell a lie. You can always depend upon her word, and trust her implicitly. Before you know her she seems to be very cold and stern, but she has a warm, loving, grateful, and affectionate heart. Once gain Lucia's love, and you can do anything with her—but you must understand her to do this. A short time since Mrs. Payne had a box sent to her from Savannah, and in it there was a very pretty bright pink dress for Lucia, sent to her by the lady who supports her here in the school. Her name was on it, and the name of the lady who sent it. We called Lucia into the house and gave the dress to her. To see her face was a perfect treat. I think the lady would have felt herself well repaid could she have seen it. It brightened all over—there was no need for her to say how thankful she was—her face told it. She looked at the dress, turned it over, the tears came into her eyes, and at length, almost choking, she turned to Mrs. Payne; "Thank you, thank you; I'm too good for it." (She meant, it is too good for me.) I wish, occasionally, friends in America would send a little present to each one by name, it elicits so much gratitude to think they are personally remembered.

Lucia is a beautiful sewer. You could not desire anything to be done more neatly than Lucia does it. She often earns a few shillings by sewing, out of school hours, making cloths for the natives, &c.; these pay her in tobacco, cloth, &c., which is the same here as money. In all her studies she does well, and anything that she does not understand, she will not rest till she comes to her teacher to have it explained. It is a pleasure to teach her. She has no father—he died about six months ago. Her mother has been accused of being a witch, and has run away to escape the *Gidu*.

To-day, as Lucia entered a hut, I paused for an instant at the door, exclaiming, "Oh, Macbeth!" The woman to whom this hut belongs is noted for her untidiness. In the centre of the floor is the fire-place, which, I think I told you before, is formed of three circular uprights made of mortar, about six inches in diameter. Between these, on the ground, the fire is made. On this fire was a large black pot, and around it sat three withered crones, wrinkled and haggard—two with their heads shaved, and the third with her hair plaited in little tails, standing out all over her her head, looking exactly like the picture of Bellona, in our old school books. A very little imagination might make you take them for small snakes. She was leaning over a little, peering into the pot. The other two were sitting on the ground—their knees drawn up close to their bodies—a favorite position; their hands and chins resting on their knees. These were rocking themselves back and forth, making a low moaning sound. The whole upper part of the hut was filled with a dense smoke—it was only those portions near the ground that were visible. Near one of the crones lay a child, in the most crumpled up form you can imagine; from its position you would have supposed it must be a corpse just cast down, and might imagine the unseen arms to form part of the ingredients of the pot. Scattered about in every direction were a number of little bowls, pots and pans, all black. The country manufactures, baskets, bowls, pans, &c., are all black. In front of one of the women was a small wooden bowl, and she had yet the pounder between her hands which she had been using. Altogether, it was the most weird looking scene I ever witnessed. They did not rise to greet me, but held out their hands as if pleased to see me. Then, in a low dolorious voice, one of them began telling a long story to Lucia. At length Lucia rose in a hurry, without waiting for me to say anything to them. So I went to the one that appeared in the most trouble, and showed her, by my manner, that I felt sorry for her. I then pointed upward, and told them to " *Bede* Nyesoa" (pray to God), and left them. I could not persuade Lucia to tell me what was the matter. She very often seems ashamed to have us know the strange things that go on among her people. I wish she were not quite so reserved.

Another house I went to, the woman told me that *they*, meaning some of the missionaries, "used to give her tobacco, but now she been to church three, four Sunday, and she have no tobacco give; she no go again." I told her if that was all she went to church for she had better stay away—tobacco was never given her for that. Mrs. Payne, on her rounds, found a woman who said she would not come to church to-morrow. She is taking sassa-wood. Often, if they are accused of witchcraft, even if no action is taken against them, rather than suffer under the imputation, they will take it at home themselves. But when they do this they have to take it three times, if they live—two or three days intervening between each dose—during which time they do not go out.

Yesterday there was a great noise in town—beating of drums, dancing, shouting, &c. They were making a grand gree-gree for good luck. Their rice is very poor, and there is a great deal of sickness and death among them. All the devil doctors, from a long distance round, were present.

The Bishop is much better; able to move about his room again.

REVERIES.—" Lord increase our faith." Sometimes the deep ignorance, darkness, and degradation of the people, seems to have a most saddening and depressing effect on the spirits.

It has been a very cloudy day to-day. This evening,

about sunset, I sat looking out upon the mighty waters, when the clouds thickened and deepened very fast; a heavy squall was coming up. One cloud was very thick and heavy, and seemed almost to touch the waves, which rolled in wild confusion, dashing and breaking on the rocks, and on each other, in their mad fury. The scene appeared to me so much to resemble the moral or spiritual condition of the people—in wild confusion dashing on the rocks of superstition, destroying and being destroyed; their gree-grees and *sassa* destroying both soul and body, while a heavy cloud of gross ignorance broods over their minds. Yet while I sat sadly gazing at it, gradually the scene began to change; it was slow, oh! so slow; but from the train my thoughts had taken, you cannot imagine with what intense interest I watched it. At first there appeared the faintest streak of light on that heavy cloud, and as it slowly increased, the cloud became gradually lifted up and rolled back, till at length the intense blackness remained only on the edge of the horizon. And where the first faint light had appeared it gradually brightened, and brightened, till just in that little spot the cloud rolled away for an instant, and the moon appeared, struggling feebly with the surrounding darkness, and apparently vainly endeavoring to make her light visible. For a time there seemed a great struggle which would gain the victory, darkness or light. For a time the thick clouds would roll over the moon, and it would seem as if her light was entirely put out—that the darkness was too thick for her to penetrate; but gradually you would see those clouds become less and less, till there would only light fleecy ones pass over her.

For, though they appeared dense and heavy at a distance, as they approached nearer and nearer to her, they became brighter and lighter. At length she had formed a bright little spot around her, while the rays issuing from that spot spread in every direction, and her gentle beams had subdued, in some measure, the tumult of the waves. Yet still she shone with a very pale and feeble light; she was not half full, and therefore, was not turned entirely, but only partially toward the sun, and so she but feebly reflected his rays. I kept gazing with eager, anxious eyes on this scene, for I had in my own mind personified it. The moon was the Church of God, struggling through clouds of affliction, darkness, doubts, ignorance, and superstition, to shed a few rays of light on benighted Africa. And often when that light has been dimmed, obscured, or apparently put out, it appears again, gradually piercing and dissipating the darkness, reflecting the rays of the "Sun of righteousness." Her light is so feeble and dim, because she only so partially reflects his beams—she is not turned wholly unto Him.

After service, when we came out of church, the moon was sailing calmly and peacefully in the heavens—not a cloud to be seen. It seemed to me a very pale, but a very holy and pure light. So may it be with the "Church of the living God." May her light gently but surely dissipate the clouds of darkness, vice and superstition; and however pale, and weak, and feeble her radiance, yet may it all be reflected from the "Sun of righteousness," and may she daily and hourly turn more and more toward Him, so that she may be constantly on the increase, till her light shall irradiate, not only this continent, but all the dark places of the earth.

STORES FROM HOME.—My box has arrived. Many thanks, kind friends; many little kind remembrances from one and another. You cannot imagine how good anything from home tastes—and as to the pickles, I will only say you would have had your pay for them could you see us enjoy them. Though we can learn to take with a thankful heart such things as we can ordinarily obtain here, yet we can enjoy creature comforts when we get them as well as any one. We do not, any of us, belong to the school of stoics.

The Bishop came out into the parlor to-day. It is so pleasant to see him about again. We are a small family —we cannot spare one. Mr. Payne is sick to-night, however, with fever. So we play a perpetual game of see-saw—one up, the other down.

TRANSMIGRATION. — These people have a strangely mingled creed. They believe somewhat in the transmigration of souls, and that the spirits of the departed like to hover round their former haunts. Therefore, though they do not hesitate to kill every species of animals outside the town, they will kill none in town, for fear it might be a spirit who would harm them. I cannot understand what difference being inside or outside of the town, can make, but I suppose they do. The Bishop heard a man addressing a Guano (a large species of lizard, quite savage) that was lying along his fence: " I pray you go away; please let me pray you go from here." He would not touch it, though he wanted it gone. The spirit, he thought, knew what he said, hence his politeness.

Rumors.—We are growing very short of rice—if we do not have supplies soon from somewhere we shall be badly off. So many children, and nothing to give them to eat; but we must have faith. " The Lord will provide." Mrs. Payne down with the fever again, and I am troubled with boils.

I believe I told you that in the war two years ago, between the natives and the colonists, at Cape Palmas, the colonists burnt the native towns, and made them move across to the other side of the river. They never have liked it there, and though they have built some new towns, they have never seemed settled, but always say they are coming back. We hear a rumor to-night (how true it is we do not know) that the natives have declared war with the colonists. Poor Mrs. Hoffman will be in a great fright if it is so; but she need not fear, they would not touch anything belonging to the mission; " The Lord our God is with us."

Mrs. Payne and myself constant chills and fever again. This it is that breaks down the constitution. Chills and fever all the time, at all seasons of the year, no frost to break it up.

All quiet at the Cape. Strange it is how our feelings change. I used to think that it would be impossible for me to sleep in a room in which I knew any one had breathed their last. There is not, however, a bedroom in the mission in which the last enemy has not appeared.

But, thanks be to God, robbed of his sting, through Jesus Christ our Lord, it has only been to open the portals of everlasting day. I never think of those that have left us with the feelings I used to fancy I should associate with the place of their departure, but I rather think of each room as the gate of heaven. May the place of my departure, wherever it may be, be such to me. "Living or dying, may I be the Lord's." Oh! here in Africa, if in any place, we ought to try to realize that " to live is Christ's and to die is gain."

Music.—Yesterday (Sunday) I was very ill all day. Calomel again—it seems to be the only remedy. Mrs. Payne ill also, so they had no ladies at table. (I believe I have forgotten to mention that Mr. J. Wilson, our teacher in the boys' school, and Mr. J. Barber, our printer, both colonist young men, take their meals with us). The Bishop sent us word, however, that he was so well he was eating enough for us all.

Last evening, while lying in bed, I was listening to nature's melody. The humming of the insects, grasshoppers, katydids, and others, such as we have not at home; the soft low sighing of the cocoanut trees; the shrill yet melodious notes of the night birds, and the deep low base of old ocean's ceaseless roar. It was music, sweet music, arising to the " Giver of good." And then I thought of the heathen towns around whence no sweet melody arises; no hearts are tuned to sing His praise, " Only man is vile," and a sadness was fast creeping over my spirit, when suddenly from the school-house, which is just at the end of my piazza, and where evening service is held, burst forth in triumphal tones, as it seemed to me, from sometime heathen lips, the glad song of praise, "It is a good thing to give thanks unto the Lord." Oh! how instantly it changed the current of my thoughts, from sadness and despondency at the great work to be done, to joy and gratitude for what God has already wrought here.

Mrs. Payne has just received another box. Her friends are very kind. These people live in a constant state of fear, the one idea of witchcraft forever haunting them—either the dread of being witched by others, or being so accused themselves. They believe that each one possesses the power, but it is only a few that use it, and they are only accused of being witches when it is supposed they use the power they possess. Even long after they become Christians they have a secret dread of this. It is one of the hard things to root out.

A Pleasant Day.—I have had a very pleasant day in school to-day, but to explain it I must go back. Mr. Hoffman, once a month, has all the Sunday-schools from different stations in his vicinity meet at St. Mark's church. He catechises them, talks to them, etc., and recently they have all formed into little missionary classes, like ours at home, and they bring in their contributions once a month. When Mr. Williams was here he was very much pleased with the plan. Before he went away he begged the children at the Cape, and those here, to write to his children, at Monrovia. He thought it would do them good to correspond. But I must tell you who I mean by his children. Every Sunday, after afternoon service, when he goes home to his house, all the children, big and little, of every class and denomination, that choose to collect, come to his room. He talks to them, prays with them, and they sing together, and they have a very pleasant meeting, for he loves children, and loves to "feed Christ's lambs," and they love him very much, and gather in crowds into his room, to be fed with the sincere milk of the Word. These are his children, with whom ours are to correspond. There were a number of letters written from our children and from those at the Asylum. Last night we received an answer from him and from several of his children. This morning I took his letter with me into the school-room—the children had become very fond of him while he was here—and read it to them, Mrs. Gillet interpreting. When I want all the little ones to know what I say, I am obliged to have her interpret for me. He spoke of his children having formed themselves into little missionary classes, and the pleasurable feeling it had excited among them. I had to stop and explain it all to our children, and immediately there was such a burst of enthusiasm. They must try and do the same; they must try and give something for their little heathen brothers and sisters. Some of the elder girls can, occasionally, earn a trifle by their needle. They are good sewers, and in whatever way they can they will try and give their mite to send the good news farther. It will be but *a mite*, indeed, that can be given, but it is the heart God looks at. So we formed the school into one class, the "Anna Payne Class," and we shall have our box to begin on Monday next. I have told the children that if either of them put tobacco, or pipes, or whatever they may receive as money, in the box, I will take it out and put money in its place. May God bless our feeble effort. Every cent put into that box will be hardly earned.

DAWBA.—We have had a very painful occurrence to-day. *Dawba*, one of the Christian natives, of whom we all thought so highly (he seemed to be so deeply interested in all religious things), has been proved to be a thief. He had stolen a sheep, and some of it was found in his house. We all feel so sorry; we thought him such a good man. He is very poor and sickly. I do not know how he will pay for it. May God give him true repentance.

The "palava" is entirely settled at the Cape. No thoughts of war. They have banished old Dawba from town. It seems he is an inveterate thief, and all the time he has been making a profession of religion he has been carrying on his thievish propensities. What a bitter disappointment it is to the missionary to see such a case of hypocrisy, and yet they, like other ministers of the Gospel, must expect some such trials always. In all places the evil one is busy at work " sowing tares among the wheat."

Chapter Thirteenth.

ENTHUSIASM.

I NEVER earnestly desired the gift of writing, I mean both the mechanical and mental powers, but more particularly the latter, as I have done since I have been in Africa. Oh! that my pen could be formed and tempered in the "fire of the altar." That it had a point which would write on the hardest heart. But I must remember "the race is not to the swift, nor the battle to the strong." I have heard it said that if we only feel earnestly in our own hearts, in any cause we are pleading, we shall make others feel it too. And yet how strange, in the cause of religion, enthusiasm is pronounced fanaticism; aye, often even by professors of religion themselves. We must be moderate, calm, and cool. The man who sees his neighbor's house in flames, and his wife and children perishing, would rush eagerly to the rescue, but the Christian, who sees thousands about "to dwell with everlasting burning," must stand calmly by. His fellow Christians, as well as others, telling him it is not his duty to expose himself to injury. He who should see a blind man walking on the edge of a precipice, liable, at any moment, to fall and be dashed to pieces, and did not hasten to his rescue, even though at some risk to himself, would be thought a weak coward, worthy only of our contempt; yet, he who runs a slight risk to his own health and personal comfort, in seeking to save many from the "gulf of fearful perdition," is a fanatic. Would that men would have a little more honesty, and call things by their right names. Is that sailor a *fanatic* who, obedient to his captain's command, in momentary peril of his life, hastens aloft, amid the howling storm and tempest, to use measures to save the ship from being dashed upon the rocks? Yet, he is such who ventures his all to save others from eternal shipwreck. It is not fanaticism for a man to set before him one earthly object of ambition, whether it be wealth, fame, knowledge, or any other earthly goods, and to pursue this one object with all his powers. Oh, no! this is all lawful, and right, and even praiseworthy. But let their one end and aim be the adding new subjects to the Redeemer's kingdom; the seeking and finding precious jewels, to shine for ever and ever; the desire to carry forward the triumphs of the cross; to add fresh laurels to the Saviour's crown; to diffuse knowledge in the dark places of the earth; those who do this are fanatics. May we pray to God, earnestly, for more of these fanatics to come forth to Africa.

This morning, instead of our usual prayers, we were all collected in the church, to attend the baptism of another of our older boys. He has only been in the school about a year. He is eighteen years old. The Bishop is very particular in watching the conduct, and duly examining the knowledge of those who make a profession, before he allows them to come forward. It is the young —those who are trained in our schools, who for years have been under Christian teaching and example—it is they must be the hope of Africa ; for those who become Christians after they are advanced in life, it is such a constant struggle, with the wickedness around and within them. Life-long habits of sin and guilt to be continually fought against, with, by no means a full, strong, and clear notion of the holiness and purity of the religion of Jesus. It is to our schools we must look ; it is those who have been educated there that we must send forth as teachers and preachers ; and yet think, with their Bibles in their hands, of their Saviour's last command (in the strong, imperative mood) : " Go into all the world, and preach the Gospel." Hundreds and hundreds of young men in America, professing to be followers of Christ, can read again and again that passage, "*Go*," and yet not see that the Saviour addresses them. No young man, outside of the ministry, seems to think for an instant it is his duty to give up worldly gain and worldly profit, to obey Jesus' command to " Go, and teach all nations." Not one can hear the Saviour's injunction to the young man in the Gospel addressed to himself : " Go, sell all that thou hast, and come follow me." We want teachers, as well as pastors. Are there none, not one, of our professing Christian young men, who can give up all worldly aggrandizement, that they may obtain a crown, adorned with many jewels, gathered from Afric's burning sands ? Our pastors have now more than they can do ; they have vowed solemnly to devote themselves to the work of preaching. Oh! that they may have their hands held up. Oh! that the Spirit of God, which has been so abundantly poured forth on our land, may awaken many to come forth to assist the pastor in "feeding the lambs of the flock." May that message sound in many hearts: "Go, ye." Oh! that Zion would awake, and put on all her strength for the conflict, that her young men may come forth as an army, glorious with banners.

LETTERS.—I must give you some account of a gift we have received, at Christmas-time, by the "Stevens." Miss Williford received a few Testaments from a little child in Philadelphia. No name was given, with the wish that they should be given to some of the children here. As they had just received a little Christmas token each, Miss Williford thought she would not give them to the children then, but reserve them for a short time. When the "Stevens" came out this last time, she brought a few more Testaments, and a number of other pretty little books, with this note:

PHILADELPHIA, *March* 8, 1858.
MY DEAR LITTLE CHILDREN:
I heard that a vessel was going to sail for Africa, and have been saving some money, with which I determined to buy some books to send you. My little sister thought that she would like to give some of her money to buy a few little books, to send you. She is nearly four years old. We have a map of the African mission, which has a map of the Grebo country, and a great many pictures; and, when I look up at it, I often think of you, and love you very much. The books that were sent to you, about January, 1857, were bought from the money saved by a

little boy—who had died just before, "who always showed great love for the heathen." I want to speak about him; he was my dear little brother; and if you remember getting them, I wish you would let me know, through the "Carrier Dove," which I take.

I remain, ever your little friend,

JOHNNY R———.

I took the little books and the letter into the schoolroom, I read it, talked to the children a good while about it, and had the note, and what I said, interpreted to them for me, by Mrs. Gillet (my assistant in school), for the benefit of those who did not sufficiently understand English. I wanted them thoroughly to appreciate the self-denial that is practised very often by our little darlings at home, who have been taught that most beautiful law of love: "My neighbor is everybody—all my fellow-creatures." The children, even the very smallest, listened with great interest. It would have given you great pleasure, if you could have looked in upon us; and when I called the six elder girls, and gave them the books that had been purchased by the money of the little departed one (and that perhaps he was permitted to know that now they were receiving his dying gift), there were tears in the eyes of all; and some were sobbing. They will value those books, not only as being the precious Book of God, but as having other sacred associations attached to them. I think, if little Johnny could have been there, he would have been quite sure his brother's gifts, at all events, were appreciated. The older girls always see the "Carrier Dove," and they thought they would like to thank Johnny themselves; so I let two of them write. One has never attempted to write before; the other has written once or twice to her friends here. These letters I shall send to the "Carrier Dove."* I would say these notes are entirely their own, only they sat by my side, and would ask me if each word was right, as they wrote. This is one answer.

My little Friend:

We all feel very much pleasure for your little Testaments, which you sent us. We thank you very much, and very much obliged to you for your kindness towards us. Again and again, more thankful to our heavenly Father, who had put it into your heart to bestow on us such nice books. I think we must have kind friends in America; they often send us nice little presents; we thank them in our hearts very much, though we know not how to tell it you in English words, but our hearts feel it. We know, for our teachers have told us, that many little children in America save their pennies, that are given them to buy candies and play-things, and send them to us. We cannot pay them, but God can. I hope God will ever bless you.

Your true friend,
Lucia Byrd.

This is the other letter that was written in answer:

My dear little Friend:

I know that you love me, and I love you, too. When I see your little books, which you sent unto us, then I

* They have since been printed.

know you love me; for when we love any one, we like to think of them, to please them, and to do them good. One of my companions has written you a letter, but I thought you would like to know that there is more than one of us who lived once without God, are thankful that we have kind friends, who come here to teach us about our Saviour, and that we have more kind friends in America who love us, and think of us, and pray to God for us. May God, my Father, and your Father, ever bless you. So prays your thankful friend,

JOSEPHINE WILLIFORD.

JOSEPHINE.—Suppose I tell you something about the last writer, and it gives me great pleasure to speak of her. She is a good, dear little girl, about fourteen, and has a very pleasant face and form. She is very dark, but not black; and has a very bright, sweet smile. She is a member of the Church, and strives earnestly to walk answerable to her Christian calling. She is a very studious child, of bright intellect; and, though the youngest, stands first in her class. In school, she never has to be spoken to for laughing, playing or talking. She is an excellent sewer, is very neat and clean in her person, and very particular about her clothes, that they should fit neatly, &c.; for, while we endeavor to discourage anything like pride or vanity in dress, at the same time we feel that a proper regard to their appearance, is necessary to inculcate self-respect. They are, therefore, never allowed to make their appearance in the school-room with soiled or torn dresses, unwashed faces or hands, or uncombed hair. Josephine will make a fine woman, if God spares her life.

African Cemetery.

THE GARDEN GRAVES.—We have a beautiful garden. The Bishop is very fond of flowers. The first thing in the morning he plucks a tiny boquet for Mrs. Payne and myself, which we wear through the day. This is to show he has no "palaver" with us. Every species of flowers, that can be raised here, are cultivated. The children need to have their tastes elevated, and their love of the beautiful encouraged. But there is one spot that I love best in the garden. In one corner, under the shade of some lofty trees, are the graves of the missionaries. The coral plant, and the beautiful mimosa, grow in rich luxuriance around. Mrs. Payne's grave is the last that has been added to those already here. The low moaning of the trees, and the constant murmur of the waves, sing their unceasing requiem over those graves. Here their ashes shall peacefully repose, till the trump on the resurrection morn shall call them forth, to greet, oh! with what joy, the many who, through their instrumentality, (perhaps, for many generations) have been brought home to God ; and then they, as having "turned many to righteousness," shall shine as the stars, for ever and ever.

> There's a sacred spot, near the ocean's strand,
> Safe guarded and held by a Mighty hand,
> Where, in calm repose, lay a noble band,
>   Asleep in Jesus.
>
> Forth, far from their own native land, they came,
> To teach to the heathen that precious Name
> That they love so well ; to ignite the flame
>   Of love to Jesus.

And here they are laid; the ocean's loud roar
Their requiem sings, but disturbs them no more.
Yes, sweetly they rest; their labor is o'er,
    At home, with Jesus.

Close in our view do their loved forms lie;
To them it was glory—'twas bliss—to die!
Man may forget them; their record's on high,
    Inscribed by Jesus.

And when the archangel's last trump shall sound,
To wake from the dead the sleepers around,
Who, through them, with joy everlastingly crowned,
    Sing praise to Jesus.

Joyfully, then, their voices they'll raise,
All joining the song of exulting praise,
To Him they all worship; "The Ancient of Days,"
    Redeemed by Jesus.

THE MISSIONARY BOX.—We commenced with our missionary box to-day, and had fifty cents put in—more, a great deal, than I had expected; for you know that there are but very few of these children that ever have a cent, and when they do, it is very hardly earned. We also determined on something else to-day. Every Tuesday afternoon (it is the only one that either the girls or myself can possibly spare), we are going to collect all, both girls and boys, that will come from town, and see what we can do in the way of instructing them. It will be but little, of course, in such a short time, but still it will be something. I am to be superintendent, the elder girls assisting me. Thus I want to teach them to become missionaries in turn. They are all willing to try to do what they can.

THE GIRLS' SCHOOL.—The Bishop and Mrs. Payne are gone to the Cape to-day, so I am "all alone in my glory." We commenced our school, within a school, to-day. We had forty-seven little heathen, only one of whom had even the vestige of a rag on. They are of all ages, from four to fourteen. I have twelve teachers, each industrious and earnest in their work. Each one had been to town, and collected her own class, most of them children in some way related to her. Our children, as soon as they know their Saviour, seem so anxious to teach Him to others; even the little things, five or six years old, when they go to town, among their companions, will repeat to them their little hymns and texts, and tell them God made them, and Jesus, the Son of God, came into the world and died for them, to save them from being punished. I had told my teachers that there was one thing I must insist upon—that the children all had clean faces and hands. I went into the school-room about three o'clock, and there were about twenty little urchins sitting quite demurely; but when I went toward the back door, there was a most amusing sight. There stood a very large wash-tub, and between one and two dozen little specimens of humanity, each one waiting for his or her turn to be—well, it did not seem like washed; it was more like rasping. This process was superintended by two of our young ladies, real go-ahead youngsters, about fourteen years of age, who felt themselves exceedingly large in the momentary power they possessed. They enjoyed it vastly, and the children submitted to it with all imaginable patience. Poor little ones! God grant that they may be washed in the fountain open for sin and uncleanness. After appointing them their separate places, I called one of the older girls beside me, as an interpreter, and made her tell them that there was one God, who made them all and took care of them all, and that they must pray to Him. She then taught them a few words of prayer, making them all repeat it till they knew it. This, she told them, they were to say night and morning. I then told them a little story, which much pleased them. Then, distributing primers to the teachers, there was soon a perfect bedlam—so many voices repeating, in the highest cadences, A, B, C, &c. Before closing, I made them all learn the first verse of "Happy Land," which the Bishop has translated into the Grebo language. But when they attempted to sing it, it was truly ludicrous. They soon got the tune, but as to the time, it was nowhere. I talked to them again, and then dismissed them, with a short prayer. So our school has begun.

PATIENCE.—It is very difficult to get any work done here. The natives have no idea of the value of time. We have to learn patience. Mr. Dorsen is here again. This is the third time he has been up to try and get men to carry down plank for the repairing of his house (about twenty miles off his station is), but again he is disappointed. Last night a number of men promised him to go; this morning they refuse. Several "devil doctors" are in town, and to-day they are going to make a big gree-gree, and offer sacrifices to the devil. All, therefore, are forbidden to go to sea, to fish, to go out of town, or to do any kind of work. So Mr. Dorsen has had to go home, disappointed again. The Bishop and Mrs. Payne have come home to-day. He has preached at eight different places in the three days. In town, to-day, I felt almost disposed to be angry at the hardness and depravity of the human heart. It is slow work, the work of faith—teaching these people. Oh! for more of the Spirit's influences. I often come home, thanking God, "Who hath made me to differ." It seems almost impossible to believe that the Anglo-Saxon race were ever so far sunk in barbarism.

SUPERSTITION.—I was asking the Bishop to-night what the sacrifice to the devil was for yesterday. He said, "The people believe the spirits of the departed (the Kwi) keep watch about the town, and when the people do anything they do not like, they send trouble upon them. Now, at this time, their rice is very bad, and they can catch no fish. So a demon doctor told them that the spirit of one of the head-men, who died about six months ago, was angry with them, because there are so many witches and bad people about town. So they must sacrifice to appease him." Poor people! whom "the devil leads captive at his will."

We just hear that an English cruiser has taken a so-called French emigrant ship, but in reality a slaver, and has carried her into Sierra Leone. We had our afternoon school to-day, and, upon questioning the children, I was surprised to find how much they remembered of what they had been taught last week.

CAPE PALMAS —Mrs. Hoffman not at all well. She

fears she is going to have the fever; and as Mr. Hoffman and Miss Ball are still away, I started off very early this morning, to be with her in case of her being ill. I, however, found her much better than I expected. I shall remain a day or two. The Bishop came up with me, stopping on the way to preach at two towns. We had heard that the American frigate Dale was anchored off the Cape; and as the Bishop was well acquainted with, and had received many little acts of kindness from, the captain and officers, he came up purposely to see them; but just as we arrived, we saw the vessel start off, under full sail. The Bishop returned home again this afternoon. I fear the journey has done me no good, as my fever is very high again.

Mount Vaughan.—Feeling better again to-day, I accepted Mr. Marshall's kind offer of his little carriage to take me to Mount Vaughan. Mr. J. Thompson (a colonist) went with me. We had three native men, two to draw and one to push us, and we went along very nicely. Mount Vaughan is about three miles from the Cape. A very good road has been formed between the two places, lined on either side, for some distance, with very beautiful trees—palm and others. The situation of the mission-house is very fine, on the summit of a high hill, which slopes down to the road, the slope completely covered with young coffee and orange trees. All the trees and shrubbery were destroyed during the late war, as well as the buildings, so that these are quite young. The house is a fine large one; it has a very extensive view, and, indeed, it is altogether a lovely spot. The mission stations, so far as I have yet seen, are all of them selected with great regard to beauty of locality. Mr. and Mrs. Crummell were quite pleased to see us. We only had time to make a short call, but we enjoyed it much.

HOME.—Finding Mrs. Hoffman so much better than I had expected, there was no need to be absent from my work, so I am home again. It really is worth going away, for the sake of the welcome on our return. Mrs. Hoffman has had a letter from Mr. Hoffman. The vessel they are in would not stop with them at the Cape, so they are on their way to Monrovia, and will have to remain there till some vessel is coming down the coast. They are both (Miss Ball and Mr. Hoffman) much benefitted by the voyage.

CRUELTY.—Last Wednesday, before I left home, Bedell, one of our native teachers, from Rocktown, was here to tea. He told us that the Sunday previous a little child of three years old had been missed, and the people were afraid that he was witched. Yesterday we heard that a witch man had carried him away, and buried him. The poor little child has been found, having evidently been buried alive. You see a witch is really another name for foe, or enemy. As yet they have not discovered who did it. On Saturday, Doctor D'Lyon, with Mr. Thompson, were visiting a heathen town, near the Cape, when they called the Doctor to a woman who had just fallen down dead, with apoplexy. She was busy about her work, when she suddenly dropped dead.

Of course, the people supposed she was witched; and when her friends began to weep and mourn, they were shut up in a hut, it being believed that some of her own near relatives had done it. The Doctor explained to them the nature of the disease, and told them that many died of it in our country; but they turned a deaf ear to all he had to say, and probably several will pass through the sassa ordeal for this.

A poor woman, living in Fishtown, had an only child, whom she loved very dearly. Last week it was taken ill, and died. She was instantly accused of witching it, and the heart-broken mother was condemned to death. Surely these people live all their time in bondage, being subject to the fear of death. None are, for an instant, safe.

CRAZY MAN.—We heard rather a singular incident while we were stopping to rest at Graway. King Wier (I find he is Paddock's father), at whose house we were, told us that there is a crazy man in his town; and this crazy man came to him the other day, and said to him: " I see the spirit of your father; I see the spirits of your brothers. They come to me; they say you go for see King Wier. You tell him, we say he must mind God's things; they be true things. You must do good fashion; you must leave country fashion. You must keep the Sunday—you must make your people keep the Sunday —so you no come to hell. We be in hell. You no come there." This has alarmed Wier very much, and he says he means to make his people keep Sunday. He seems to feel very serious about it. What if God has employed the instrumentality of a crazy heathen man to effect this great object (the observance of the Sabbath), that the missionary has so long been endeavoring to accomplish? This crazy man never himself *believed* in the Gospel, though he has frequently heard it preached.

> "By weakest instruments, and most unlikely means,
> Full oft are great events produced."

NYA.—There is a poor young man in town, a Christian, named Nye, who has had a dreadful leg for a long time. At length, the Bishop persuaded him to have it amputated. Dr. Fletcher* came down from the Cape to-day, to assist Dr. D'Lyon. They gave the man ether, and he was utterly unconscious till the limb was off. They say " kobi" (foreigners) are great devil-men—they can do everything. The astonishment at the effect of the ether is boundless.

BEAUTY.—They have a legend among the people, that when God first made man, He made the black man and the white man. The black was the oldest brother; and Nye-soa (God) came and asked him which he would like —a beautiful country, and a beautiful person, or great powers of mind; he choose the beauty of person and country. Nye-soa then asked the youngest brother, the white man, the same question. He choose mental powers; that's the reason why the black man is so handsome, and the white man know so much. But the first sight of us, thinking we must be fearful lepers, is, probably, very disgusting to them. When the "Stevens"

---

* Dr. Fletcher, a colored physician, formerly the only one here.

came out, she had one or two sick with the measles on board; it is a very bad kind, followed, in every case, by severe dysentery. It has spread rapidly all over the country, and has been very fatal. We have several down with it in the school; we shall be greatly blessed if we lose none of our number. At home, before leaving, I often heard people speak of the condition of the heathen, that they might be saved without the Gospel, "they being a law to themselves." I used to be of that opinion. But, oh! it only needs you to be amongst them to see how utterly neglected is that law of conscience which they do possess. It does not do for us to limit the boundlessness of infinite love, or the world-wide efficacy of the Redeemer's blood; but it would seem to us that, could they reach heaven, in their present condition, it would be no heaven to them; the purity and holiness required there would be misery to them; and, we know, as they die, so they remain. Oh! the millions that are going down to eternal death. May our earnest daily prayer be, "Come, Lord Jesus, take these kingdoms for thine own."

MARRIAGE.—I must tell you something with regard to the marriage customs here. I have told you that their customs are somewhat patriarchal, the headman of each family having perfect right not only over the property, but even over the persons of each member of the family. This, probably, is a great drawback to their national energy and prosperity, as no man can really call the things he possesses his own. For instance, if a member of the family dies by the sassa ordeal, the body is thrown upon the beach, and not allowed to be removed till a bullock is provided by the headman of the family, as a sacrifice to the Kwi. If the departed himself does not possess one, it must be obtained or some other member of the family. In cases of accusation of theft, or other crimes, though the sassa is not given, the bullock, for sacrifice, must be. Should there be no bullocks in the family, the next available property is a young girl, the nearest relative to the criminal that remains unsold. She is offered, then, to any man that will pay the price of a wife. This always includes a bullock, with some few other articles, amounting in value to about twenty-five dollars. She then becomes the property of the purchaser, and he may either take her immediately to live with, and assist his mother, or one of his other wives; or he may leave her with her mother till she is of a marriageable age, which, with them, is about fifteen. He then builds a new hut for her, beside those of his other wives, and takes her home, and she takes her position with the rest. Where girls are not sold like this, to settle a "palaver," they are generally purchased by some man, who may take a fancy to them. In this case, the man is expected often to make little dashes to the mother of the child. Thus it is, you seldom see a girl over eight years that is not already sold. There is no affection. The female part of the population are only so much property. A man's wealth is estimated by the number of his wives; and, strange to say, the women themselves feel it to be a disgrace, and do not like to acknowledge themselves to be the only one. On a man's death, his wives, with his other property, become the possessions of his nearest male relations. The greatest disgrace that can happen to a woman is to remain unmarried. When the Bishop first commenced the girls' school here, he took what children were permitted to come to him. But he soon found that this would never do; they all had husbands, who, at any time they chose, could come and take them away. Thus, when the poor girls had become partially civilized, and partially Christianized, they would be dragged back into deep degradation, rendering their education not only useless, but injurious to themselves. He, therefore, determined to pay the purchase-money for each child that should hereafter be brought into the school; and then neither the parents, nor any one else, would have the slightest control over her in future. But should she be a bad child, and run away from the school, and remain away, the parents are obliged to refund her purchase-money, as they have to do in the case of a runaway wife. When the girl enters the school, however, the parents always beg that she may be married, to avoid the disgrace attached to a single woman. Our children are never influenced; they are allowed to make their own selection; and it seldom happens that a girl remains disengaged over fourteen. Ours being the only girls' school, and there being several boys' schools—and the civilized and Christianized boys wishing to obtain such wives—our girls are generally in great demand. I have just received a letter from Mr. Ogden, in which he gives me the account of the price paid for a Benga wife. He is at Corisco, much farther to the south than we are. There, a man will have fifty or sixty wives. Among the Greboes, they do not often have more than six or seven.

Now, to tell you what is the price of a Benga girl: 20 small bars of iron, 1 gun, 1 brass kettle, 1 coat, 1 shirt, 1 chair, 1 hat, 2 caps, 1 cutlass, 4 knives, 1 umbrella, 1 chest, 4 wash-basins, 6 plates, 4 empty bottles, 1 keg of powder, 1 iron pot, 1 brass pan, 10 brass rods, 10 pieces of cloth, 5 mugs, 1 small looking-glass, 1 jug, 4 pins, 5 needles, 5 fish-hooks, 2 razors, 2 pairs of scissors, 8 bunches of small beads, 2 pairs of ear-rings, 1 pocket-handkerchief, 3 padlocks and keys, 4 pipes, 10 heads of tobacco, 1 piece of cloth for her mother, 1 silk handkerchief, 1 small bell, 1 tumbler. This is the usual price. You see a Benga wife is much more expensive than a Grebo, and there they understand better the uses of articles of civilization.

AMUSEMENTS.—We have twenty on the sick-list, but they are doing pretty well. The doctor came down to-day. He has amputated the hand of a poor woman; she has suffered dreadfully with it. He is likely to have plenty of practice.

I will give you a sample of our evening's amusements. By the time tea and prayers are over it is generally ten minutes past eight. Then Mrs. Payne and myself reach out our sewing—the only time we really give to it. The Bishop sits in his library, off the parlor—every one having to pass through it to go to him. He sits there making up accounts, writing orders, and attending to wants, these last not few or far between. Generally Mrs. Payne and myself attend to any that may come requiring our assistance, as they may happen to apply to one or the other of us. But I never noticed how many such applications there are, till last night. Mrs. Payne had a number of business letters to write to the Cape that must go off this morning. You can form no idea of the amount of such work that has to be done here; providing supplies, &c., for all the other stations round us. So as Mrs. Payne had so much of that work to do, I agreed to attend to every petitioner that should come. Well, I was scarcely seated when in came a native man, with a large piece of flesh completely torn out of his leg. That had to be dressed and attended to. Of course, after every such thing the hands require ablution. After he was gone Valentine came in for some medicine for the baby. Then comes one of the girls who has lost her mat that she sleeps on. This has to be inquired into, and orders given for another to be provided. Next follows one of the school-boys who has cut his toe badly with a rock—that must be dressed. Then three of the girls come in, one after the other, for a dose of camphor. I find a few drops of this an excellent medicine here. Then four of the little boys begging for pins, and a man from town begging for a little molasses for his sick wife. Then Harry Bacon to say his spelling lesson. And lastly Mrs. Bristow, our cook. Mrs. Payne always hears her a reading lesson in the Bible, and explains it to her, in the evening; but to-night, on account of Mrs. Payne's letters, I do it—but I have been obliged to keep her waiting a long while. So passes the evening. Where is our sewing? Usually we do not notice these interruptions so much when both are on hand to do that which may be required. How do you like our evening's amusement? This is a fair sample.

SICKNESS.—So many down with the measles—the school-room looks quite desolate. Many who have friends in town have gone home to them for the time. They always keep fire in their huts, and the children like the heat when they are sick. It relieves us of a great charge—so many being ill. But though they are dying all round us, none belonging to the mission have yet been taken. I have been confined to my room again for two or three days. I find I do not regain my strength after these attacks as I did at first. But I can have my classes come to my room, even when very sick.

Mr. Hoffman and Miss Ball have just arrived at the Cape in a little coasting vessel. They are much benefitted by their voyage.

THE EARTHQUAKE.—Our summer has commenced in earnest—it is very warm. The doctor is down again to look after his patients. (I forgot to say, the doctor's home is at the Asylum.) He says Mr. and Mrs. Hoffman are coming to-morrow to make us a visit.

We had an amusing little incident last night. I had been taking opium, and it made my head very stupid. In the middle of the night I was partially aroused by the house shaking violently. The second time I muttered to myself earthquake; so the same, the third and fourth time. With the fifth time it was very severe—it aroused me a little more, and a picture I had seen of the earthquake at Lisbon came up distinctly before me, and I recollect saying to myself, "Oh, it will not hurt us so much, as our house is all of wood," and then I knew no more of what happened till this morning. What do you suppose our earthquake was? The Bishop and Mrs. Payne had been very much frightened, and got up to see what was the matter. It was the poor old horse—he had been tied to one of the wooden pillars, on which the house is supported. There is no foundation under the ground—the house is built on pillars raised above the ground, as most all are. Well, the poor horse had fallen, and the rope was twisted round him; and there he lay, pulling and kicking vigorously at the post. You may imagine our house is not the most splendid mansion in the world, that a one-horse power can have the effect of an earthquake upon it—for I was not the only one in whose brain visions of such a disaster had their place. But there is nothing like opium to make one philosophical. The Bishop went down to extricate the animal from his perilous position, for he had nearly hung himself. The poor beast lay panting and groaning as if in the last agonies. As he could not make the horse get up, the Bishop thought he was very ill, and he came up directly to get some medicine for him. He mixed a dose of castor-oil and something else—I forget what—and soap-suds, and he found it to be a most effectual argument—the moment the bottle, with its contents, was inside the animal's mouth, he was up in a trice. I expect, if we could get him to give us his opinion on the subject, he would be a decided homœopathist. Allopathy does not suit his taste. But he prefers keeping his opinions to himself. I hope, however, the next time he undertakes to perform feats of gymnastics and circus tricks, such as climbing a pillar or drinking out of a bottle, he will have a waking, not a slumbering audience.

THE COMET.—I have been very ill again for several days. Mr. and Mrs. Hoffman have been here, but I was only able to leave my room once to see them. While they were away Mr. Hoffman and Miss Ball visited the German Lutheran Mission, down the coast. They were delighted—but they have written the account of this themselves.

I have been sitting up to-day, and this evening the Bishop helped me out to take a look at the comet. It is perfectly splendid—fully realizes all my preconceived ideas of it. I have never seen one half so beautiful. I do not know whether this latitude would have the effect of making it appear more plainly. But it is so very brilliant, and its tail so long and bright.

The people are in great trouble about the comet—they say it always portends dire misfortune.

How very grateful in sickness are the little luxuries sent us by loving hands! The appetite fails, and it needs to be stimulated to enable us to gain our strength. Our friends may be well assured their kindnesses are always received with grateful hearts.

It is very strange where these people have obtained some of their notions. I was reading to-day of God's anger with David for numbering the people—and it is very singular, but the Greboes will not number their tribe, or town, or family—they think some harm will happen to them if they do so. They always, likewise, have a great aversion to having children twins; for they say the elder will always have to serve the younger.

The measles seems like a pestilence; there is scarcely a house, either in the native towns, or in the colony, but where there is one sick. We have just heard that Mr. Geoffry Thompson, the brother of Mr. T. Thompson, at the Asylum, died last night of the measles. He was a very fine young man, a teacher in Mr. Hoffman's Sunday School. He has left a young wife and three children.

We hear that the English mail steamers are going to stop at the Cape every month. This, it is hoped, will give an impetus to trade, and materially benefit the place.

GENEROSITY.—While Mr. Hoffman was at Monrovia, they had a missionary meeting of all denominations, Hitherto there has been a great deal of sectarianism among the colonists, and it has been the constant effort of the missionaries to unite them. Mr. Williams' efforts, for this effect, have been indefatigable, and, at length, he has got all the children of the different schools, to unite to endeavor to support a teacher among one of the heathen tribes, about fifty miles back of Monrovia. Mr. Hoffman pledged that his Sunday-school should send them ten dollars. So, as soon as he came home, he told his children what he had promised for them, and that they must go to work now, to make up the money. So the children at the Asylum, and the boys at the Harris Station have gone to work vigorously, to cultivate vegetables, that they may sell them, to put the money in the missionary box. I went into the school-room and began telling the children about what all the others were doing for the spread of God's word, and, suddenly looking up, I perceived that a number of the girls were in tears. Upon inquiring the cause, one of them said, "The boys and others can work and get money to give to our brothers and sisters, who know not God, but what can we do? We have no gardens, we no work and have money." "Well, girls," I said, "I know you have very little time, and I have very little, but we will see what we can do. Those of you that wish, come to my room on Saturday mornings, and I will find you the materials, and teach you, and you shall make some little specimens of fancy work. We will send them up to Mr. Marshall's store, at the Cape, and whatever he sells them for, you can have to put into the missionary box." This was gladly acceded to, and our work began. And now, while we are upon the subject, I will give you one of the results. Lucie worked very diligently, and finished a very pretty bead bag, to hang against the wall. It was done very nicely. It was sent up to Mr. Marshall's store for sale, but he admired it so much that he sent it on to Monrovia, to the State Fair (an institution similar to ours), which was being held there at that time. After exhibition it was to be sold for the benefit of the mission. Well, a certificate was given, and the third prize granted to Lucie. The prize was a little gold dollar. After its reception I took the certificate and the dollar into the school-house, explaining its meaning and why it was awarded to her, and telling Lucie to keep the certificate always, as it would be pleasant for her to see in future. They had not seen a gold dollar before, though they had silver pieces. I told them its value, and it was passed round for all to examine. Upon returning to my room, after school, and opening the missionary box, I found there the little gold dollar. I was very much surprised, and thought certainly that Lucie could not know the value of it, as it was more than she had ever had in her life, and I thought it would not be right for me to allow her to give it without being aware of the amount of the sacrifice she was making. I, therefore, called her into my room, and said, "Lucie, my child, do you know the value of this piece of money? I was very glad to see you had given it for God's cause, but before I consent to take it you must know its full value." She knew the value of a shilling, that is, how much she could purchase with it, so I laid eight shillings before her, and told her, her dollar was worth those; was she willing to give it all? She nodded her head. I then told her that it would buy her just such a dress as the one that had been recently sent her, with which she was so much pleased; or it would buy her so many bright head-handkerchiefs (of which they are very fond), or so many aprons. To all this she shook her head. At length I saw poor Lucie was full; she was almost sobbing, and she said, "Missionaries love God, and love poor men much; they leaves their country, friends, all their fine things, to come to teach us so we go to heaven; and then you think we no love God or our own people, so we work little, little bit for them." This was a great speech for Lucie, she is so reserved. "Yes, Lucie, I am glad God has put it in your heart to love your people, and gladly will I take your gift; I only wanted to be sure that it was entirely with a willing heart it was done." Christians, let each one of us pause and ask ourselves, in this Christian land, have any of us ever known such an instance of self-denial for God's cause? Have not many, who have given their twenty, fifty, or a hundred dollars, reason to *blush* when they think of this one dollar?

I was telling the children a little anecdote I recently heard, that I think it would do us all good to remember. "A congregation of free blacks, in one of the West Indies, hearing that their brethren, in another island, were utterly destitute of the Gospel, determined to try and do something for them. They, therefore, called a meeting of all the Church members, and three resolutions were passed.

"' *First.*—That every one should give something.

"' *Second.*—That every one should give according to his means.

"' *Third.*—That all should give willingly and cheerfully.'

"A secretary was appointed, to sit at a table to write down the names and amounts given. After several had been to him, one very poor man came up and laid down a shilling, twenty-five cents our money. The secretary received his money and marked down his name, with a ' T'ank you, broder.' The next man that came up was known to be one of the wealthiest men among them. Seeing what his neighbor had given, he, likewise, laid down a shilling. The secretary took it up and returned it to him, saying: ' Broder, dat be 'cording to de furst resoblution, which say, ebery body he gib something, but it is not 'cording to de second resoblution, which say, ebery body gib 'cording to his means; I can't take it, broder—take your shilling.' The man went back to his seat with his shilling, but, after a little time, pride overcoming covetousness, he again went up to the secretary's table, and this time laid down a pound, about five dollars. The secretary looked up in his face, and again handed him back his money, saying: 'Broder, dat be 'cording to de furst and second resoblutions, but not 'cording to the tird, him say all must be given willingly and cheerfully.' The man buttoned up his pockets and marched back, very indignantly, to his seat, but by and by a better spirit took possession of him, and again he approached the secretary, and this time with a smiling, cheerful countenance, laid down his pound. This time the secretary said: 'I take him now, broder, cas' dat be 'cording to de furst, and de second, and de tird resoblutions.'"

This is the doctrine I want to teach the children, to give, however small the mite, with a willing heart. And would that all Christians would learn and practice "the three resolutions." There is an English vessel anchored off here this evening.

STRANGE VESSEL.—This morning the head-man from town came in. He appears to be very suspicious of the vessel that is anchored out here. He says, that though she carries English colors, he is sure she is no English vessel, but he is persuaded she is a slave vessel from all he saw on board. They want Kroomen, but he has forbidden any men, from his town, to ship on board of her. He could not well give his reasons, but he feels persuaded she is a slaver.

This afternoon Mrs. Payne and myself were in the

parlor, when one of the strangest specimens of a white man presented himself at the door. The Bishop was away preaching at one of the towns. The man, therefore, gave us to understand that he was the captain, but not expecting to see ladies had not dressed himself. He was without shoes, stockings, or coat. He, however, seated himself, and commenced a conversation, with an air of perfect nonchalance. We spoke of his vessel, and said we had heard that it was not an English vessel, though sailing under English colors. "Oh! no, ma'am; she was built in Nova Scotia, but we sailed from New-York. We can hire Nova Scotia vessels cheaper than we can get them in New-York." "Yes, but you sail under English colors." "If there is one Englishman on board we can hoist English colors. I am the only Englishman." "Pardon me, but I know the English tongue; I do not think you are one." "Well, you see, ma'am, I am not; I was born in New-York, and so were my parents, but I have been to Liverpool several times, and so I swore that I was an Englishman." "How could you do such a thing?" "Oh! bless your heart, ma'am, don't you know a Yankee will do anything for money?"

We expressed our sorrow at hearing such language. He then went on abusing the English for daring to have the right of search, and said that one vessel belonging to his owners, a firm in New-York, had just been seized and carried to Sierra Leone, and that another had just got into a muss with a British cruiser. He stated, too, that he was going directly down the coast where eight thousand dollars worth of goods, we much suspected human chattels, was waiting for him. Of course, all this tended to excite our suspicions still more. I suppose he thought we were so far out of the world that we could not harm him. After awhile he went away to trade with the natives, giving them rum and tobacco in exchange for palm-oil. The effects of his visit were soon visible. One of the finest young men in town was so drunk he was like a crazy man.

In the evening, when the Bishop was at home, he came again. We had found out then that he was only one of the hands on board; the captain being a Portuguese, and all the rest either Spanish or Portuguese. The Bishop asked him: "How it was that he had imposed upon the ladies, passing himself off for the captain?" He answered, with the coolest impudence: "Bless your heart, sir, why I pass off for anything or everything." Such are the men that come forth from a Christian country to these poor heathens. Oh! say not that the missionary ought not to come forth; rather ought he "not to count his life dear unto himself."

If this vessel is such as we suspect, we can only pray that God will frustrate the machinations of the wicked. When the vessel set sail she hoisted the American flag. A little farther down the coast she had the Spanish flag up. And again still later she was seen under Portuguese colors. There surely must be something wrong to need this.

Music.—Our music to-night. How much I should have liked some of our good people, at home, to have heard it. Those, I mean, who are so fond of Sunday opera music; the hearing one or two person take God's name in vain in his own house; making his house a house of merchandise, (not to show off their cattle for price, but their vocal powers). Many, I believe, that are true Christians, have not thought what a crying sin it is. But how I wished that they could have been with us at our service to-night. I do think that they would have felt that they would rather praise God themselves than hire others to do it for them. Our evening congregation numbers about one hundred and fifty. Mr. Jones, our native deacon, understands the science of music, and he takes pains to teach it to all in the schools. To-night, when the Bishop gave out the thirty-ninth psalm, Mr. Jones struck up a most exultant jubilant tune, and I do not think there was a single voice mute. They sang with the voice and the understanding also; apparently " singing, and making melody, in their hearts, unto the Lord." Only think what supreme absurdity it would have been for us to have had one or two high-flying singers stand up there to-night and sing *not with*, but *for* those poor ransomed heathens, these words:

> "Oh! 'twas a joyful sound to hear
> Our tribes devoutly say,
> Up, Israel, to the temple haste,
> And keep your festal day."

Our music was truly sublime. It carried the heart with it. I do believe that church music, as we have it at the present day, is a device of the arch enemy, and a very effectual one, too, of abstracting directly the good seed that may have just been sown. Perhaps I speak strongly, but I feel strongly on this subject. I know it is doing so much harm. I fear if our Saviour were to come to many of our temples now, many would be scourged thence, to whom he would say, "Make not my Father's house a house of merchandise." Show not off your wares here—"carry these things hence." If ever we reach Heaven, I do not think that we shall wish to hand our golden harps to others that they, for us, may make melody before God, or that we shall wish others to sing for us the new song, "To Him who hath bought us with his own blood, and made us kings and priests unto God," &c. Our services to-night would have touched the heart of any one coming from our own more favored land. Here, surrounded on every side by the depths of heathen darkness, is a little band come forth from that darkness into marvellous light. At night none of the town's people come, as our services are all in English. Only those attend attached to the Station, numbering about one hundred and fifty. As each one comes in, he or she, kneels, not sits, reverently for a few minutes in private prayer. In the united prayers and all the responses, not a voice appears silent; all seem, at least outwardly, engaged in solemn worship. I suppose this struck me more to-night than usual, as the Bishop's text was, "Worship God in the beauty of holiness." And certainly if the spirit as well as the letter of our services is carried out, it is, indeed, the "beauty of holiness." God grant that we may all learn to praise him on earth, so that when we shall cease to praise him here we may help to swell the full hallelujah chorus above.

Mr. T. Thompson has just lost a sister by the measles, and is himself very ill with it. He feels sorely God's afflicting dispensation. A brother and a sister both taken in one week. Many of our children are still very ill, but we have yet lost none.

CARES.—There is so much to be done that we have no time for selfishness. We must forget our aches and pains and weariness, if we would be of any use. The Bishop and Mrs. Payne are hoping to return home in two or three months. They both need it much. Since school to-day I have been busy cutting out shirts. Hitherto, Mrs. Payne has attended to all in the sewing department, and I suppose one of our new sisters, who is coming here, will superintend that, but Mrs. Payne will probably not be here to afford her the benefit of her experience. I must learn all about it, so as to give her the necessary information. Or it may be, that I shall have to take charge of it myself. At all events, I must know all about it. We have two very sick children, one quite a little one. We much fear that we shall lose her. Mrs. Gillet is very good, kind, and attentive to them. Many and multifarious are our duties, but how much pleasure, too, in feeling that we may, perhaps, be able to remove a little of he load of misery, both temporal and spiritual, from those for whom Christ died.

The Greboes have a very pretty expression I heard to-day. When any one is angry, using strong or hasty words, they say to them, " Wora, woro ni na," " Throw water on your heart." This language is very figurative.

SUPERSTITION.—One of the principal men in town is very ill with measles. Of course, they say he is witched.

Now, to be effectual, it is supposed that a good many of the witch's incantations must be performed in the neighborhood of the hut where the person whom they wish to injure is living. Therefore, it is very dangerous for any one to be found out of doors at night alone. This also is the reason why they try to hide their sick. Last night a party of the Sedibo (soldiers) went out in the night time to see if they could find the witch. As they came near the sick man's house, they declared that they saw a man, and that, as they approached, he instantly changed himself into a cow before any of them could recognize him. They believe that witches have this power; as they also believe in the transmigration of souls. Now, they will go to the devil-doctor to find out who this man is

THE ARMY.—Infant baptism this morning in church. How the Bishop's heart must glow with gratitude to God! It was a child of one of the villagers. Father, mother, and sponsors all natives. May God's work here " go forward." Pray for us that the Spirit may be poured out upon us without measure; upon pastors, and teachers, and people; that there may be a shaking among the dry bones. We know not how much of the present success may be attributed to the prayers of Christians at home. You cannot think how trifling and vain appear all former occupations in comparison to this. I wonder at God's great goodness to me, unworthy as I am, that I am permitted to labor in this the most noble, the most glorious cause, the world ever saw, that of raising human beings from the lowest depths of misery, degradation, and vice into the "glorious liberty of the sons of God."

I often look at our kind, gentle, loving Bishop, and think what martial hero of the highest renown is to compare with him. For more than twenty years he has been a leader in the advance guard of the army of the "King of kings." Fighting manfully against "principalities and powers, against spiritual wickedness in high places." Marching steadily onward, and invading the enemy in the heart of his own dominions; never being daunted by the number or skill of his adversaries Often standing almost alone in the battle field, and this not for his own fame, glory, or emolument, but, if possible, that he may wrest from the enemy some precious gems that may shine forever in his Saviour's crown; that he may gain some rich spoils, not to adorn himself withal, but that he may lay them as trophies at the Saviour's feet. May many more such soldiers of the Cross soon join him! Each hard-fought battle is not recorded on earth, but the "Captain of our salvation" knoweth them that are his, and the Saviour's precious promise is, "To him that overcometh will I grant to sit with me in my throne, even as I also overcame and am sat down with my Father in his throne.

LETTERS.—News from home; when they wrote, the death of my father was hourly looked for. A few lines from himself—the last he will ever write on earth. Reposing alone on the love of Christ and the atoning efficacy of the Redeemer's blood, death must be gain. I feel assured he is safe at home. Many, many kind tokens again from loving friends. Thanks, thanks to all—nowhere can gifts be more thankfully welcomed and appreciated.

Fish.—The Bishop was telling us to-night of a very pretty little custom here. The first fish that are caught in the fishing season, they bring all home and make soup. Then all the children in town are called and it is all given to them—no one else tasting it. They think that being generous, especially to children, will bring them good luck. The same thing is done with the first fish caught in a new canoe. The feast is for those who cannot repay them.

Faith.—The Bishop has started with one or two workmen to-day up the river to *Nitie Lu*. He wants the workmen to cut timber up there for building a house at the station. He says he may extend his journeyings back a little farther to the Mountains of the Moon. May God preserve him and bring him back in peace and safety to us! Dr. D'Lyon was to go with him, but he sent word this morning that he had fever and could not possibly go. It is up among the Webo tribe, where those men were so cruelly murdered and eaten a short time ago, that he is going.

As I was bidding the Bishop good-bye this morning, I asked "if he was going alone?" and I supposed that my manner expressed some little fear and sadness, for he turned round quickly and said, "Sister Harriet, I am going in my Father's country, and about my Father's work." Oh, what a different tone those few words gave to the whole tenor of my feelings. Would that I had the faith that he and his dear wife have.

I am getting very, very weak—the fever hangs on me so long. The man I spoke of that was so ill with measles, is still very low. To-day they have accused two of his wives of witching him, and made them take the sassa, but both have recovered from its effects.

THE SABBATH LAW.—A very pleasant thing has occurred to-day. The villagers have, for a long time, been trying to persuade the towns people to pass a law prohibiting work on the Sabbath. The Bishop, though, as you may suppose, longing earnestly for it, has forborne to urge the matter too strenuously, fearing if made to please him, much against their will, it would only be broken continually, and that would be worse than having no such law. To-day the Christian villagers and towns people have had a meeting, and the law has been passed almost unanimously by the Sedibo—these are the soldiers, or chief part of the citizens. The law runs thus: "No person is to work on Sunday. If they go fishing their fish is to be taken from them; if they go to the bush, their wood, or whatever else they may bring home, is to be taken from them and carried to the mission house for the use of the children there." This is their own law. They had a long "palaver," however, before it could be settled. *Kadi*, the son of the former king, was spokesman for the villagers. I will give you a specimen of the discussion, as we afterwards heard it:

Townsmen.—"Well, but if we do not catch fish on Sunday, or go bush, what will we do to eat?"

Kadi.—"The Bishop does not give us food, all us

boys in village—we no work Sunday, yet we always have food. God give us food when we mind his day."

Townsmen.—" That be true; you boys in the village catch fish plenty; you shoot deer plenty; we no find them; 'spose we want bit meat, we come you."

Kadi.—" Yes, God mind us. Now this sickness (measles) come, he go all over country. *You* make much greegrees. Keep him off all towns; but plenty people and children die all towns. All children have it here and at other mission stations; big people have it; many sick, plenty, we afraid they die, but God say no! he take care of them."

And by God's providence it is so—not one attached to the mission stations have died, while there has not been a town without some deaths from it. Such were some of *Kadi's* reasonings. May we not trust that God's spirit is among us?

LETTERS.—I mentioned, some time ago, that the children of our mission and those of Mr. Williams' Sunday School, corresponded. I will give you the exact copy of a letter, written by one of our boys at this time to Monrovia.

DEAR BRETHREN AND SISTERS IN THE LORD:

Having an opportunity I drop you a few lines to inform you of my health which is quite well at present, and I hope that these few lines may find you all in joying the best of health. Dear friends I have never seen your face but I love you in my heart. And I have seen your teacher and I was much pleased to see your teacher visited us. I been with him from (he meant to) neiborhood countrys which are about some miles each from cavalla where we made our settlement. I was interpreter, and Bishop Payne was with us. I delighted much in his preaching he is good preacher of christ's crucifixion. My dear friends I will make appendage of few words before I make the conclusion of my letter. I will tell you something about the country people how they acted on sunday, and how they make agreement of keeping the sabbath. Now they make agreement to keep the sunday and they are trying now to keep the Lord's holy day. I must ask you did they are able to keep the sabbath for themself without some one helping them. No Sir they are not able. What we must do before they are able to keep the Sabbath. We must pray to God to sent his Holy Spirit on them that they may know that there is a God in earth and who made heaven and earth and all things. I am very glad to say that you must pray for us, and we will pray for you. I complete to talk you about cavalla, and I am very glad to tell you something about Graway people which is some miles from cavalla. The towns are on the beach I and Mr. John Wilson going there every Sunday. They are not like cavalla people. They did'nt care fore sunday we must pray for these people that God may sent his Holy Spirit among them that they may know the God of Jacob. Let us fight under the banner of Christ and let us put our whole trust in christ because he is our leader. Bishop Payne and his wife are well but Miss Brittan is not well. I have much to say but time permitted me not. Please excuse my last writing.

Yes, friend,   E. J. P. MESSENGER.

This is one of our older boys—he is an excellent interpreter. I have so many letters before me that my only difficulty is in selecting from among them. I will give one other now—at another time, perhaps, I may give you more.

HOFFMAN STATION, CAPE PALMAS.
REV. AND DEAR SIR :

It affords me more gratitude to present you an information of our Sunday School opened in at St. James' Church in Hoffman Station. This school contains about fifty boys and twenty-five girls under the care of Mrs. Harris. The former is conducted by Rev. C. C. Hoffman, Mr. Harris, and the eldest boys at the Station Myself have a class in this school contains of about twenty-five boys from the towns, as attendance of the school. We who are the eldest boys have formed ourselves a classes call William A. Muglenburg's missionary Society. This class is teaching by S. B. D'Lyon, M. D., after recite our class before Dr. hears our own lesson. The demeanours and behaviours of these pupils are more encouragement to us and we hope something will come out of this undertaking. Though we are small in number, yet we hope that God will do whatever he pleases.. For there is no restraint to the Lord to save by many or by few, and again have not I commanded thee ? Be strong and of a good courage. Be not afraid, neither be dismayed : For the Lord thy God is with thee withersoever thou goest. Therefore the followers and the labourers of Christ cannot be afraid to do good, and to deliver the souls from darkness to the glorious light of Redeemer. My God raise up more labourers to carry this light among the dark places, to disperse darkness and dispell the devil from this land by the name of our high Priest Jesus Christ. My God grant that we shall take a possession at last. My kind regards to you and to children I remain yours unworthy servant

S. W. SETON.

Rev. E. T. WILLIAMS

These letters surely show " what spirit they are of."

HARRIETT.—I want to tell you something about Harriett Vaughan, one of my girls. She is about the same age as Lucie, and in their studies they are just on a par. She is very black, and not as pleasant looking as many of the others. Yet I have a strong partiality for Harriett. She is a member of the church, but, poor girl, she suffers much from her own temper. She is very impulsive and very passionate, and so often sins in that way. And then she really suffers for it, for she is so sorry and bitterly repents before God her sinfulness.

There is a great deal of clanship here, and almost always an enmity existing between the different tribes, which constantly vents itself in spiteful words, and petty, malicious acts. Harriett belongs to a different tribe to the most of the girls, and they are continually teasing her. Harriett seldom shows any temper to her teachers. With her is exemplified the truth of those words of Scripture, " A soft answer turneth away wrath." Whatever storm she may be in—and she is a perfect tornado—if I go to her, lay my hand on her arm, and quietly utter her name, she is still in a moment. Were I to speak loud and cross to her, it would only make her more angry still. I have never known her to disobey me in the least. She is exceedingly affectionate; and, though so passionate, she would not really do an unkind thing, or hurt any one, if she could help it. She is engaged to one of our Christian young men, named Seton, from Hoffman Station. You see our girls are happier in that respect, than any of the others in this country. They are not sold for wives to any man who wants them; but they can choose their own husbands. These husbands are Christians, who have no other wives. So you see it is very important that our girls should be well taught the truth of God's word, so that they may assist their husbands. Now, I want to tell you something that happened in school. On going into the school-room, after the bell had rung, all the girls were in their places, but Harriett was standing up vociferating and gesticulating wildly and fiercely, whilst many of the others were laughing, sneeringly or mockingly, at her. Of course, on my appearance the tumult subsided; but during the opening exercises of the school, she would constantly turn round from one to another of the girls, muttering between her teeth, and with the expression of the fiercest rage. I took no notice till after the first class had finished their Bible lesson, then, when the others retired, I bade Harriett remain, as I wished to speak with her, and the following conversation took place: "Harriett, my child, what is the matter?" "Nothing, ma'am." "Oh, yes! there is something the matter—are you sick?" "No, ma'am." "But I think you are." Harriett, looking up with surprise, "Oh, no, ma'am, indeed I am not!" "But I know you are, my child; you have the worst kind of sickness, a disease in your heart—sin, you know, is the disease of the soul—have you not that to-day, Harriett?" She hung her head, but made no reply. Our conversation was all in a low voice, so no one else heard us. "Can you not tell me what is the matter?" No reply. "My child, I know not who was in fault in the commencement of this trouble; I only know that whoever else has done wrong, Harriett has. She professes to be a follower of the meek and lowly Jesus. Has she acted like such? I cannot look into your heart, and see what is the matter; but there is One that is looking at it this moment. Go to Him, Harriett, "go and tell Jesus." He, you know, is the great physician. If you are wounded by the unkindness of others, tell Him: He can comfort you, and can give you the heart to bless, and not to curse, your enemies If your sickness is entirely the sin of your own heart, you know that His blood is the fountain open for sins and uncleanness. Go to Him at once. Ask Him to wash you in that fountain; whatever it is, whatever troubles, you just tell Him at once; the very telling Him will relieve you. You need not move from where you stand, only lift your heart to Him. He is looking with a loving, pitying eye upon you now. (A pause for a moment.) And now, Harriett, I tell you what I want you to do for me. Mrs. Gillet is not well, to-day; she cannot come in school. I want you to take her place for me, and teach the little ones." She looked up, with a start of astonishment. On account of her hasty temper,

I had been afraid ever to trust her before to do this. I put into her hand Mrs. Gillet's rod, which she occasionally used, saying: "Take this, Harriett; you must use it, if you are obliged to, but remember those children are Jesus Christ's little ones. You are teaching them for Him." She took Mrs. Gillet's place, and I watched her closely, without her perceiving it. She was as gentle, and as loving, and as kind, as it was possible to be. After school was over, I had occasion to go up into the girls' dormitory. On passing Harriett's door, I saw it was closed to. I gently pushed it open, as we always want there to be a free current of air. Harriett was kneeling at her chest, her hands clasped, her face upturned, the tears streaming down, and her whole soul evidently absorbed in earnest prayer. She did not see me, and I quickly closed the door and retired. Does not God give us many joys, many encouragements in our labor?

PENALTY.—I have adopted a mode of punishment, which answers very well. Whipping I cannot bear; yet those of us, who would be wiser than Solomon, too often find out our mistake—for it is as true now as it was in his day, that "foolishness is bound up in the heart of a child," and some means must be taken to get rid of it. So, when any of our little ones have quarrelled, and come to blows, whether it be in or out of school, I tie the one hand of each of the contending parties together, and they are obliged to go about a longer or a shorter time thus linked together, according to the nature of the offence. I find this a far more effectual punishment than whipping.

JUSTICE.—A short time ago, one Sunday morning, the Bishop witnessed quite a ludicrous scene. It seems that, for a week or so, the boys had constantly missed little articles, more particularly food, from their school-house, but could not detect the thief. This morning they were all in the girls' school-house, at prayers, when one of the elder boys, not feeling very well, retired to his own school-house. There he caught a native boy, from town, in the very act of running off with a quantity of their rice and plantains, that were to serve for that day's dinner. He had them all wrapped up in a cloth. The schoolboy seized him, and held him fast till the rest of the boys returned, after prayers, when they inflicted a most singular punishment upon him. The Bishop, after breakfast, was walking in the garden, plucking some flowers, when, on passing the boys' school-house, he heard them singing a tune he did not remember to have heard before. He entered, and went up into the dormitory, where a singular sight presented itself. A native boy, about fourteen or fifteen, was hanging by his feet and hands, tied to a beam in the ceiling, while placed on his stomach was a large cloth, tied up, filled with the things he had stolen—rice, plantains, &c. The boys were all sitting round, singing the most grave and solemn hymns, with faces that looked as if they were at a funeral. Upon learning what was the matter, and that the culprit had been tied up in that painful position for over two hours, the Bishop thought the demands of justice were fully satisfied; he, therefore, bid the boys untie him, and let him go. At the same time he did not reprimand them for executing this specimen of Lynch law, as the boy was known to be a most inveterate thief, and they had often suffered from his depredations, and it was but right that he should pay the penalty of his guilt. They had adopted this mode of procedure in preference to whipping him, which they would have done at any other time; but they knew that on Sunday they dare not make any noise on the mission premises. The punishment has been very effectual; he has never dared to show his face in these parts since.

LEGENDS.—I will mention here one or two legends that I have recently heard. I wish that I understood the language better, so that I could hear more of them. One of the negro legends is this: About two hundred miles up the Cavalla river, there is a dense forest; the trees and underbrush grow very thickly everywhere about for miles, except in one spot, where there is a space of about half an acre in circumference, with a sort of pathway leading to the river, which is perfectly bare and destitute of either trees or herbage, and nothing will ever grow there. It presents a most singular appearance among the surrounding luxuriant verdure. Well, the legend about this place is, that, in the forests, on this river, there used to reside an immense dragon, that would rush out and devour every canoe, with its contents, that attempted to pass down the river; canoe and all would be swallowed at one gulp. For many years the people had tried every means to destroy him, but without effect. At length they hit upon the expedient of placing a live goat, which, by its bleating, might attract the dragon's attention, in a canoe full of red hot stones, and send it floating down the river. As soon as the dragon heard the bleating of the goat, he rushed out, and swallowed the goat, canoe, and all. But though he could digest both canoe and goat, the red hot stones were more than he bargained for. With most fearful roars, he crawled up the bank of the river, into the forest, and at length laid down and died. But the ground wherever he crawled was so injured by the intense heat, and the poisonous saliva and melting grease that flowed from the animal, that nothing has ever grown there since. Such is one of their stories. Another is this: In the vicinity of the Congo and Loango rivers, the Gorilla monkey grows to an immense size. The natives are more afraid of it than of any other animal. It sometimes grows to the height of seven feet, and is very strong and ferocious. On the Loango river they show the site of a large town, which has been entirely destroyed, and left in utter ruin. They give this account of its destruction: A man and his wife went out one day, from this town, to work in their field. The woman had a little infant, which she laid down to sleep in one corner of the field. Presently the child began to cry; the mother looked up, to go to it, when she saw a large female Gorilla rush out from the wood, seize the child, and begin to pet and fondle it. The woman screamed to her husband, who immediately took up his gun and fired at the monkey. The poor animal dropped dead, and the child was saved, uninjured. But the deed must have been witnessed, and summary vengeance was executed. That night, when the inhabitants were all asleep in their huts, they were alarmed by most unearthly yells and screeches. A whole army of Gorillas had beset the town. They were all armed with immense clubs. They pulled down every house, and killed more than half the inhabitants. The rest escaped to the different towns around, and they never have had the courage to return and attempt to rebuild the town. They all believe that monkeys can talk as well as men; but we do not understand their language.

THE MERMAID.—One of our missionaries says that he has seen an animal up the river, which he thinks was probably the original of the ancient mermaid. It is an animal of the seal species, covered with fur, and though not resembling a woman, yet the head and breast are very similar to those of a monkey. On the head the hair is a little longer than elsewhere. It is a warm-blooded animal, amphibious, and comes on the shore to suckle its young. Its arms and hands are merely elongated fins, but with these it holds its young. It often utters a cry, like a woman in trouble. It is very difficult to get a correct view of it, as it is very shy, and dives out of sight at the approach of any one.

THE WITCH.—You recollect my mentioning a man in town very ill with measles, and that they had given two of his wives sassa-wood. He still continues very ill. He is a relation of one of the villagers, Robinson; and it is a great compliment they pay to Christianity, that they will always trust a relation, when they are ill, if he is a consistent Christian, when they are afraid of all the others. So, *Kraw* still continuing ill, they brought him up to Robinson's house last Saturday. They all say he is witched, and every one is on the look-out for the witch or witches. The power of imagination is very strong. If a sick person thinks himself to be witched, and the witch is supposed to be caught, the sick man will very frequently get well. Since Kraw has been there, Robinson's fence has been broken down every night, although each day he has mended it afresh. This has confirmed their idea, that some species of witchcraft is being practised against him. Last night we heard a gun fire close beside us. Upon inquiring the cause, we found that Williams, one of Robinson's neighbors, had gone out into his garden, and he saw a man pulling down Robinson's fence, and then dancing and cutting up all sorts of antics (part of their supposed incantations). Whether they have any such power as they claim, we cannot decide ; but we do know that Satan reigns triumphant. They think they possess the power. The desire is in the heart; murder is in the thought and wish. Williams, when he saw this man, crept back, unperceived, to his house, seized his gun, came out again quickly, and shot at him. His gun missing aim, the witch-man, of course, fled. But the sound of the gun had aroused all in the neighborhood, and villagers and schoolboys were soon in pursuit. They could not overtake him, however. Immediately a town meeting was summoned, at which all adults, male and female, are bound to appear (you see they have some laws), that the Sedibo may see that all persons belonging to their town are present. One man and one woman were absent—a most suspicious thing, none daring to be out at night, for fear of being accused. A meeting was summoned again very early in the morning. The same man was absent, but the woman appeared. The wife of the missing man was questioned, and it was found that he had gone out a short time before the gun was fired, and had not been seen since. The woman who was absent last evening was then summoned, and she stated that the man (she is not his wife) came to her hut (which is at the end of the town) last evening, and he asked her to come to him in a little time, outside the town, and bring him his cloth, which he left in her care. It is one of the necessary parts of their witchery that their cloths shall be left in the house, and their incantations must be performed by them in a state of perfect nudity. When the woman heard the gun fire, she ran to meet him with his cloth; he snatched it from her, and ran away. Such is her story. They will keep her securely, as an accomplice, till the man is caught, when both will suffer the *gidu* ordeal. Now this is evidently a case of malice; there is no doubt of the wish and desire to kill, whether there is the power or not. This morning, when I went into the school-room, I found my little girl Josephine crying bitterly (a very unusual thing; you rarely see one of the children cry). I asked her the reason, but could obtain no reply; she only continued weeping. After the opening exercises, she came to me, and said: "Please let me go to town a few minutes." "Why, Josephine, my child, you know it is against the rules; and for *you* to ask it, I am surprised. But what is it for?" There was a fresh burst of tears. "Oh! please, please let me go." I immediately went to Mrs. Gillet, to see if she could tell me the reason of Josephine's request. She told me that "the witch-man was Josephine's father, and she was in such anxiety about him, she wanted to hear if he had been caught." Of course, I gave instant permission. She returned in about half an hour. He had not been found. Josephine has no mother, and her father she is very fond of. He is a fine, intelligent man, and at one time the Bishop supposed him to be almost a Christian; but, alas! alas! for the hardness of the human heart. After school was over, I was sitting alone in my room; I heard a gentle tap at the door, and Josephine came in. "May I stay here a little while?" "Yes." She took a little bench and placed it at my feet, with a book in her hand; but I soon saw she was not reading; the tears were falling fast upon its pages. I had been reading; I continued to hold my book in my hand, thinking what I should say to comfort her. You cannot think how we learn to love —how our hearts are drawn out towards—these "little ones" of Christ's flock, who are gathered in from "the highways and hedges." I laid my hand on her head. "Josephine, my child, I, too, have lately lost a father." She looked up with streaming eyes. "Oh, yes! but he die believing God's Word; he die praying to Jesus; God take his soul, and, no matter how bad he been, he Saviour wash him in His blood—take him heaven. But my father, he know God's things, but he no mind them. He know them in his head, but he no mind them in his heart; he no do them. He take sassa; he die; he no go to heaven." Then, after a little pause, she begged me to pray with her, that her father might not die by the sassa-wood, but that he might be spared a while longer, that he might hear God's things more, and have time to repent. Poor child! she left me feeling a little more comforted.

Josephine's father has escaped to another town. When once there, he is as in a city of refuge. He cannot be taken thence; but if found outside it, he will be caught immediately, even though it may be years after the supposed offence.* Most always, however, rather than endure such an imputation, they will probably take the poison—in presence of a few witnesses—and then they may return to the town. There is another punishment here for lesser crimes. They cause the culprit to dip his or her hand in a pot of boiling palm-oil. You will see quite a large number of the people with one hand disfigured by this; for after it gets well, it leaves large white scars. The women are generally pretty well treated, the men being afraid of them, as they believe that women are more powerful witches than men. Occasionally, at night, however, you will hear fearful shrieks and the sound of blows; it is a man beating his wife; but this is rare. To-day one of the girls brought me a very large handsome beetle. It was alive. She had found it in the woods, and had stuck it in her hair, to bring it home to me, its claws sticking fast in her wool.

CHURCH.—To-day (Sunday) we saw the effects of the law that has been passed; the church was full to over-

* He afterward returned and took the sassa himself, but escaped a fatal result.

flowing. It was a very orderly, attentive congregation. In the afternoon there were over four hundred little town children in Sunday-school. Our children had to turn teachers.

When we come out of church, in the mornings, I always go into the girls' school-house, and distribute to them their Sunday-school lesson books, and books to read, and often stop a few minutes and talk to them. To-day I was speaking to them of the delight of seeing such a full church, and what pleasure it must have given to those among them who are Christians, to see their friends coming to hear about God's things. While I was speaking to them, one of the girls who stood beside me whispered: "May we sing?" "Oh, yes," I said. "What shall we sing?" "Praise God, from whom all blessings flow." And, think you, was not that one little verse of praise and thanksgiving, which sounded as though it came from overflowing hearts, issuing forth from sometime heathen lips, as welcome incense to the ear of the Almighty, as the splendid harmony that peals forth from the fine-toned organ and well-trained choirs of our great cities? I think so. Kraw is a great deal better. Certainly, imagination has had a great deal to do in his case.

SICKNESS.—I have had constant fever for weeks; a sort of remittent, no chills but burning fever and headache. I have not the slightest appetite, and I am growing daily more weak. Yet I do not give up. I still keep about my work. Mrs. Payne fears I shall become utterly prostrated, and is telling me if I do not soon get better

I must take a short voyage on the coast. I hope not; I cannot endure the thought of leaving my work for a day. We are beginning to think about the examination again.

To-day Laura brought me her Bible and told me she had selected the chapter she wished to learn. It was Ezekiel's vision of the dry bones. Upon questioning her, to see whether she understood it, she said that it seemed to her as if her people are the dry bones, and this Sunday law is the prophet telling them to stand up, and now they only need the Spirit to blow on them that they may live. I was rather surprised at this in Laura; although she is a member of the church, and, I think, tries sincerely to do right, yet she is very thoughtless, and loves laughter and frolic far more than her book. But when she applies she can do very nicely. She is very dark, really black, but with a bright, happy expression; always cheerful and smiling. Such is Laura Gertrude Benjamin. I give these little notices of the different girls, as, perhaps, they may be interesting to those (if such should see them) who take an individual interest in them; our children being named and supported by special individuals or societies.

The doctor is down again. All our children are well now, but many of the people around are very ill. Mrs. Payne sent for him on my account, but I hope I shall not need his care long. It is so pleasant in our sufferings to feel that all are meted out by a Father's hand, and none are sent but what are absolutely necessary.

> When Satan tempts my tortured mind,
>   And trials thicken fast,
> I love to think upon that night,
>   On earth my Saviour's last.

Oh! what a scene of gloom was that
　Which burst upon his soul;
Oh! what a tide of sorrows then,
　Did o'er his bosom roll.

In that dread cup of wrath he drank,
　Was mingled every woe;
And 'twas his Father's hand that struck
　The most afflicting blow.

But owning still the hand divine
　Which had infused the cup,
He humbly bowed his head and said
　"Shall I not drink it up?"

'Twas love divine inspired his heart,
　And made him well content;
Nor death, nor hell could shake that love,
　Or cause it to relent.

Oh! may that love inspire me too,
　'Tis all I ask below;
Let it with purer fervor still
　Daily to Jesus glow.

Then painful as may be my lot,
　My happiness shall be
To drink my cup, to take my cross,
　"My Lord, and follow thee."

Chapter Fourteenth.

MONROVIA.

WEEKS have passed since I have written in my journal, and again I have to render great thanks to my Heavenly Father for restoring me to a certain measure of health and strength. Mrs. Payne's threat of sending me for a voyage was fulfilled rather quicker than either she or I anticipated. After the slow fever of which I was complaining has lasted for some time, the patient will suddenly run completely down. I was really very ill for weeks, but would not give up, though using every remedy, as I expected when I came here, to labor on in weariness, pain, and weakness. But without my knowledge Mrs. Payne had sent for the Doctor. I was still up when he came, but in a few hours was taken much worse, and he and Mrs. Payne thought that nothing but entire rest and utter cessation from care and labor would do me any good, and also, that it was necessary that, for some time, I should be under the doctor's constant care. So they determined that I should go up to the Asylum for a time. The doctor sent for bearers, hammock, &c., and waited over a day that he might go with me to take care of me. I was really very ill. For a week after reaching the Cape, I was very low—just a low, constant fever that they could not break. I was perfectly helpless, both the doctors attending me. At length it was decided that

I must go on a short voyage, it was the only thing for me. I must go on the very first vessel that came in, wherever she was going. Providentially, as it seemed, a little vessel came in that night; she was going in two days to Monrovia.

It was instantly determined that I must go in her, particularly as Dr. McGill, of Monrovia, is considered one of the best physicians in Liberia. Mrs. Carrol, my former nurse, and who has been nursing me now, was to go with me to take care of me. I begged and implored at first not to be sent away, but at length I felt that it was my duty to use every measure for my restoration; that I was utterly useless at present with no prospect of gaining. The doctors also told me that in no case would they let me attempt to resume my duties till after the holidays, which will commence in about three weeks. So, at length, I agreed to go. They sent, in great haste, to Mrs. Payne for some clothes, and the next day we were on board. All vessels being obliged to anchor some distance from the shore, and not being well enough to sit up in the boat, I was carried in my hammock into the boat, and in that lifted on board and carried to my berth. The doctor and Miss Ball saw me there and then left me.

So now fancy me, the only white person on board this little vessel, captain and sailors all colored. Mr. Ashton, the teacher of one of our stations, a colored gentleman, came up also with us for the benefit of his health. My poor nurse was so dreadfully sea-sick that she was perfectly helpless. But there was a bright, sharp little native boy on board, who, though he only understood a few words of English, waited upon me very well. I was carried up and down and laid upon the deck, and soon began to feel the reviving effects of the sea air. God is very good to us; the people are so kind. On the third day out my fever began to break. I was too ill to be the least sea-sick. When we arrived here I was still very weak. We came directly to the Rev. Mr. Gibson's house; he is now settled quite comfortably here. They received us very kindly for two or three days after our arrival. I could not sit up, but the doctor gave me hopes of being out in a few days. Actee, one of the girls from the Asylum came with us, thinking the change might benefit her. She is suffering from a disease not unfrequent here, called the sleepy disease. We much fear for poor Actee. I was recently very forcibly struck with the beauty of that passage, "He shall sit as a purifier and refiner of silver." I was reading that the ancient alchemist, when he wished to obtain a metal of perfect purity, would place it in his crucible over an intensely hot fire to purge away the dross, and according to the amount of dross, or worthless matter, and the purity he required in the metal, so it must be subjected again and again to different degrees of heat, of shorter and longer duration; he, the refiner, sitting and constantly watching it, bending over and looking into it, till the instant when he could see his own image clearly reflected therein. Then it would be directly removed from the purifying heats, as needing them no more. And is it not thus that Jesus, the Great Refiner, does with his people? He says: "I will purge away all thy dross and take away all thy tin." While we are here on earth he finds it necessary to place us often in the furnace of affliction, but he himself regulates the exact proportion of the heat, and he bends constantly over us watching to see that we more and more nearly reflect his image. May all his professed followers grow more and more into his likeness!

Visitors.—Mrs. Benson, the wife of the President, and some of the other ladies have been to see me. I do not know how long I shall be detained here, the arrival of vessels is so uncertain. My present business is to seek to regain my health. I may, perhaps, have to stay till the Stevens arrives; she is expected in three or four weeks. She brings a fresh reinforcement for our mission.

Sunday-School Celebration.—About a week after my arrival at Monrovia, the Sunday-schools had a grand gala-day. I wrote a full account of it to the Sunday-school I love; I will, therefore, just insert the letter.

Monrovia, *December* 8, 1858.

My dear Children:

I will tell you something very pleasant—something that has made my heart glad—and I wish much that I could impart some of my own glad feelings to many of the warm hearts and true friends of Africa, who live in America. I can but very poorly express what I wish, but still I will try and tell you something about the pleasant scene I have witnessed. I arrived in Monrovia in time to be present at the Sunday-school celebration, which after this, I hope, will be held as an anniversary. Children, I have been at many a Sunday-school anniversary at home, and I have enjoyed it as much as any child of you all—for I think there is no more pleasant sight on God's beautiful earth than children's happy, smiling faces—but I never felt at one of our anniversaries as I did at this. It was not calm happiness only, but a deep, holy joy, which every Christian who looked upon that scene must have experienced. The feeling that the time was fast hastening on when the whole earth shall be the Lord's, and when

> "The King who reigns on Zion's hill,
> Shall all the world command."

The school belonging to the Methodist church had held anniversaries before, but this year all the Sunday-schools were to unite together to form one band; and, as there was no church large enough to hold them all, they were to meet in the government square, a large square just opposite the President's house. It was a bright, lovely day; the sun shining gloriously. It had, at first, been appointed for a previous day, but that being wet, it was deferred till Monday. The children had been very much disappointed; but when I witnessed the bright sun on Monday, and knew how much everything had been refreshed by the clouds and showers we had received, I could not but think how often the "Sun of righteousness" appears more glorious and beautiful to the Christian, when he has just passed through the cloud or the storm; and I could not but pray that the dark, thick cloud, which had so long enveloped this country, might soon be dispersed by the rising of that "sun" whose beams are just beginning to gild its horizon. But I must go on with my story. Near the centre of the square are several large, noble trees, that form a delightful shade; in the centre of these, a little open space was left for planting the banners; and, around that, a number of mats were laid, in circles, for the children to sit on—outside these, again, seats were placed for visitors, with at one end a raised platform for the speakers. When the church bell rung, the children all marched from their different schools to the square, and were ranged in the circles according to their numbers. The Presbyterian, being the smallest, had the inner circle, with a banner bearing the words, "He shall gather them in His arms." The Episcopal came next in size; they, therefore, took the next circle. The motto on their banner, "One Lord, one faith, one baptism; one God and Father of *all*." The Baptist came next; their motto, "Suffer little children to come unto me." The Methodist took the largest circle of Christian people; their motto, "Feed my lambs." In the very centre of the circle was planted a large banner, with the words, "The Sunday-school Army." Can you imagine what sweet, pleasant ideas this suggested? There were a number of different regiments, each having its own colors and its own officers; each one having its own appointed post in the field, there to fight manfully; but each forming a part, and a most essential one, of the "great army;" all fighting under the one great banner, and being marshalled and led forth by the one "Great Captain of our Salvation." Was it not a glorious "review day?" Here was a company of over four hundred children, with bright, happy, intelligent faces, all dressed in their best, looking so joyous; the children of Christian parents, who, from infancy (most of them), had been taught to know, to fear, and to love their God; to read His Word and sing His praises; and as they took their seats beneath the shady trees, you could not but feel that it was a beautiful picture, and that the eye of angels might look with delight on such a scene, and say, " Of such is the kingdom of heaven." But stop! What's this? What makes your heart to beat so violently, your temples throb, and your whole frame to be convulsed for an instant with deep emotion? There is a buzz, a stir, among the children. Hush! hush! What is it they say? " The Congoes are coming! the Congoes are coming!" Immediately a long file of men, women and children, headed by eight or ten Liberian ladies, enter the square : though now for some time under Christian care and treatment, their hollow eyes, protruding bones, and emaciated, cadaverous appearance, are heart-sickening. Is there aught so vile as man given up to the lust of gain? Look at these poor victims of the love of gold. Well may we pray to be kept from covetousness. I thought I had seen specimens of human suffering and emaciation before, but I pray my eyes may never look upon a sight like this again, and if such is their appearance now, when for weeks everything that can be, has been done for their relief, what must it have been when in the midst of their sufferings? The men and boys were all dressed in check shirts and pantaloons, with straw hats; the women and girls in straw bonnets and dresses of every kind, description and style, from fringed and flounced bareges to loose gowns, second-hand clothing that has been sent out to them by government — of course, there is not the slightest appearance of a fit among them. Their appearance was very grotesque, but the consciousness of what they were, with the deep pity that filled every breast, instantly suppressed the mirth that their appearance might otherwise have excited. They had also each been furnished with a very unnecessary article, in a pair of shoes apiece. These, also, had been sent out to them. There is an old and very ridiculous proverb "Of furnishing a side-pocket to a toad," and, really, you could not help thinking of it when looking at them. Those who did wear their shoes could hardly walk in them, but the most of them were wiser, carrying their shoes, as an ornament, in their hands. And who are these Congoes? Ah, dear children, I dare say you all can tell. You must all have heard of that company of poor creatures that were torn from their homes and huddled together on the deck of the "Putnam" slave-ship—carried across the Atlantic, away from friends, and country, and home, to be sold into life-long slavery.

Sickness, disease and death, were busy among them. Still the man-stealer felt that he had a *valuable cargo*. Think of it, children, calling human beings a cargo! Yes, he had, indeed, a *valuable* cargo. A cargo of immortal souls bound for eternity, each one of which was worth more *than all the world*. But it was not in that light the man-stealer valued them—no! he only looked upon them as so many working machines.

Pray for these wicked men, children! they forget

what God says in the twenty-first chapter of Exodus and the sixteenth verse, "He that stealeth a man and selleth him, or if he be found in his hand, he shall *surely* be put to death." Pray earnestly, fervently, for them; if ever men needed the prayers of Christians, they do, that God may forgive them; for oh! their sins are of the blackest dye. But Christ's blood can wash away even their sins. Well, the Putnam, you know, was seized by one of our men-of-war, and the poor Congoes, those who still lived—many had died—were released and placed in safety at Savannah, till the Niagara was made ready to bring them here. This was a far more noble work than the Niagara's late glorious achievement. In that she laid a chain by which, it is hoped, man may communicate with man, and which will greatly increase the happiness of the world at large. By the last she has laid one line of the chain—the other end we hope to reach to heaven—by which man may communicate with God, and by which the kingdom and dominion of the "Prince of Peace" may be greatly enlarged, for, properly instructed here, these poor creatures may, at some future time, go back to carry the "glad tidings" to their own dark land, and thus may God make "the wrath of man to praise Him." We have these poor Congoes here now. The American government will provide for them for one year, and many of the ladies here are devoting a portion of their time to instruct them. At the end of that year what is to be done with these poor Congoes? The people here, however willing they might be, are too poor to maintain them. They are now among Christians. They must be taught God's Word. Cannot the different denominations of our several missions take charge of these poor, helpless creatures, far away from home and friends? It would be impossible to send them to their separate homes, as they have been stolen by the tribes on the coast to sell to the white man. Their homes are, many of them, far inland and hundreds of miles apart. Therefore, they must find a new home—and shall they not be taught of that home prepared for them in heaven? The Presbyterian mission have authorized Mr. Williams to take eight of them into their mission school. Would that some at home would undertake to support eight or ten in our mission schools. Can it not be done? It was our countrymen tore them from their homes, and, therefore, our country owes them a debt. Perhaps you will think how much I beg. Yes, I do; but I want to tell you a fact that has startled me very much. I was reading a book, lately written by a clergyman in New-Jersey, called "Primitive Christianity Reviewed," and in that I saw it stated, " that the poor Hindoos in India, gave more each year for the support of the temple of *Kaloo*, one of their idols, than is given by all the Protestant churches of every denomination throughout the world, for the spread of the Gospel. Does it look as if we *really believed* in our religion and obeyed its commands as they do theirs? What luxury do we deny ourselves to send the bread of life to those perishing with hunger? If the rich man among us gives his fifty or a hundred dollars, he thinks he has done a great deal, forgetting that the first Christians gave their all, and he thinks it is very hard to be called upon soon again to give, forgetting that God's mercies are renewed to us each day, and that we should offer a daily oblation.

But oh dear! thinking of these poor Congoes, I have forgotten all about the anniversary; where was I? Let me see, they were coming in with their teachers; those ladies who go on Sundays, and what other spare time they can find, to teach them. They carried a banner with the motto, "All flesh shall see the salvation of God." Then followed the Kroomen from the town close by the landing; their motto, "Ethiopia shall stretch forth her hands unto God." Lastly came a company of men, women, and children from the Vey towns, across the river, where a little church is being built, their motto, "Come over and help us." This completed the different regiments, or companies of the army; was it not a noble one, numbering in all, eight hundred and ninety-eight? On the platform were all the different clergymen, the President, Ex-President, with other of the gentlemen of the colony. There were likewise present the captain, surgeon, and lieutenant of an English steam-frigate, that had just anchored. Then commenced the exercises, opened by prayer, then an excellent address by the President, speaking in strong terms of the duty of African Christians to the heathen around them. To call attention to this duty, by the sight of these poor degraded ones, was the very object had in view in getting up this celebration, as it has been much neglected by the colonists. Then the children sung "I want to be an angel," then prayer by the Rev. Mr. Henning, the Presbyterian minister. Between the addresses the children sang "There is a happy land," "Who shall sing if not the children," and "The Sunday School Army." The Rev. Mr. Williams gave us an eloquent address, appealing most powerfully to the sympathies of all present in behalf of the poor Congoes. He then spoke to the children about the Station that they as a body, all schools combined, are going to establish among the heathen up the river, and he asked the children, "If they would not try and begin that mission on the first of January 1859?" One unanimous Yes! answered. It was a joyful and a joyous shout, and appeared to come from the heart, I know it *went* to mine. See, children, the missionary spirit is at work here. The "glad tidings" is being spread farther and farther; may God speed it, till "all the ends of the earth shall see the salvation of our God." The English captain, by much persuasion, was induced to say a few words to us; they were indeed but few, but they showed how much the scene had touched his heart, and that he was truly a Christian man. Rev. Mr. Gibson followed with a very pretty little address, after which, cakes were distributed to all. Then the Baptist minister made a short speech to the Congoes, through an interpreter. He, the interpreter, was formerly a re-captured slave, but he has been living here many years, and is now a Christian. After a short speech to the Kroo and the Veys, the army commenced to march; it was all arranged so nicely, there was no confusion, all marched in one procession through the town, and at length, as each came to their own church, the divisions filed off and were dismissed. So ended the celebration, but not, I hope, its effects. It was gotten up with earnest prayer, that it might be the means of promoting *union* amongst the different denominations, and arousing them to a zealous discharge of their duty to the heathen amongst them. We were glad that those officers of Her Majesty were with us, it was their first landing on African shores, and it could not fail to give them a pleasant impression, and show them what the Missionary of the cross is effecting. This union, and life, seems to be attributed under God, to the unwearied efforts, and never tiring labors of this servant of Christ; his name is never mentioned but it calls forth loud expressions of love and praise. He and Mr. Wilson, have labored here for years, often fainting but not discouraged, though their work seemed fruitless, but now, God grant them an abundant harvest, and that they may see of the fruits of their labors. For a year Mr. Williams has been alone, all alone in his work—may God soon send him faithful fellow-laborers. Mr. Gibson has recently taken up his abode here, and they labor heart and hand amongst the poor heathen. Children, you are all part of the "Great Army;" you must be active, warlike soldiers. You must fight manfully. God give you grace to overcome all your foes, prays your loving friend.

I forgot to tell you one important little item, while the children were eating their cakes, a collection was taken up towards defraying the expenses of the station to be established up the river. It amounted to seventeen dollars

PATIENCE.—I have had some very pleasant conversation with Dr. McGill. He was formerly, as many others of the more respectable part of the community were, an ultra abolitionist, and almost hated the white man. Can you wonder? He had not yet learned the blessed law of love, his Saviour's command to love his enemies. And not being himself a Christian, he did not wish to have the white missionary to come to Liberia; he thought they could do very well without them, and he rather opposed than aided them in their efforts for the public good. But his feelings have greatly changed. By their earnest, "*patient continuance* in well-doing," they have won not only his respect and esteem, but his love and gratitude. He feels that the young men that have been educated by the Presbyterian missionaries in the Alexander High School at Monrovia are the men, and the only ones, on which their country can depend for statesmen and for men of intellect, in whatever capacity they may be needed. And all are waking up to the truth that "knowledge is power." He spoke in the highest terms of the labors of the Rev. D. A. Wilson (whom I have just mentioned) before his wife's health compelled him to leave, hoping they might soon return to them. And also his praises were freely bestowed upon the only white missionary now amongst them, the Rev. E. T. Williams, Presbyterian. He confessed how he had formerly misjudged them, had looked upon their every act with a jaundiced eye; but their holy, blameless lives, their unwearied patience, under ingratitude and unkindness, and their constant labors, had forced him to love them in spite of himself. God grant that "the love of Christ" may likewise soon "constrain him" to devote himself entirely to Him. He is a kind, generous man, and even when most opposed to the missionaries coming here, has personally been ever ready to aid and show kindness to them. But coming from such a source, is not this a high testimonial to Christian worth? Mrs. Wilson's name is never mentioned here, but with the kindest expressions of love. Oh! that all who bear the Christian name, would " live as becometh the Gospel."

SPEECHES.—This day, the first of December, is the anniversary of a great battle, fought between the natives and the first colonists; they celebrate it somewhat as we do the fourth of July. The people all meet in the Methodist church, it being the largest. We went over to hear the orations. I never heard better. Ex-President Roberts gave a most excellent one. In it, he presented a concise history of Liberia to the present time, from its first founding. And, truly, the names of its first founders deserve to be remembered; they were as much martyrs for the sacred cause of liberty, as any whose names fame has made known to the world. Aye! and more so, for they were poor, ignorant, unlettered men. But they *were men*, and noble ones, too. It would be a good lesson for all who despise the colored race, if they could but visit Africa. They would learn to know themselves, and feel humbled before God, for their injustice and cruelty. For we ought to feel it; we, at the North, are not free of the charge. The intelligent, educated, colored man, feels the slight and contempt of the northerner, more than the slave does the stripes and chains of the South. We are apt to talk about *their* cruelty, but ah! how few of us look at home! In the evening, we went to what they call the Lyceum, or Young Men's Debating Society. Rev. Mr. Gibson and Mr. Bliden were to deliver addresses before them. The company assembled were *ladies* and *gentlemen*, if beautiful dress, elegant manners, and true courtesy and politeness, form ladies and gentlemen. And many were there white as myself, and who could, without the slightest suspicion, have passed off as such. Indeed, had you seen them anywhere else, you would never have dreamed that they were aught but white. The President and Ex-President are both noble looking men. Ex-President Roberts is a white man, with very light hair, which curls tightly all over his head; this is the only trace of his origin. I took him for the captain of one of the vessels lying out in the harbor. The present President Benson is jet black, but he is truly a noble looking man. The addresses, this evening, were exceedingly good. God help and speed Liberia, and the Colonization Society, to which they all appear so grateful.

UNCLE SIMON.—Now I am going to introduce you to one of the finest old gentlemen, and one of the best Christians, you ever knew in your life. His real name is Mr. Simon Harrison, but I always heard the Bishop and every one speak of him as Uncle Simon, and by that name he is generally known. Now just think of Mrs. Stowe's "Uncle Tom," much better educated, polished, and refined, but retaining all his simplicity, and you will begin to have a little idea of Uncle Simon. But I will begin at the beginning with his history, what little I know of it. Uncle Simon was a slave in one of the Southwestern States, but when quite a young man he became possessed of that true "liberty wherewith Christ makes his children free." He became a preacher among his people. His heart was so full of love that he was compelled to

"Tell to all poor sinners round
What a dear Saviour he had found."

At length Uncle Simon was sold—sold to an Indian. Still here he forgot not the commands of the Word of God, " Servants, be obedient to your masters, not with eye service, as men-pleasers, but in singleness of heart as unto God." He was here in the neighborhood of a mission station, and in a little time Aunt Nicey, the cook there, became his wife. Though his present master was a poor Indian, he was a kind, good master, and at his death he left Uncle Simon to his daughter, stating, as he had served him so faithfully, he felt sure he would be faithful to his child, but with the injunction to her that when she became of age she should give him his freedom. This was done. Uncle Simon then, with his wife, lived for a time at the mission station, among the Cherokee Indians, they having to provide and look after the meals of the children. At all the mission stations it is necessary to have some responsible person, who, out of school hours, attends to the personal comforts and wants of the children. After remaining some years at this station the missionaries advised him that it would be better for his children to be in Liberia—he has two young sons—so about four years ago they came out here.

The Presbyterian mission has bought a piece of ground about twenty-five miles from Monrovia, up the St. Paul's river, quite on the top of a hill—a most lovely spot. A number of colonists have settled in this vicinity. Here they have put up a tiny little church, and a small house for Uncle Simon. This, it is hoped, will form the nucleus of a large mission station. Uncle Simon is the catechist or pastor of the church. That is, he performs all the offices of a minister, except administering the sacraments. He has never been ordained. Hitherto they have only had a day-school held in the church, of which a young man, a colonist, of the name of Melville, is teacher. Now they are building a school-house (native style); and the Congoes Mr. Williams has taken are to form the commencement of the heathen school. Mr. Melville is to be the instructor, and Uncle Simon and Aunt Nicey are to take care of them. God grant that from this little mountain-house streams may issue forth that shall make glad the City of our God!

Well, Uncle Simon, hearing that I was here ill, came down the river, and before he saw me he went to the doctor and told him he thought it would do me good to be up at his house for a little time—that as Mr. Williams had to be up there for a week or two to attend to the mission business, he would see I was taken care of, and they could make room for me, nurse and all. The doctor told him that nothing could be better for me—that the inland mountain air would be a far greater change than that on the coast, only he must take very good care of me. This the old gentleman promised to do, and then came to me—his face glowing with happiness and benevolence. I loved him the moment I saw him. As I sat looking at, and talking to him, I could not but think if the holiness of character and the partial measure of the graces of the Spirit that is possessed by Christians here, imparts such a loveliness and beauty to the countenance now, what will it be when we shall " see the King in his beauty," and when " we shall be like him, for we shall see him as he is." Oh! for the transforming power of divine grace! Afterward the doctor advised me by all means to accept his invitation, thinking it would do me much good, and should any vessel come, in the meantime, going to Cape Palmas, he would inform me.

In speaking of Uncle Simon, the doctor said: "Oh! Uncle Simon's word, at any time, is as good as a bond." Would that all Christians acted so, that all men might take knowledge of them, that they have been with Jesus. We shall go up to Uncle Simon's next week.

COMPANY.—Mr. and Mrs. Gibson and myself were invited to tea at Dr. McGill's this evening. We went a little after seven, and one after another the ladies and gentlemen began dropping in, till there were about twenty-five couples. Among these were the President, the ex-President, and their wives, with other dignitaries of the place. I had a very agreeable conversation with both the above named gentlemen. Mr. Roberts has been a great deal at London, at St. James' Court, and has been pronounced a fine statesman. The rooms in the doctor's house are very large—a very handsome saloon being on either side of the entrance hall. When tea was announced, each gentleman conducted his lady to her place; and we sat down to an elegantly laid table. The company was of every shade of color, from white to jet black.

SUNDAY.—Mr. Gibson preaches, at present, in the little school-house occupied by Miss Williams (our colonist teacher here). It is in a very dilapidated condition, but we are in hopes the Stevens will bring out the materials so that the new church can be proceeded with vigorously. The foundation is laid, and Mr. Gibson is very energetic—he will hasten matters as fast as practicable. May God grant that wherever our Church is planted, it may " be built on the foundations of the Apostles and Prophets, Jesus Christ himself being the chief cornerstone." I am still very weak—little cessation from fever. I admire Mr. Gibson's character more and more each day. He is a devoted Christian. I hope he will be the means of much good.

Uncle Simon came down the river after us to-day, but as the Legislature is sitting now, and the President is to deliver his message to-morrow, we wished to wait to hear it, so we have made every arrangement to go on Thursday.

St. Paul's River.—The delivery of the President's message is again postponed. We wished much to hear it, but as every arrangement had been made for our going up the river to-day, we could not well defer it. It had been very wet in the night, so we hardly thought we should be able to go to-day, but about ten o'clock it ceased to rain, and as everything was prepared, we thought it best to proceed. You recollect travelling here is not like at home, where you can start off at a moment's notice.

We had a delightful day. It did not rain but it was very cloudy—that serving only to render it the more pleasant. We had a very nice row-boat belonging to Dr. McGill, with an awning completely covering it. We had six oarsmen, and our company consisted of Mr. Williams and his little colored boy, Dennis, a Miss Mallary, the colonist teacher of one of the Presbyterian Mission-schools, at a place called Clay Ashland, about twelve miles up the river, my nurse, and myself; these formed the passengers. They had very kindly arranged an extempore bed for me, with pillows, &c., so I could lie down in the boat. Mrs. Carrol, my nurse, takes good care of me, too; packing and unpacking, and taking the sole charge of everything for me. I am in a fair way of being spoiled. How apt we are to forget the countless mercies, and ever to remember the few wants! Would that we more often tried to " count up our mercies;" then what ascriptions of gratitude and praise should we not constantly offer to the " Giver of good." The St. Paul's river is very beautiful. After leaving Monrovia, we pass through a mango swamp, which extends, on each side, for several miles. It is these mango swamps that create the malaria that is so deleterious to the health. A species of fly is also found among them whose bite is very poisonous. But in passing through them they are very pretty. The mango is, I suppose, a species of the banyan, whose branches falling to the earth take root and then spring up again, forming almost impenetrable groves, except for wild beasts. You can imagine snakes and alligators of every description hid in these coverts. After passing the mangoes the scenery becomes very varied. Vegetation is very luxuriant. Large trees of every kind growing close together, their foliage of almost every hue, beautifully contrasted and intermingled. The cotton tree, which, in some respects, resembles the American elm ; its wide spreading branches high in the air. Then comes the bloody dragon, a plant that grows some twenty or more feet high, with a thick stalk, and leaves some five or six feet in length, all set thick with sharp prickles, the stalk also being so covered. It bears a large fruit, not good, of the size of a pineapple, but it looks like an immense thistle head. It forms an impenetrable barrier both against man and beast, as in passing through it, where it grows thickly, anything would be torn to pieces. It grows, however, only near the water side. Then there is the rattan, with leaves resembling a large species of fern, which pushes its slender form up to fill any interstices between the other trees ; and frequently, towering above all the rest, you will see a lofty palm, its naked trunk pushing up or out wherever it can find room, surmounted by its beautiful crown. Besides these there are infinite variety of trees, full of all-colored flowers, the names of which I have not yet learned. While pendant from each and every one of these are many species of wild vines ; these intermingling in graceful confusion with the other foliage, gives an air of marvellous beauty to the whole.

Birds of splendid plumage are here and there discerned among the branches, adding, by their brilliancy, to the high coloring of the scene. In different places on the river, it is cleared away. You then see little cottages appearing, surrounded by their plantations of cocoa-nuts, bananas, plaintains, coffee, cassada, and sugar-cane. On one of the plantations they have a steam sugar-mill at work. We stopped to obtain some of the expressed juice to drink ; it was very refreshing.

About four o'clock in the afternoon we arrived at a place in the river where there are many rapids, and, except in very high tide, no boat can ascend higher. In high tide they can go up as far as Uncle Simon's, but no farther— even canoes find it difficult to ascend much higher, though the river is over a mile wide and several hundred miles in length, yet it is so shallow. We stopped at a little landing belonging to a Mr. Washington, who has a very nice plantation on the river, and we sent a man on in a canoe to see if the tide was high enough that we could pass.

While the man was gone, Mr. Washington came down to the boat, bringing us, as he said, a little lunch, consisting of some beautiful bread, sardines, and bananas. It was very kind of him.

Uncle Simon had seen the boat coming up the river, from his house, which is on the top of a high hill, and he came down in a canoe to meet us. He said the water was high enough, that we could get up to the upper landing, where he had a hammock in readiness for me, as it is a mile to his house, up a very steep hill. He has a nice little house, but our rooms are only separated in some places by mats. We are living in primitive style. But the old people are so good and kind. Uncle Simon says he would soon make me well and strong if I was living with him. We are now on the extreme edge of civilization, no house or civilized man between us and the great desert. Here a heathen school is to be established, which, it is hoped, will send forth its light in all directions. May those words soon be literally verified : " How beautiful upon the mountains are the feet of him that bringeth good tidings, that publisheth salvation." It is the desire to draw the sons of the chiefs, of the principal tribes around, into the school, that so its influence may be extended. God prosper this undertaking.

The mountain air is delightful and exhilarating. This must be a healthy spot. Uncle Simon is praying so earnestly that white missionaries may be sent to help him here, and he says he has faith to believe they will come. Oh! that God will answer his prayer, and send many laborers into this field. The harvest is great, but alas! how few are the laborers. Uncle Simon is so earnest, simple minded, and devoted.

I made an acquaintance yesterday, whose intimacy, for the future, I should wish most respectfully to decline. It was the mango fly. I had been warned about it, and had been on the watch, but one of them eluded my vigilance. I was bit on the ancle. I had hardly noticed it at the time, but it is very painful now, being much swollen and inflamed. Aunt Nicey is a very kindhearted old lady, and as to Uncle Simon I am quite in love with him. How true it is that the Gospel precept, "to do to others as we would have them do to us," makes the most polished gentlemen. We come to this country to work, and whether in one part or the other, the moment our health permits, we must work. "The field is the world." It is the vacation now, so a band of the little ones come to me from some of the houses around, each day for an hour or two, just to read and talk about the most important things in the world. How I love children; how much they teach us!

We had a beautiful Sunday. The little church is directly across the road. It was pretty well filled with colonists. Strange feelings were excited in worshipping in this little mountain church on the extreme edge of civilization. Oh! that Zion may soon "lengthen her cords, and strengthen her stakes," and "cast forth her branches like Lebanon." A few of the natives from one of the towns in the neighborhood (those who are helping to build the school-house) came in after church, and Mr. Williams taught them for an hour or so by an interpreter. When the missionary comes forth here it is, indeed, like the sower going forth to sow—the seed is scattered far and wide—who knoweth the result?

DRIVERS.—Aunt Nicey called me out this morning to see a line of the drivers making their way along. She was fearing and yet almost hoping that they would take the house in their course, for though sometimes, for two or three days, your are obliged to give the house completely up to them, yet they rid it so entirely of all other vermin that it is a great comfort, and as soon as ever they have accomplished this, their mission, they depart. These ants are of a shining-dark brown color, about half an inch long, and they march along in regular files like soldiers, about eight or ten abreast. About every sixth row another ant, jet black and a third as long again as the others marches either beside them or between the ranks, like a captain. He never marches with the others, nor two of these together, unless they appear to be consulting. Well might Solomon tell us "to go to the ant and consider her ways and be wise."

When they come to any impediment in their course the whole army halts, and a number of these large black ants collect together as if in consultation, and presently a detachment will be sent off in a different direction as if to explore. You may stand close to these little creatures and watch their actions for hours, if you do not disturb their line, but tread on them or in any way disturb their line of march, and woe betide you; they swarm upon you in a moment and you never care for a similar greeting again. I have been told that their manner of crossing a little rivulet that is too deep for them to wade, is very singular. They will pause on its edge, and after a number of the captains have apparently consulted together, three or four of them will place themselves side by side, standing upright on their hind feet; others will climb upon their shoulders and lock their fore feet in the fore feet of the first, with their heads placed on their heads. A third set now climb on those, locking themselves with the previous ones, these will throw their bodies out horizontally, their middle claws entwining round each other; others again join to them till the obstacle is spanned. Upon this natural bridge the whole army crosses over. When the bridge breaks up a number of its component parts always perish; a few thus sacrificing themselves for the good of the whole. I watched these little creatures for a length of time, and could only think, what must the Infinite be!

A Curiosity.—I had an amusing scene this morning. It is a rare thing for a white lady to be seen up here. I believe never more than one or two have ever been here; therefore one is quite a curiosity. White gentlemen have been much more frequent. Well, one of my little colored girls, who comes to read to me, asked me this morning to please to let her brush my hair, as she used to do for her ladies at home in America. When the head aches it is often a great relief, so I was very glad to have her do it. We went and sat down on the piazza, and I took a book to read while she did it for me. But in less than a minute I had a dozen or more natives standing around, with eyes and mouth wide open with astonishment. I have a great profusion of hair, as yet, apparently uninjured by the fever; it is very long and very thick: and as the child passed the comb easily through it their wonder knew no bounds. They clapped their hands, laughed, shouted, and called to all who were near to come and see this marvellous sight. Then one of them, the head man, who could speak English a little, said: "Mammy, may I touch him?" I told him, "Yes." He came upon the piazza quite near me, and then put out his hand toward my hair and drew it back again several times, like a child in approaching the fire. He was very much afraid to touch it, and when he did at last venture his fears did not seem much removed. The softness of the hair, with its smooth, shining appearance, made him think of snakes. They could not tell what to make of it. It was really an amusing sight to see them. They stood watching the whole process of brushing, combing, braiding, and putting up the hair, with the most intense satisfaction, and then asked if they might bring their wives to see me.

POVERTY.—I have seen something to-day that made

my heart ache, and yet it should lead me to deeper gratitude to my Heavenly Father, for all his gifts to me. The poor colonists when they first come out here suffer, oh, so much! They are taken care of and provided for for the first six months after their arrival. This is full as much as the Colonization Society can afford to do. Then they must take care of themselves, and this many of them have not the slightest idea of doing. They never have been used to thinking for themselves, and are as helpless as children. They probably have no money, and very little furniture or clothes; and many of these, perhaps, have been brought up as house servants on a plantation—not used to hard labor or hardship. To them the change is very great. They suffer much, but their children will reap the advantage. Curtis Wright,*

---

* I give the names here, as I think, should any one feel disposed, when, at holidays or other times, from the abundance with which God has blessed their basket and store, they are selecting their gifts for their own little ones, to spare a trifle to purchase a little gift for those who cannot repay them, they may know those to whom the veriest trifle would be highly valuable. There are eight little girls, here on the St. Paul's river, varying in age from ten to fifteen, who have not one of them had a new dress probably for years, yet they are always neat, clean, and whole. They all can read and write beautifully, and have exceedingly polite and courteous manners, and truly Christian parents, yet oh! the depths of poverty. Two of these Christian parents are widows. Are there none who, by occasional little gifts, will make the widow's and the orphan's heart to sing for joy? Any trifle sent to them to Uncle Simon—to the care of the Rev. J. L. Wilson, Presbyterian Mission Rooms, New-York—will reach them. As also for our own children, anything sent to any of them, by name, to the care of the Rev. S. D. Denison, Bible House, New-York, they will obtain. Think of it, friends, a thousand gifts to the children at your home will not call forth half the delight that one, particularly if sent out specially, will there. You may never have the satisfaction of seeing it, but recollect the promise of Christ to those who love His little ones.

one of the children who comes to read to me, a very pretty light-colored girl of about fourteen, asked me to-day to go in with her to see her mother. I went with her. Her mother is a widow, with four children living home with her, of whom Curtis is the eldest. She has one daughter married, but able only very slightly to assist her mother. They are all very light-colored and very pretty. Mrs. Wright's house is a small log-hut, the logs none of them larger than a child's arm. These are placed as close together as possible, but with nothing to fill up the interstices or to exclude the night air, except just at the head of the bed, where a small piece of matting is hung up as a protection. The roof is thatched, and projects a long way over the side, so as in some way to shield the side from the rain. There is a place for a window with a shutter, but no windows here; indeed I forgot to say that there are no windows anywhere in Africa, except at the mission houses and a few of the more wealthy inhabitants, and most of the churches. There are no windows at Uncle Simon's or at the little church, only places for them and shutters. They are too great luxuries.

Mrs. Wright's furniture is not very costly, consisting of an old bedstead with a patch-work coverlet; one large and one small chest, and two or three boards nailed up for shelves in one corner. On these there are a Bible and two or three school books belonging to the children; one plate, cup, and knife, and a small pot. This, with a little tin pail (that holds about a quart, with which they fetch water from a rivulet about a quarter of a mile distant, down a steep hill), completes the furniture. When we went in, Mrs. Wright was lying on her hard pallet reading the Word of God. She has had a dreadful ulcer in her leg for over nine months. She has been trying to do everything for it. It is the most fearful looking sore you ever saw, and terribly painful. She would be able to do some sewing if she could only get it to do, but the people are too poor to have anything to make. Uncle Simon sends her her daily food, and the children live upon what they can cultivate themselves, rice and cassadas; and yet even these children occasionally put something in the missionary box, for they will go out into the woods and get peanuts, and sometimes they can send them to Monrovia and get a few pence, which is gladly and joyfully put in the box. What sacrifices, what self-denials do we make at home for God's cause? What lady among us would ever think that she could go with one ring the less, or one flounce the less to her dress, or what man will go with one cigar the less, that so the Gospel may be spread? And yet see these poor children; their peanuts would help out their scanty pittance of food, but they are freely given that the "Bread of Life" may be carried to those "perishing for lack of food." Mrs. Wright spoke with the greatest cheerfulness, and with warm expressions of gratitude and thanksgiving to God for giving her such good friends—not a single murmur or complaint; and her wants and sufferings had to be inquired into for you to know them, I left that lowly hut, having learned lessons of gratitude to God, and of deep self-abasement and repentance at my want of faith, love, and gratitude.

The Mite.—In giving we often think our mite is so small it cannot possibly do any good, but you know the old proverb:

"Mighty oaks from little acorns grow."

Now think, ten little pennies will buy a Testament. Now just count and see how many leaves there are in a Testament, and see how many of those leaves one penny will buy. Now I will tell you what one of these leaves may sometimes be worth: worth! why more than all the world, for is not one soul worth more than all the world?

I heard this little anecdote related by a missionary the other day: A large caravan was travelling the great desert in the northern part of Africa, and among them was a Christian missionary. He did not know that among all that people there was one who had ever heard of Jesus. One evening, when about to rest for the night, he heard a great bustle in the back part of the caravan; upon asking the occasion of it he heard that a sick man had fallen off his camel and was supposed to be dying. He immediately went to the poor sick man, who was lying on the sand. No one knew who he was, therefore nobody took any notice of him, or did anything for him. They had not learned that their " neighbor is everybody—all their fellow creatures." The missionary found he was dying; he raised his head, bathed it, and gave him some water to drink. Then, as the dying man opened his eyes for a moment, the missionary said to him, in the Arabic language: " Brother, you are dying; have you any hope?" The dying man clasped his hands and exclaimed: " None but Jesus—none but Jesus." The missionary said: " Thank God; where

Only one leaf—its worth.

did you hear of Him?" "Here, here, only here—precious Jesus," said the man. He then pulled out of his bosom a torn and soiled leaf of the Bible, and fell back dead. The missionary took the leaf and found these words marked, "God so loved the world that he gave his only begotten Son, that whosoever believeth on him might not perish, but have everlasting life." The dead man was taken up and buried in the sand. No one knew anything more about him. But he is known in Heaven; there too is known how and by what instrumentality he obtained that little leaf that told him of Jesus. How much was that leaf worth?

THE CREEK.—This evening we took a walk to the creek, it is a very beautiful way to it. You have to go down a deep narrow pathway, through a dense forest, the trees towering up on all sides to the height of eighty or ninety feet, all most gracefully festooned with wild vines. The trees meet above the rivulet of pure limpid water (the best and coolest I have tasted in Africa), which flows with an ever murmuring sound; this, with the notes of the strange birds and insects, fall with sweet melody on the ear. I do not know whether the scenes are really more beautiful here than at home, or whether it is that the heart is in different tune, but certainly they have, at times, an overpowering effect. Some of the children went down with us to the water, but, for a few minutes, we stood quiet and speechless. We then spoke of the grandeur of that scene and the beauty of that spot, where the white man's foot, probably, never before rested—and the exquisite glory and beauty of this earth, when the Son shall claim the "heathen for his inheritance and the uttermost parts of the earth for his possession." Then in the depths of these wilds, which had never heard the Saviour's name, we sang—

> "From all that dwell below the skies,
> Let the Creator's praise arise," &c.

And then was poured forth a most earnest prayer for the poor heathen around, that light may shine in upon their darkness, and that this wilderness and solitary place may soon "rejoice and blossom as the rose." Truly it was a magnificent temple of nature's own erection in which we were worshiping

LEOPARD.—This morning I saw a native boy, about twelve years of age, who had some dreadful wounds in his side. Last week, he laid down to sleep, in a field very near here, when a leopard sprung upon him, seized him, and was carrying him off when his cries brought a number of his friends to his rescue. Poor boy, he will carry the marks of the teeth and the claws to his grave.

TRAVEL.—There was a congregational meeting to-day, for the election of an Elder for the little church. We all went to the church, and I could not but observe, how needful it is to have "the wisdom of the serpent," combined with "the gentleness of the dove," in him who has to preside in such meetings; here, particularly, where there is very great jealousy, in many of the colonists, of white influence. Poor people, they have not, many of them, the least power to rule or guide themselves, and yet disdain to be guided, even for their own good, by the whites. This afternoon a man by the name of Ash came in, on his way to Monrovia. He has just returned from an exploring expedition. He, with a Mr. Seymour (both colonists), have been up into the Mandingo country. He thinks they have traced the river, the St. Pauls, to its source, and he believes, allowing for its windings, it must be a thousand miles in length. Its whole length, however, is like our Mohawk, so full of rapids that it is not navigable, except by canoes, and in many places not even by them; the natives frequently having to wade and carry their canoes. Ash seems to be a very intelligent man. He and Seymour were sent by the Liberian government, who paid their expenses, as they wish to open a communication with the interior tribes, for the purpose of trade. These men have been absent about nine months. They have met with kindness in every instance save one, and that, he says, was their own fault. It appears it is the custom among these natives, if any stranger is received kindly among them, when he wishes to proceed farther, for the king or headman to give him guides, and a sort of passport through his dominions, to the king of the next tribe; he will do the same, and so you can travel safely from tribe to tribe. The king of the tribe with whom they were staying being absent, on a warlike expedition, and they wishing to proceed, they left his dominions without this passport; in consequence, they were attacked, robbed, wounded, and scarcely escaped with their lives. Ash was offered as a slave, his value set at the rate of one gun; all these tribes make slaves of their prisoners. At length, however, he escaped and reached again the town of the friendly chief he had left. It does seem as if God is opening this country as well as all others, for Missionary enterprise. Are there not those who will come, and enter in, and take possession " in the name of the Lord ?" Ash says, that the natives, up there, appear to be ignorant of the value of ivory, and yet that there is some there that it would take seven or eight men to carry. In many other respects they are far more civilized than those on the coast; their religion is a corrupt sort of Mahometanism. The most of them can read and write a species of Arabic, and have portions of the *Koran.* Writing paper was almost worth its weight in gold. They raise cotton, and have a way of spinning, weaving, and dyeing cloth. Round the towns they have palisades, or mud walls, from thirteen to fifteen feet high, and eleven or twelve feet thick. The walls of their houses are made of mud, the floors likewise, and at one end of the hut a narrow ledge of mud is elevated above the rest for a sleeping place.

FEASTS.—We have been visiting some of the poor people. Most of their houses are just one room, they are formed of very small logs, set upright, quite close together, and then covered inside and outside by a species of matting which they make here. These do seem very comfortless to me. But we often forget that what would be utterly destitute of comfort to us, from the way in which we have been used to live, is almost luxury to others. God appoints our lot, our sorrows, and our joys more equally than in our shortsightedness we are apt to imagine. When Mr. Williams came in at dinner, "Oh," he said, "I have something to tell you, but I must wait till you have dined." I wish I could give you his graphic description. There is a strange looking little native boy, that comes about the premises a great deal, for the occasional food he may receive. The child gives you the idea of deformity, and yet you cannot tell why. He has staring red hair; this, on one perfectly black, you may be sure, is very singular in its appearance, but it is by no means uncommon. Mr. Williams was out looking at the progress of the building the school house, when he saw this little urchin bending down over a fire made in the ground, apparently very intent on something. On drawing nearer he observed that the child had something wrapped up very carefully in some leaves in his hand. These, which looked like long white worms (a species of which they use for food), he was turning over very carefully; selecting the fattest he held it on a stick in the fire, till it was partially roasted, and then eating it with great gusto, smacking his lips, and apparently taking an epicurean enjoyment in his food. The process was repeated again and again with infinite relish. Upon looking a little closer, to observe the nature of the animal, Mr. Williams perceived that it was not a worm, but the entrails of the chicken we had for dinner, which the child was eating with so much relish. I am afraid our chicken would not have tasted quite so nice had we heard this before dinner.

The native women have a custom of cramming their children. They begin when their infants are only a few days old. They will have about a teacup full of soft boiled rice, and holding the infant on their lap, with their fingers they will poke the rice down its throat, then with the hand rub the throat and the stomach to force the rice down—the poor child crying most piteously all the time; this is continued till the whole of the rice has been forced down. The mother, meanwhile the child is crying, smiles and looks on most complacently, thinking she is doing the best thing for her child. After the stuffing operation is completed, the child is rubbed all over with palm oil, and then laid down for an hour or two before the fire. You must suppose the child who lives through this ordeal must have a tough constitution. They are very good children, you rarely hear one cry except when undergoing this operation. This is a daily process.

Last night I was awakened by hearing quite a scuffling and scrambling in my room. But as in the next room to mine, which is only separated by a mat, a hen with a brood of young chickens rests under the bed for fear of snakes out of doors, I just thought, perhaps she had mistaken her quarters, and found her way into my room, so I quietly went to sleep again. When it was daylight I called to my nurse, who was sleeping on a sort of couch in my room, to look on the floor between her couch and my bed. There lay the cat, very quietly purring away, while beside her lay the bloody remains of a snake, which she had partly devoured. Whether she had brought it in to devour, or whether it had found its own way in, and she had killed it there, I know not. From its appearance then it must have been from four to five feet long, about as large round as a child's arm, and of a beautiful bright blue color. Mrs. Carrol, in great horror, flung it away, so our gentlemen did not see it to be able to recognize the species. I felt very timid after that, though I did not say a word, as when we are placed in such circumstances, it is our duty to try and overcome our fears, and not to torment all around us with them, when it is not in their power to allay them. It is so sweet always to feel, in every circumstance, that there is an "eye that never slumbers or sleeps," constantly watching over us, and nothing can harm us but by His permission, and if he allows it we know it is for our good, and with his protection

> "On the lion, vainly roaring,
> On his young, our foot shall tread,
> And the dragon's den exploring,
> We shall bruise the serpent's head."

Oh, for perfect faith, and trust in our Almighty Father's love!

PLEASURE.—On Sunday an Elder was ordained, and Uncle Simon preached from the text, "He was made a curse for us." What deep earnest love he has for his Redeemer. He has not had much of man's teaching or learning, not much of worldly knowledge, but he has been "taught of God." His library is the Bible, and he illustrates and explains it by itself beautifully. He has the true wisdom. His fervent, earnest prayers always carry you to the foot of the cross. I am daily learning lessons. Oh, may they be remembered!

The air is very balmy and refreshing; it must be healthy. I have not had a touch of fever since I have been up here, but still I am very far from strong. I hope my voyage down the coast may strengthen me. It will be rather longer than it was coming up, as the "Stevens" has to stop and land passengers and freight at several places. We are looking for her now, hourly; so to-morrow we leave here for Monrovia, to be in time to welcome our new friends. We are looking anxiously for them. There is to be a meeting of Presbytery at Sinou, about thirty miles above Cape Palmas, so a number of the Presbyterian clergymen will go down in the "Stevens" with us. This afternoon we took a walk down to the river. There are several large rocks out in the water, under the shade of some beautiful mimosa trees, which tower up some seventy or eighty feet above the water. We went out and sat down under the shade of these trees on the rocks, and talked of the wonderful works of God, displayed here in all their grandeur, and then of loved ones at home. Poor Mrs. Carrol (my nurse), though, was in momentary dread of snakes; her fears were almost ludicrous—mistaking every withered branch or pendent vine, for the object of her terror. Here we had quite a little Bethel—reading some beautiful selections of God's Word — singing those precious hymns, "Guide me, oh thou great Jehovah," and "How firm a foundation," and praying for the heathen around us, the missionary friends coming to us, and for *all, all* we loved at home. Truly, we could feel that our God was with us—that "the Almighty dwelleth, not in temples made with human hands," but "wherever two or three are gathered together in his name, there will he be to bless them." In travelling through this wilderness He often gives us manna to eat, and refreshes us with springs from the pure river of the water of life.

Aunt Nicey was telling me that there used to be great quantities of monkeys about here, but wherever civilized man takes up his abode, the lower animals have to give place before him. She says, that some time ago she saw some natives catch a monkey, and while it was living, put it on the fire and roast it, and then they ate it, skin, entrails, and all. She said the moans and groans of the poor little animal were so like a child it made her sick. " The tender mercies of the wicked are cruel."

MONROVIA.—We came down the river to-day in Uncle Simon's canoe. It is a very large one, and he arranged it quite comfortably for us, making seats and backs with boards, and putting in pillows. A heavy thunder storm came up while we were on the water, but having umbrellas we did not get much wet. A clergyman's office here is no sinecure. I will give you an idea of *some* of Mr. Gibson's duties. Every third Sunday morning he goes across the river, in turn with others, to preach to the Kroo and Veys—this is at seven o'clock. Then he has service every Sunday in the morning and evening at his little church, or rather school-room, here, and then he has Sunday School in the afternoon—this he is obliged to superintend. He, in turn with the others, preaches Sunday afternoons to the Congoes. Oftentimes, on the Sabbath, besides these duties, there are the sick or funerals to attend, so that frequently he has barely time to catch his meals. Through the week he has an evening service and an afternoon prayer meeting, besides preaching twice in the heathen towns. Then he has to attend to the building of the church, and most of its secular affairs. I have just mentioned a few items. You see our laborers have a chance " to wear out" here, but not " to rust out."

I have made a few calls to-day. I am very much pleased with Mrs. Benson, the President's wife. She is a quiet, lady-like, unassuming woman.

THE STEVENS.—Early this morning we heard that the " Stevens" had arrived, bringing a noble band of missionaries. I received my letters, giving me confirmation of my father's peaceful death. Safe at home, safe at home! Christ being *all*.

This afternoon, after reading my letters, our new friends came to see me. There were Rev. Mr. and Mrs. Stone, of the Baptist mission. They are going considerably farther down the coast, to Abbeokuta. The Rev. Mr. Syes, of the Methodist church; he was formerly out here for many years. He has now been sent out to look after these Congoes, see what is to be done with them, &c. Miss Kilpatric, also of the Methodist church, is come out again (she had to return home, some months ago, on account of her health) to take charge of her school up the river, where she has labored most perseveringly, the only white lady. And we have quite a reinforcement for our mission; the Rev. Messrs. Rambo, Messenger, and Hubbard, with their wives. We surely have cause to " thank God and take courage." The " Stevens" brings a number of passengers, among whom is the Rev. Mr. Burns (colored) who has just been to America to receive ordination as a Bishop of the Methodist church. We hear he is going to be married immediately to the young lady who has had charge of Miss Kilpatric's school, in her absence.

It will probably be two weeks, or more, ere the "Stevens" leaves here, as she has much freight to discharge. So many little kind mementoes from loving friends! oh, for grateful hearts!

CHRISTMAS DAY.—This morning, at the breakfast table, a little package was laid by my place; a strange boy had brought it, but no one knew from whence. On opening it I found a number of letters and a beautiful book from a dear friend at home. On the inside she wrote, wishing me a happy Christmas, she little thought I should receive it Christmas morning; but it remains a mystery to me how it came, for all from the ship disclaim any knowledge of it. But I have it, many thanks, kind friend. All our friends, from the ship, were on shore, and after service, we were invited to different places to dine. In the afternoon we all met at Dr. McGill's and went in a body to the National Fair, which is now being held in what is called the Palm palace, a building constructed in the Government square for the purpose. This is the second fair, only, that has been held, and it is very respectable. There are samples of cotton, sugarcane, fruits, vegetables, and flowers, country cloth, and chairs, looms, tools, &c. There is one very beautiful wardrobe, made of a wood they call bastard mahogany. After we had remained here till we were tired, we accompanied our friends to the boat. Miss Kilpatric and Mr. Syes remain in Monrovia—she returned and took tea with me

SUNDAY.—Mr. Messenger preached in the Presbyterian

Church—Mr. Rambo preached for Mr. Gibson. In the afternoon we had a Missionary meeting. Mr. Russell, an Episcopal clergyman from up the river, gave us a very interesting account of the work amongst the natives there. There are about thirty towns in his vicinity, which he visits, each once a month, preaching in all. In most of these they have built a little hut, which they call the church, for him to preach in when he goes there, and they all of them are crying out for God men " to go teach them," that they " want to leave country fash, and to do God fash," and they are begging earnestly for teachers. This seems to be the cry now amongst them all. May God hasten the time when we shall say " Great is the multitude of preachers." Miss Kilpatric is going up to her school to-morrow

THE CONGOES.—Some of our friends, from the vessel, come on shore each day; I enjoy their company much We have had letters from Cavalla; both the Bishop and Mrs. Payne very unwell again, they have concluded to return to America by the Stevens. It will be a sore trial to me, their leaving, but they need the change much. I spoke of Mr. Syes, the colonization agent, he came out now in the Stevens. He invited us all (the white people) to dine with him to-day at his boarding house. Mr. Gibson's house being near the boat landing, when they come on shore, all collect here. About eleven o'clock all were assembled and we went up to his house; we had a very pleasant day, but I fear I am going to be ill again. I have a great deal of fever, and yet am so weak. After dinner we went up to the Receptacle (the place provided by the Colonization Society for the emigrants on their first arrival), where the poor Congoes are lodged; they were eating their dinners—corned beef and sweet potatoes. The poor things are beginning to recover somewhat from the effects of their ill usage, though still they look deplorably; they have all now nice clothing and seem quite happy. Mr. Rambo addressed them through an interpreter, and Mr. Hubbard prayed fervently for them. They then sang for us one of their native songs, one man standing up and leading them, and as they sang, he went through a great variety of most graceful manipulations, all imitating him, and as the gesture was changed the note was changed. There was not much melody, I must confess, in their song, but the *time* was most accurate, and would have done good to the heart of a music-master, and that from two hundred at once. The Congoes are young; I should not think that there is one among them over thirty. The interpreter is a recaptured Congo, who was brought here about fourteen years ago; he is now a Christian, and, to his great joy, has discovered an *own brother** among the new arrived. Oh! that I had an eloquent pen that could touch the heart, and make others see these scenes as I see them. We must pray that friends may be raised up for these poor friendless ones—that they may be taught the knowledge of the only *true friend*

THE GOSPEL.—Mr. Gibson was telling us to-night, that when the Bishop was up here, some time ago, he

---

* A mother's child. Others are called my father's son or daughter, but a mother's child is a brother or sister.

preached from the text, "Woe is me if I preach not the Gospel." He was heard by a young man of the first standing, and good education, who is doing an excellent business. He is a member of the Church, and that sermon made him feel that it was his duty to give up all, to preach the Gospel to the heathen. He has been struggling with conviction, all his family opposing him, but now he has determined to give up all for Christ, and he has written to the bishop, to know what course he must pursue to obtain a theological education and prepare for the ministry. Is not God amongst us when the Africans, themselves, are waking up to their duty to their brethren, and devoting themselves to the work? Pray, pray for the Missions, pray earnestly; we know not how much of the success in the work here, is in answer to the faithful prayers of those at home. God has promised the blessing—"Yet for all these things will I be inquired of by the house of Israel, saith the Lord."

SICKNESS.—So there is a break, in my journal, of twelve days again. Our Heavenly Father constantly teaches us our weakness and our need of daily dependence upon Him. The commencement of this year has been ushered in, to me, on a bed of sickness, pain, and languishing—where will its close find me? Oh! for growth in grace and preparation for the eternal world. In reading the account of the building of Solomon's temple, we find that not an axe or a hammer was lifted up upon the temple itself, nor the sound of it heard, but each separate stone was cut, and carved, and wrought, and polished, beneath in the earth, ere it was fit to take its place in that sacred pile; and is it not so with the heavenly temple? Must not each living stone which is to occupy a place in that holy building, be cut and polished, and wrought into fitness and meetness, for the position it is there to occupy? No sound of the workmen's tools will be heard there; it is here, on earth, that each stone is to be prepared for its future place, in the "building of God, the house not made with hands, eternal in the heavens." May our prayer be, not that we be spared the process of preparation, but that each stroke may only render us more beautiful and fit us the sooner to take our position there.

So much kindness has been shown me in my sickness, oh! for a thankful heart. The principal people of Monrovia have shown every kindness and attention to the Missionaries. We have all been invited out to dine every day, and though I could not accept the hospitalities, the others were enabled to do so. On New Year's day there was a grand pic-nic given to the united Sunday Schools, the expenses entirely defrayed by one or two gentlemen. It was held on a lovely spot, near the point of the cape. They had a delightful day. To-day we were invited to the President's; it being very near, I was enabled to go. We sat down to dinner, about forty of us; everything was in excellent style—a very fine display of cut-glass, silver, damask, &c., and a very pleasant company. Before going out this morning, a basket was brought me; on opening it, I found a large, beautiful, iced cake. Miss Kilpatric had sent it me from up the river. Bishop Burns, of the Methodist Church, was married yesterday, to her assistant teacher. She has been busy making cake and did not forget us, probably thinking it would be nice on board ship (we leave in a day or two). "Little deeds of kindness, little acts of love," what beautiful flowers they are, springing up by the way side.

FRIENDS.—We dined with Bishop Burns and his bride to-day. We spent a pleasant day, and, before parting, had a delightful prayer meeting. When I reached home I found Uncle Simon had come down the river, expecting the vessel would sail to-morrow. She does not, however, till Monday. Aunt Nicey had been thinking of something to send me, so she sent me a pretty little rice bird, but it looks very drooping; I fear it will die. The little children I had gathered together sent me many messages, and much love, and wrote me three or four little notes. Dear children, I may never see them again. Mr. Syes is going down in the Stevens with us, with about eighty of the Congoes. These he is going to distribute at different points down the coast as far as Cape Palmas. I feel very sad to-day, the doctor tells me he fears that I shall have to return home to America. This constant fever has so broken me down, he fears I cannot regain strength here. My voyage back to Cavalla may, perhaps, strengthen me. It would indeed be a bitter trial to leave my work here—but God knows best. Poor Artee does not seem much benefited by her voyage. The doctor fears she is incurable. It is a strange disease, this sleepy disease. It is often hereditary; the person suffers no pain, but constant heaviness and stupor. Eating, drinking, walking, no matter what they are doing, they will fall asleep; then it seems as if the brain gradually softens and the person becomes slightly deranged, and after two or three years the whole frame becomes gradually weakened and they expire. Artee has troubled us so much by her strange way of acting lately, but it was a relief when the doctor told us it was her disease. She was a fine girl ; one of the most promising at the Asylum. But this is an affliction sent from the "All-wise."

THE STEVENS.—So I have said good-bye to my kind friends at Monrovia. When saying farewell to Ex-President Roberts, he said he was sure they would soon send me to America, as he thought I was not fit to remain in Africa at present. I laughingly told him he was a "bird of ill-omen" and he must not croak (I little thought he would be so true a prophet.) The Stevens is a very fine vessel ; she is very much crowded with passengers. The captain told us to be on board to-night, but we are not to sail till to-morrow. The Congoes are not on board yet. How it troubles me, the thought of the possibility of my having to leave my work. I feel as if I could willingly die here, if such is God's will, but to leave! Well, we know "the Lord doeth as he will among the inhabitants of earth."

We have a very pleasant company on board. Quite a band of ministers. They conduct family worship in turns, though of so many denominations, there is never a jarring note. All are "one in Christ Jesus." Our captain seems a rough old customer.

BASSA.—We anchored off Bassa. Mr. Rambo went immediately on shore to pack his furniture. Before his return to America, this used to be his station, but now he is to remove to Rocktown, so he wishes to remove his furniture. Mr. T. Thompson has been ordained and appointed to this station.

We all dined on shore at the mission-house to-day. It is a very pretty house, and lovely location; but it is said to be very unhealthy. Here in the garden, entirely alone, lies the grave of the first Mrs. Rambo, a most lovely women. At first it gave me a very sad feeling to view that lonely grave, but in an instant came the remembrance that her white-robed spirit had joined the countless multitude which no man can number, bought by the precious blood of the Lamb.

Some native women came round us at the house, particularly admiring our hair, and Mrs. Rambo kindly let her's down that they might have the satisfaction of examining it. Mr. Williams showed them his watch, with which they were much delighted. He then told them it was like a man, showing them the works. He said while those works were good the face was all right, the hands moved right, and the watch told the truth, but if those works inside were bad the hands did not move right, and the watch did not tell the truth; so if a man's heart inside him was good his hands would do good; he would act right and his mouth would speak right and true things; but if his heart was wicked and bad he would say and do all bad things. He also told them that the watch sometimes got wrong, out of repair—then it must go to the watchmaker's to be made right, so our hearts get wrong, out of repair—then we must take them to God in prayer to set them right. He told them this so simply and easily, that they seemed to understand and appreciate every word. The gentlemen had appointed service in the afternoon, but as it was a two miles' walk, along the beach, to the little church, none of the ladies went; we, therefore, returned early on board the ship. I have had very high fever again for the past two days.

Sinoe.—We put into Sinoe this morning. All our Presbyterian brethren are gone on shore to attend the conference. The Stevens will remain here two or three days; by that time conference will be over, so Mr. Williams and Uncle Simon will go on in the Stevens to Cape Palmas, and then return in her. She will be there two or three days. Uncle Simon wants to visit some of our native schools to observe the management of them.

Mr. and Mrs. Rambo and myself went on shore this morning. We went first to call on the Rev. Mr. Green, the Episcopal clergyman, and his wife. He has a very pretty little church, in the Gothic style; it is his own designing. We went in to see it; from there we went to the Presbyterian church, it was the closing of the conference. This is quite a large building. We here heard several excellent addresses, and then went to dine at the house of Mr. Priest, the minister. In his garden there is a splendid lemon tree that covers an area of over thirty feet, and it produces the largest lemons I ever saw. We left Sinoe in our boat about four o'clock, and our vessel got under weigh again at six.

Chapter Fifteenth.

HOME.

WE anchored off Cape Palmas last evening, and soon were safe at the Asylum, and I am sure our new comers must be satisfied with their reception. The Bishop has come up to-day to welcome all. He, with all the rest, remained to transact some business and to settle the abodes of our new friends, but I came down home; Home! how pleasant a word it is. Mrs. Payne was much disappointed at my appearance. She hoped to see me looking quite well, and she thinks I hardly look any better than when I went away. Mrs. Gillet and all the girls came to meet me, some distance along the beach, but it growing dark before I arrived, they were obliged to return home, thinking I should not be here till to-morrow. About eight o'clock I stepped into the school-house, and I almost thought I should have been torn to pieces. Only think of forty-two girls with their teacher all crowded round you, each one trying to give you the first hug. I had to make my escape very quickly again, but it is pleasant to feel you possess the love of these poor children. I desire to thank God for it.

MRS. GILLET.—I have not described her to you. She is a tall, large woman, very dark, but with a very good-natured, smiling, pleasant face. She was brought into the school many years ago, a little naked heathen child; as ignorant and degraded as any among them. Now she is a Christian teacher, in every way thoroughly well suited to the position she fills. She teaches and explains the Bible well to the children, showing them clearly the way of salvation through Christ. She is kind and affectionate, while, at the same time, she maintains good discipline and makes the children obey her. She has a nice little bed-room off the school-room, fitted up very neatly; there she can oversee the girls at all times, being with them night and day. I have sometimes gone into her room, where she would be sitting, neatly dressed, reading or sewing, and her own mother would come in to see her, a perfect heathen, wearing only a little cloth (they do not like to wear more clothing, many of them). I think how painful it must be to the daughter to see her own dear mother still so far away from the true God.

Mrs. Gillet has been telling me that during the holidays she has been up to visit Brownell, one of our native teachers; who, with his wife, is up at Nitie Lu, a hundred miles up the Cavalla river. Here he has a little school, which has been established about a year The boys in this school, one year ago, were perfect heathens, had then never even heard the name of God. Mrs. Gillet says to see them at prayer it is so pleasant. They all kneel, with their eyes fixed on their teacher, and no matter what happens they never look away from him. She asked one of these little boys how it was when there was any strange noise out of doors that he did not turn his head to see. He answered, "If we turn our heads to see, then our ears will follow our eyes, and our hearts will follow our ears, and God says we must pray with our hearts." May we not learn lessons from poor African children? Mrs. Gillet's husband was a very fine young Christian man, a good Krooman. One of the French emigrant vessels tempted him and several others of our young Christian men, with the promise of high wages and a speedy return, to ship on board of her about four years ago. The Bishop strongly advised them not, telling them what he believed to be the character of the vessel. The temptation, however, was too strong, they thought he must be mistaken. They went, but have never since been heard of. I fear she is widowed for life.

ORDINATION.—Mr. and Mrs. Hubbard, and Mr. and Mrs. Messenger, are appointed to reside at Cavalla; Mr. and Mrs. Rambo at Rocktown. The Bishop has concluded not to return by the Stevens, but to go by the next English mail steamer; then, he will be able, in the meantime, to initiate our new missionaries a little in their work. This is an arduous post, particularly for new comers. May they have grace given them, and strength according to their day. Mr. Hubbard was ordained on Sunday. Mr. Rambo came down to be present. May he be a faithful soldier of the cross. The Stevens has left.

THE MAGIC LANTERN.—I forgot to mention a pleasant circumstance that occurred a little while ago. Some kind gentleman has sent us out a magic lantern, with scripture pictures; and Mr. Hoffman was showing it to our children, any of the natives who chose to come in, and explaining it to them, when he came to the picture of Christ as a babe at Bethlehem; whilst explaining this he paused for a moment, when instantly a number of the children struck up singing that beautiful hymn:

> "Salvation, oh! the joyful sound,
> Glad tidings to our ears."

No one had told them to do this; it seemed as if it burst forth involuntarily from their lips. It did sound so appropriate, it truly was singing from their heart. May this word, "salvation," soon be glad tidings of great joy in all the nations of the earth.

ILLNESS.—Since writing last, I have again been led by my Father's hand down to the "border land," and for two or three days to stand, as it were, on the very edge; but "thanks be to God, who giveth us the victory through Jesus Christ our Lord," I was enabled to bow with submission to his will, and say, "my Father, thy will be done." In health, I always have an instinctive horror of death, yet, when in the "dark valley," the "King of terrors" loses most of his hideousness. Now, when doubts, and fears, and Satan's legions beset me, I could put them to flight with these two passages, which never left my mind. "Simon, Simon, Satan hath desired to have thee, that he might sift thee as wheat: but *I* have prayed for thee, that thy faith fail not;" and again, "He ever liveth to make intercession for us," and I felt it to be impossible for *His* prayers to fail. But it has pleased the "Lord and Giver of life," again to raise me up from what all thought to be my bed of death. I am just able to sit up. The Bishop and Mrs. Payne at first spoke of my returning home with them; but now, it is hoped, that after this severe illness, the worst I have had in Africa, that, perhaps, I may be better than I have been at all. If it is God's will, I hope it may be so, for it is the one earnest desire of my heart to labor for Africa. Mrs. Hoffman is just taken with fever; as yet it is slight; some have it very lightly, we hope it may be so with her.

FUNERAL.—Last night the girls had a visit from the *drivers* in their school-house. What a noise and hubbub there was; Mrs. Gillet had to desert her room, and give them entire possession of the lower story, but they did not go up stairs; this morning they have disappeared. Eliza Hutchings, the wife of one of our native teachers, formerly a scholar in the girls' school, came to the village a week ago, very sick of dysentery, a very prevalent disease now. The doctor has been carefully attending her, but she died last evening. Her end was peace. Last week, this time, I lay very low. Why was I spared? She was buried this morning; she was placed in a neat deal coffin, and carried into the church, where the funeral service was performed. It was very sad to see the poor mother, as she followed the coffin, at times embracing it with frantic cries and gestures. She is a heathen, and her manner was in striking contrast with the subdued grief of the Christian relatives. *She* had no hope.

DEPARTURE.—The evening after the Bishop and his dear wife left us, I again had a severe relapse, probably owing to excitement consequent on their departure. I had promised them, ere they left, that should I be ill again, I would take the first opportunity to return to America; as if I could not labor, I should only be an additional burden. All our new missionaries have had occasional attacks of fever, though, thanks be to God, none of them had yet been dangerously ill. I fear I was very rebellious to God's will. I was not willing to give up my loved work; I felt as if I could die, if it were God's will, but not leave there. How hard we often find it to say in *all* things, "Thy will be done!" I left Africa in the next English steamer after the Bishop and his wife, hoping that we should take them up at Madeira, as they were to stay there for a month. Here is an extract from my journal, written out at sea :—" Yes! I have had to leave Africa, it may be forever; at times, I hardly think I shall live to reach home. God knows best, but ah! it was a sad and bitter trial. I love my work, I love my children, and they love me, but ' God's ways are not as our ways.' I have been ill, so ill; high fever every day; but every alternate day the pulse would be up to one hundred and thirty, accompanied by four or five hours' vomiting and retching, with utter prostration; each of those days we all thought that death would take place. But God mercifully spared me; every kindness and attention was shown me; all that could be, was done for me. One week the doctor scarcely left my bedside; I shall ever remember with gratitude his kind attentions. My poor children would come quietly into the room without making a sound, and stand looking at me, with such sad countenances, sometimes the tears stealing silently down their cheeks; and if I would give them anything to do, they seemed so happy, to rub my feet or hands, bathe my head, or fetch me water. Poor children, I never knew how much they loved me before. Three days, when I was very ill, Mrs. Gillet stayed in my room all day, leaving Lucie in charge of the school; and as for poor Lucie herself, every moment that she could spare, she was in my room. The villagers, men and women, used to come and look in every day at the door. If able, I would speak to them; if not, they would just look at me sadly, and go away. I had not been aware that they had so much affection in their nature. But it is not often that it has such an opportunity of being tested, as a serious illness here is seldom of long duration. At length I told Mr. Hoffman that I would leave by the steamer; it had been a bitter struggle to me to decide on this; but he, with others, had proved to me, that it was like committing suicide to remain. By leaving, there was only the shadow of a hope that I might recover, but if I remained, it was utterly impossible. The doctor took me up from Cavalla to Cape Palmas, though much fearing I should not survive the journey. Many of the natives, particularly the Christians from the towns, came to 'look me' before I left; and my children followed me for miles. May God bless them, and send them one far more efficient than I have been, to teach them. When the steamer arrived, I was carried on board in my hammock, my nurse going with me, to take care of me. Little, I believe, did any one think I should live to reach the shores of England; and I could not even look a farewell to my beloved African home. Two days before I came on board my fever was broken, and the sea breeze immediately began to revive me; in a few days I could leave my close state-room, and lie on a couch in the saloon, or be taken for a few minutes on deck. I was obliged to send my nurse on shore at Sierra Leone, to return by the first opportunity to Cavalla, as the charges are so high on these vessels that I could not bring her on, and my strength was returning that I could begin to help myself. To-day, I am considerably better, so I can scribble a little with a pencil, as I lie on the sofa. Every alternate day, though, my fever is still very high."

PASSENGERS.—The steamer is a fine one, but our sleeping accommodations very poor, and the attendance miserable. We are rather crowded and have a medley set on board. One colored girl, who is very rich and very homely—she has received an excellent education in England. She is from Fernando Po. Two or three of the gentlemen on board pay her great attention, and to see the airs and graces and the spoilt ways and ridiculous behaviour of the young lady, is at once sad, yet amusing. I often think it would be a lesson to some of our flirts if they could see themselves thus caricatured. Then we had three quadroons on board—they went on shore at Sierra Leone. They were very beautiful and graceful—just enough African blood in them to give a warm glow to their skins. They have amused themselves sitting on deck, drinking champagne, ale and port, till, each night, they were completely "how come you so." Then we have a sea captain, brought on board dying; he now looks somewhat better; there are hopes he may recover. We have two doctors, one from the navy, the other in the army, neither of them have been here a year, but both of them obliged to return from ill health. Doctor D'Lyon placed me under the care of the army doctor, but since the first day I came on board he has been so drunk all the time that he has not been near me. The other has prescribed for me. Then we have quite a number of army officers—all going back for health. One has his wife and two little sickly children with him. Then there are three Spanish gentlemen from Fernando Po: the Spanish consul, the captain of the frigate, and one other. They have been but a few months there, but appear more dead than alive. What can it be that makes this climate so fatal to the Saxon race? We have one American gentleman, one French lady with her child, besides many others, colored and white.

SIERRA LEONE.—At Sierra Leone the harbor is very pretty, and presents a lively appearance. It is almost a semicircle, formed by high hills, or rather mountains, at the foot of which lies the town. The streets are wide and the houses look like good ones, but for the defacement of the climate, which gives them all such an old look, but the cocoa-nut trees thickly scattered through the town have a fine appearance. The mountains in the background are very broken and picturesque, but almost entirely barren. The government house and barracks

are situated on the summit of one of these hills; they are very fine buildings, and rising behind them is a high hill, the only one covered with foliage. Vessels can approach the shore much closer here than at any port in Liberia, and we saw as many as fifty lying at anchor; among them three English steam frigates. The scene is very pretty—so much activity and bustle. The lighters plying continually between the vessels, carrying coal, produce, &c., and the little skiffs with their gaily dressed company, combine to enliven the harbor. Then there are several varieties of gulls, which seem contending with the fishermen which shall have the largest portion of the finny tribes with which these waters teem.

We lay off here three days; one of those days I was very ill indeed; I did not think I should live till night, but in consequence of a water-pipe having burst, my berth was flooded, therefore I was obliged to lie on a couch in the saloon. That day I was quite heart sick, almost in despair. I was alone, far from home or friends, death staring me in the face, and—what had never troubled me before—thoughts of a watery grave haunted me, with the thought that I had no one to tell to those I love, how I had departed. I felt as if man and God had forsaken me. But that evening God sent a " good Samaritan" to me. An English missionary of the Wesleyan Church (I know not his name) came on board to see a sick friend, and, seeing me look so ill, he inquired who I was, and came and sat down beside me, and he did not leave me till he had " poured in the oil and wine into my wounds," and till he had carried me, in spirit, to my Father's house—had shown me the precious "balm" there, and left me in charge of the "Great Physician." Oh, for more of that Christian love to go about doing good. May he always be comforted in his hours of tribulation by the "Great Comforter."

THE GAMBIA.—We are lying in the Gambia river, off the little town of Bathurst. We anchored here yesterday at noon, and are to leave at two o'clock to-day. This is a very hot place—low and sandy; between the streets of the town the loose sand is up to the ancles. The houses here are not so defaced as elsewhere, but there are very few trees. Altogether, it appears to me, it is the most uninviting place I have seen on the coast. The natives are Mahometans—much more civilized than elsewhere. They are tall, well-made men, and their loose, flowing robes and Turkish caps, mostly white, give them a graceful and even majestic appearance. They remind you of the Moors in their palmiest days. The women's clothing is of every color of the rainbow. Here, at the Gambia, is a species of monkey called the dog monkey. It is about two feet high. Its nose very much resembles that of a dog, and it barks just like one. They are very savage—if a man, when out alone, should fire at one of these monkeys, he would never escape alive, as they always go in troops, and if one is injured they all immediately try to revenge him, and one man alone has no chance with them—they will bite him to death.

Mr. Ward, the American gentleman on board, has been very kind to me. He has brought me some tamarinds and oranges from shore—they are very grateful in fever. He came on shore and up to the Asylum at Cape

Palmas, and went on board the steamer in the same boat with me. He has told me since, that he did not think it possible I could live to reach the vessel. He has been travelling for five years. He is excellent company, quiet, gentlemanly, and full of information. He was speaking to me of the natives farther down the coast, where he has been. At Fernando Po, he says, they are the most debased and degraded set of beings he ever saw, and not even social in their habits. They do not congregate in towns, but they place their huts in the woods far apart from each other, and, unlike the rest of the people on the coast, they are not polygamists.

THE JUJU.—On a small island, near the mouth of the Niger, the people have some strange customs. They have a large town of about three thousand inhabitants; their huts are built within mud walls, with the streets crossing each other at right angles. At every corner there is a creature stuck up, like our scarecrows in America, with a gourd for a head, and dressed up with cloths, shells, beads, &c. This thing is called *Juju*, and whatever is devoted to it is also *juju* (sacred.) Thus the little animal called the Iguana, a species of lizard, which elsewhere is eaten, here is allowed to increase and run all over the island. At one end of the town there is a temple dedicated to the Juju. It is higher than most of the other houses, with an arched doorway, the sides and arch of which are formed of human skulls. Inside the hut, at one end, is a sort of sacred altar, like the Roman Catholic altar, that, with an arched recess behind, is formed of children's skulls, the east side and floor being the skulls of adults. In the eye sockets of each a square piece of board is inserted, first painted red, and then an eye painted on it. Outside the door is a post to which prisoners are tied, and beaten to death with clubs, and then their skulls, after being dried and bleached, are used for replacing any that may have become cracked or otherwise injured. There are three priests whose business is to put prisoners to death, to take care of the temple, and attend to the dressing of the *Jujus*. It is also their business to look out for and seize anything persons may possess that is juju. For instance, any piece of cotton cloth with a distinct pattern, such as a leaf or flower, is juju. Any bottle with a label on it is juju, though the same bottle without the label is not so. The priests seize all such things, and stow them away in chests for the *Jujus'* use—dressing them and such like.

CRUELTIES.—On other portions of the coast, their customs are more cruel about witchcraft than among the Greboes. Any one, once accused of witchcraft, is burnt most cruelly. In some places a slow fire is made, and four posts sunk in the ground, at certain distances, the person tied hands and feet to these posts, and suspended over the fire, thus being slowly burnt; sometimes they are left to die there; at other times they are taken down before death, cast into the bush, and left to perish miserably. No one must pity a witch. Sometimes they torture them a different fashion: they are fastened down so that they cannot move, and then red hot coals are placed in different parts upon the body, and left to eat in. But such details are sickening.

DRUNKENNESS.—We had quite an excitement last night. Our army doctor has been intoxicated all the time, since the first day I came on board; sometimes he becomes very uproarious. The captain has tried to stop his drink, but without effect, for if he is not allowed to have a bottle of his own, he will take that belonging to others. On Sunday, he had delirium tremens, and they locked him in his state-room, with a man to watch him. He was tolerably quiet; but last evening he was dreadful; his room is very near the one which I occupy, and all the evening he was shouting and hallooing for brandy, which they would not give him; at length they forced him into his state-room, and set two men to watch him. The captain and the naval surgeon had been on shore* all the evening, and had only been on board ten minutes, when loud cries came from the doctor's state-room, " I am murdered, I am murdered, my throat is cut." The men who were with him were very much frightened, and called for assistance. He would not stay in his berth; and though they had been watching him closely, yet, with a madman's cunning, he had contrived to pull off his belt, and with the buckle dash to pieces the looking-glass; he instantly seized a large jagged piece of this, and cut his throat. He had severed an artery, and if the other surgeon had not been on board, he must have bled to death in a few minutes. As it was, they said it seemed almost impossible that any man could live, after losing so much blood; and yet, during the whole of the rest of the night, he was raving fearfully, at times shouting so loud as to be heard all over the ship. He is a little quieter to-day, but has to be

* At Bathurst on the Gambia.

constantly watched. It is a terrible wound he has given himself, this cut with a jagged piece of glass. Compare that man with the poor heathen we have left, and which is the most degraded? In looking round this saloon, one would no longer wonder at the difficulty the missionary of the Cross finds in persuading the poor heathen to embrace Christianity, when these, and such as these, are what he hears called Christians. And these here are not what would be called the low, common people, but such as call themselves, and would be entitled, gentlemen. In all my life I have never heard so much profanity, as I have these few days on board. It makes me shudder to hear them talk; may God give them "better minds." The day I first came on board, the doctor was somewhat sober, and he came to me in a very gentlemanly manner, prescribing for me, and promising faithfully to attend me. (He has not been in a condition to speak to me since that day.) Then he sat down and talked with me; and my being so ill, I suppose, made him introduce the subject of death, and religion. He sat talking with me for an hour or more, deploring his dreadful habits, his sinfulness, and wishing, apparently sincerely, that he could break away from them, could become better, could be a Christian; he had evidently been rightly brought up, and knew his duty. At the same time, he declared he knew it was impossible for one so vile as he, to break away from his sins, or to receive pardon. I talked very seriously to him, pointing him to the Saviour of sinners; the blood of the Atonement shed even for him; I spoke very earnestly, I know, for I felt so. When himself, he was a fine, gentlemanly, young man, only about eight-

and-twenty, having left a young wife at home in England, to whom he was now going. I felt great pity for him. I afterward thought, I dare say he went away and ridiculed all I had been saying to him; but at any rate, I felt that I had done right to try, and point him to the Saviour. Last night, after he had cut his throat, he was raving, poor creature, for them to "go and fetch the missionary lady, that she might come and pray with him, and tell him of Jesus." They could scarcely pacify him without doing it. Ah! man may forget God for years, but there will come a time when he will wish he had in him a friend, when no earthly arm can aid him. May this be a lesson to the poor doctor, he will never forget. I saw in a book, the other day, the motto of some German Missionary Society. I wish to make it mine. It had the device of a bullock, standing between a plough and an altar, with these words, "Ready for either." Either for work or death, as the master saw fit. And yet, if he chooses that it should be neither, but appoints unto us "waiting work," that is the hardest of all, yet we must pray for submission, and to do even that cheerfully.

TÉNERIFFE.—Early yesterday morning we came within sight of the Peak of Teneriffe. I did not see it then, however. About six o'clock in the evening, we anchored off the town or city, in the bay. As we approached the island, the scenery was very beautiful. The Canaries on either side of us, rising like giant mountains out of the sea; these, with those of Teneriffe, appearing in many places far above the clouds. The Peak, itself, had only been visible for a few minutes in the morning, after that, the clouds completely hid it from sight. As you approach Teneriffe, it looks like a long, irregular, chain of mountains; a lower range rising within the higher; and again, a third within that. There did not appear to be many trees, but the whole of the mountains, as far as we could see, from the water's edge to the top of the cones, were all terraced. We were quite a distance from the shore till we came near the town, running along horizontally with the island, but still we were near enough to discern this; as, also, the numberless pretty little villages scattered along the sides, and in the valleys, and slopes of the mountains, from the very shore up to the highest points. The houses are all either built of white stone, or painted white, which makes them everywhere distinctly visible, against their green back-ground. The town is beautifully situated; it is near the northern end of the island, where the shore takes a curve, forming a pretty little bay. In the back-ground rises the lofty Peak, its summit lost in the clouds; while to the north of the town, are innumerable sugar-loaf cones coming close to the water's edge, and rising, some higher, some lower; the lowest elevated some eight or nine hundred feet above the sea; and the valleys or depressions between the cones, sinking to the level of the town, all of them covered with terraces. The town, itself, is built on a wide, extended plain, which seems made for the purpose; and the houses being all white, it has a very pretty, clean appearance from a distance. There are no trees in the town, and being built so on a level, it was impossible to observe how the houses were constructed, though here and there we could see the handsome dome of a cathedral, rising above the surrounding buildings. The sound of the convent bells, echoed back by the hills, was exquisite melody. I should have liked to see more of the place, but it was impossible, even had I felt strong enough to go on shore. Some of our passengers will long have occasion to remember Teneriffe. It seems at the time we left Sierra Leone, the small-pox was very prevalent among the natives in that vicinity. When we were in the Gambia, we heard that this report had reached Teneriffe, and, consequently, all vessels coming from there were put into quarantine; we, however, were hoping that this was not so. When we arrived at Teneriffe, the health officer who came alongside, said that no one could go on shore, without first going to the Lazaretto (the very name has horrors connected with it), which is the same as our quarantine hospital, for fifteen days. It was in vain for the captain to assure him we had no such sickness on board; he would not come and examine for himself; and a letter the captain wanted to send to the Governor, was received at the end of long sticks, and deposited at the bottom of the boat. Well, after a great deal of trouble, and the boat going back and forth many times, it was at length agreed by the Governor, that the passengers who wanted to land there, might be let off with five days in the Lazaretto. How sorry I felt for them. There were Mr. and Mrs. Burton, teachers in the Baptist mission school in Sherbro Island, come to Teneriffe, to remain there for a month, to regain their health, and then to return to their work. Mr. Ward, the American, who wished so much to ascend the Peak, and yet had to leave for Havana in fifteen days. A little Frenchman, and the three Spaniards, one of whom has been very ill, and is only just getting about again. All these, with their luggage, had to be put into the little boat at midnight, and taken off to the Lazaretto. This is a large building situated far off, at one end of the town, close to the water's edge. The exactions there are exorbitant, and the regulations dreadful. It is a filthy hole, with only one room, which, when there are females there, is separated by a curtain. Here they have all to eat, drink, and sleep. The only article of furniture provided, is an iron bedstead for each person; if they wish to enjoy the luxury of bed, pillows, blankets, &c., each article has to be separately paid for. Each person has to pay two dollars a day for food, whatever the keepers may choose to provide; and in this case, the boatmen who row them ashore, are to be shut up with them for fear of contagion, and the passengers have not only to pay their expenses at the Lazaretto, but also the five days' hire of each boatman. Pretty expensive travelling. It is a shameful imposition, but they cannot help themselves. I feel very sorry for them. The Spaniards are raving about it, though it is their own government.

We left Teneriffe at one o'clock at night. The next morning we had an excellent view of the Peak; we must have been full sixty miles off, but there it was, towering far above the clouds, covered with snow, some distance down from the summit, glistening in the sun, the clouds appearing more than half way down its sides. The Captain is somewhat apprehensive of the same quarantine at Madeira.

MADEIRA.—We arrived at Madeira about ten o'clock in the morning. All the passengers had been for hours on deck to view the scenery, which is grand, and to breathe the balmy fragrance of the air. The island consists of a high mountain chain, terraced, and like Teneriffe, sprinkled from base to summit with pretty villages. The houses being all white, show well from a distance. When the ship anchored we all watched anxiously to see if we should be quarantined, but not a word of the kind was mentioned. We were much amused for some time watching a singular proceeding. The boys and men here are expert swimmers and divers; as soon as a vessel anchors a little boat, pulled by two boys about twelve years of age, comes along side; one of the boys manages the boat, the other dives over the side of it for small coin which is thrown into the water by the passengers on the vessel. They are most expert, no matter how small the coin, they never fail to get it, and they will come up holding it above water to show you they have succeeded. Once or twice I was quite frightened at the length of time they would be under the water.

I sat watching the boats, hoping to see the Bishop come on board, when a strange gentleman came up and addressed me. He told me he was the host of the house where the Bishop was staying; he came on board to secure a stateroom for him and Mrs. Payne, and he had requested him to inquire if I was on board, as when he left Africa he feared I should be obliged soon to follow. He requested the gentleman, if I should be on board, and be at all able, to bring me on shore. Though very weak, I determined to venture to go on shore. The beach, for some distance up, is formed of loose cobble-stones, very bad for the feet. The streets are not much better. They are very narrow, no side-walks, and they are all paved with cobble-stones set edgewise, which hurt the feet badly, but then they have the advantage of keeping the feet dry, as the water runs down between them. Their conveyances are very easy carriages set upon runners, drawn by two bullocks. It was quite a matter of wonder to me how easily and quickly these vehicles glide along over the stones, with four passengers inside. Invalids go out in *hammocks*, but to those who are well enough, horseback riding is far the pleasantest. The horses are as sure-footed as mules, and are well trained for travelling through the gorges and ravines of the mountains, where a pedestrian would scarcely dare to trust himself. The owner of the horse always goes with him, hanging on to his tail, and in this way he will keep up with him for a whole day. The scenery is very wild and grand. There is a Romish Church called the Mountain church, at the very summit of the mountain. It is an almost perpendicular road up to it, through one of the gorges. You are carried up in a hammock, but come down in a sort of basket-sled, a boy standing on it behind, to guide you. The Bishop says he came down in that, a distance of a mile and three quarters, in nine minutes. After it is once started it comes down by its own weight. The houses I cannot describe; they were of all sorts, shapes, and sizes, with sometimes a tower jutting out here and an angle there. The house of Mr. Mills, where the Bishop has been boarding, is a fine, handsome one, in the English style. The view from the top of this house is fine beyond description.

Here I met my dearly loved and kind friends, who were sorry yet glad to see me, and with them again that night set sail. Under their kind care and protection I safely reached my friends in England, with the fervent hope and prayer that if it please our Heavenly Father to restore my health, I may again go forth to labor for Africa, but if not permitted to do that, wherever I may be I hope to labor for her.

Reader, have I roused one feeling of interest, one hope, one prayer, for Africa's redemption, one desire to devote a little time, a little means, for her and her children's good? If so, my aim is accomplished: and let me once more press upon you the duty of earnest prayer for her, her children, and her teachers, then soon will she "Arise and shine."

THE END

www.ingramcontent.com/pod-product-compliance
Lightning Source LLC
Chambersburg PA
CBHW020311240426
43673CB00039B/769